# REVELATIONS

## Sandy Cohen

REVELATIONS

ISBN: 9780984621699

Library of Congress Control Number: 2010915470

Cover Photo: Creative Commons

Cover Design by: All Things That Matter Press

Published in 2010 by All Things That Matter Press

To Rob

# ACKNOWLEDGMENTS

My gratitude and thanks to Jim Hendricks, the late Oliver Land, Carolyn Maschke, and Bill Strickland, all fine writers and discerning critics themselves, for listening to and making suggestions about earlier drafts of this book, and to editor and publisher Phil Harris for making *Revelations* less clunky than it was when I first sent it to him.

# PART ONE: THE LIES

The lies fell like steady rain
                    –Shiva Naipaul

# ONE

John Steinbeck has this story about a rancher, Peter Randall, a big strapping fellow, tall and imposing, with a flat stomach and barrel chest, even as he pushes fifty. His wife, Emma, is an 86 pound, bed-ridden, bag-of-bones. But all their married life, she makes him wear an elastic harness-a sort of girdle. It's the secret of his upright bearing.

The day she dies, he removes the thing, of course, and for the first time in twenty-one years, his back is free to slouch, his stomach to distend. He confides to his cousin that Emma didn't die dead, and when he makes a pile of money the next year he has electric lights installed in his farm house because Emma always wanted electric lights.

That's the afterlife for you.

When my own wife died, I'm not really sure what I did. I didn't have a girdle to remove. But I had a life to find again. I remember staying in our same big rambling house until I sold it, but to this day I can't really tell you how long that was, maybe six months, perhaps a year. I don't remember what I did in it before it sold. How do you measure being alive? The hallways were so empty my footsteps shattered into echo. I ached with each resounding. We had no children to be brave for.

I remember forgetting little things, like where I parked my car on campus. Sometimes after class I'd pace one lot after another for hours in muddled search. I forgot whether I bought that blue patterned tie I thought about getting to go with the light blue shirt she got me on our last Hanukkah together. It turns out I bought four of them, all pretty much alike.

It's not that I started dipping into the Manischewitz or anything, but the effect was the same. What more than alcohol can fog the brain than grief? That's why this is not a memoir, but a memory, a sort-of myth. Besides, the only alcohol we had in the house, other than the two carafes of Passover wine, a dark and a light, was a half bottle of cognac Sara used for a wonderful chicken recipe she never wrote down. Like my mother's stuffed cabbage, that's another meal I'll never eat again, unless ghosts do walk, or recipes can float to us on Ouija Boards.

Seeing my distress deepening into habit, some friends and colleagues suggested I take a sabbatical and travel. I did. I went to the place of light, to Greece, to find some equilibrium in my life again. But who could conceive what I found there? Was it colossal fraud? Murder? Madness? That's where I met Abis, my life force. He brought me back, and forward, too, to that other place where Diana was, and will be, forever.

\*\*\*

I arrived late in Athens and headed directly to the little hotel a colleague recommended. Except I got lost and spent two hours wheeling my suitcase up and down the streets, asking Athenians for directions as best I could. A stranger in a strange land. Night was falling quickly when I finally arrived and checked in. I should have taken a taxi, but I was afraid. After dinner I sat on my balcony. If you looked hard to the left, you faced the Acropolis, less than one mile away. The night was cloudless and the black sky spangled. Spotlights of various changing colors and angles lit the Temple of Athena and the mountainside itself, now from this direction, now from that, and the Temples of The Other Gods as yet unknown to me. It was miraculous. I sat for hours, staring.

Sounds of laughter, strains of music drifted upward from the streets. When the breeze blew fair from across the sacred mountain, it carried the aroma of wild thyme and rosemary. When the wind shifted, there came the sounds of clinking glasses and silverware, and the aroma of Greek dinners and Greek wines from the restaurants below. I closed my eyes and took a deep breath. In that first night in the shadow of the enchanted mountain, I knew what the ancient Grecians knew intuitively, that this was a place of magic and delight. Now it was also a real place to me, too, a place of life enjoyed and magnified.

I fell asleep in the chaise lounge on the terrace, such deep sleep, and when I woke it was morning. The sun shone bright and hot and yellow. Though my side of the terrace was still shaded by the overhang, the sun had found the other side, and a red geranium in a terra cotta pot. It illuminated the flower so intensely I couldn't help but squint and smile. I hadn't unpacked or even touched the hotel bed, but had slept more restfully than I had since Sara was healthy and whole, and curled in bed beside me with her mass of dark, dark, curly hair against my chest, her hand pressed softly to my cheek.

So long ago.

I wanted to climb the sacred mountain that very morning. But my friends back home had already booked me on a tour bus to Delphi. "Don't see Athens first", they'd told me, "save the best for last." I took a quick walk-through of the Athens Museum in the morning, and by noon I was off for a day's excursion to Delphi, to stay overnight. Then back to Athens by the next evening. These were my friend's best-laid plans for me.

On the bus, I read my guidebook. "The navel of Mother Earth," it called Delphi. Apt. You climb and climb into the mountains and then look down into the round, vast, green valley, covered rim to floor with olive trees, leaves shuddering in the wind, now silver-grey, now deepest green again. The valley is at least a mile across and a mile deep. You could understand how the ancients would think this place could be nothing less than the belly button of Mother Earth, reclining in the Heavens. Opposite the Delphi shrine parking lot were the tiny temples and the ruins of the marble storerooms for the treasures of the Oracle, each shrine no bigger than a lawnmower shed. The ancient Greeks came with their apprehensions from all across their world to hear the frenzied, drug-induced shrieks of the sibyl and the sober misinterpretations of the priest.

"Should I have another baby? Should I start a civil war? Here, take my gold offering, my bronze votary. Keep them in your storehouse, sacred ones, keep them for yourselves, only tell me what to do."

"Think for yourself," the sibyl screams, "know thyself!"

And the priests listen in and tell you what you want to hear.

I step across to the other side of the temple site, walk across a field of weed and crushed marble stone and look down and down and down again below the rim: an ancient playing field for the Games for the Gods. It shimmers in the sun. Apollo of the many epithets resides here in his splendor.

Far off, on the other end of the playing field, a dog appears. It seems to be very skinny, but I can't be sure. It's so removed from me. It stops and squats, then looks behind her. Soon a man emerges from the shadows. He looks in my direction. Does he see me? He's wearing baggy white pants, a baggy white shirt to match, and a bizarre red hat. His dog turns around and points like one of those setters on the covers of *Field and Stream*. The man turns to face her. The other side of his hat is black.

I get out Sara's small binoculars to watch. The hat is the oddest, most obscene thing I've ever seen. It's as if he'd ripped the codpiece from a pair of parti-colored tights and stuffed a sock in it. A single, wilted feather hangs from one side. He looks like a fool.

With the binoculars I can see the poor dog is so underweight all her ribs stick out. Despite her anorexia, she can really hold her point. She has to. The guy's turned his back to her and doesn't notice what she's doing. Finally he sees what she's pointing to and begins to stalk. In the shimmering heat currents, I can't quite make out what they're hunting. Maybe a dying bird, quivering toes-up in the sand. But that could just be the shimmering heat currents. They're so obscuring I could just as well be seeing an old shoe, or the corpse of a weasel.

Suddenly the man dives and quick as a conjurer catches, yes, I think it is a bird, in both finger tips. Then, my God! He seems to rip it apart with his bare hands! Feathers are flying everywhere! I scream out, "Hey!" but he doesn't seem to hear. It looks like he's spreading the entrails out on the ground and leaning over them on all fours like someone reading the Sunday comics. I scream out, "Hey!" a second time, but again he doesn't hear.

My head begins to swim in the heat currents. I have to put away the binoculars and sit. Still I can't take my eyes off the scene below. The man points up toward me, but without raising his head. The dog looks up, then runs in my direction. The guy follows her in a lumbering, clumsy kind of gait, more bear-like than human. I don't think either of them has seen me, but really, I don't know what to think.

I watch until they're hidden by the overhang, then return to the main temple site and sit. I'm still dizzy and nauseated. More buses have disgorged their sight-seers. The oracle is awash with polyester. Suddenly I realize the tourists and their guides are walking right toward me-every one of them. In a moment they surround me, crowding into a tight circle. Quite loudly, I say, "What's going on?" Now they're all staring at me. Then I realize I'm sitting on the navel stone, the central place of worship. My face feels so hot it must be crimson. My head withdraws into my shoulders. I drag the shell of my embarrassment to the far side of the temple site and sit down on a piece of broken pillar as the tourists turn their attention to what their guide is telling them about the navel stone and press my hands to my face. Then I actually begin to sob so hard that from behind it must seem as if I'm holding onto a jack hammer. Who knows how long?

"Are you all right, young man?"

I look up. A semi-circle of plaid shorts and sunburned skin has formed about me like a Greek chorus-every single white-haired gentleman and lady from the Putney-Porter Unitarian Church of Wilmington, Delaware. My friends back home had booked me on their half-filled tour bus. It was a good deal, sure, but now I'm thinking, I don't deserve this. First the numbing grief, and now the tingling humiliation. I'm thirty-five years old, for God's sake, and I don't even come from Delaware.

Their leader, a tiny woman, moves forward, all earnest face and blue hair. She's a widow, originally from Delaware City, has two cats, sisters, both with bad arthritis. Her eldest daughter, June, was looking after them for her while she traveled the civilized world with her church group.

"You look like you were crying so hard your heart would break, Mr. Markovitz," she says. "What could ever be that wrong?"

By now my face must be the color of a baboon's bung. "Uh, no, ma'am, I'm not crying; it's, uh, Klip, uh, um, Klipspringer's, uh, syndrome. We sort of heave about like that if, uh, we don't take our medicine on time. No, no, really, don't worry; I've just taken it. All I need now is lots of open space and fresh air. Thanks, everyone, please, back to your temples and shrines. Really. Thank you very much for your concern."

The chorus disperses. I move off toward a grove of mixed hard and soft wood trees, looking for a hollow oak to crawl into and die. I mean I honestly at that point contemplated killing myself. I remember thinking; doesn't hemlock grow wild in these parts? What does it look like? God, what if I make a mistake and overdose on wild parsley? It would probably make the papers back home. How could I face them then? Parsley gives me terrible diarrhea. Suicide is not for the socially sensitive. How could I live with the failure?

This should be my dark night of the soul and the best I can seem to do is wear prescription sun glasses. I move further into the grove and choose a tall, straight evergreen to butt my head against. But I don't, because there's this sound coming from much further into the woods, like some kind of animal, humming. It has made me quit my angst midstream and begin to follow it through the pines and laurels. Sara's casket was made of laurel wood. Such a large coffin for such a small woman.

The animal-humming sound is gone. Then it's back again but from a slightly different direction. This time much higher-pitched, like a flute. Alive. Vibrant as a heartbeat. Despite the heat, my arms goose bump. I follow on, over and around the un-hewn marble rocks and through the darkening forest. Suddenly a man leaps down from a heap of stones right in front of me. It scares me nearly witless. Though we're no more than two feet apart, he shouts at the top of his lungs, "Hey, you! Mister!"

He has to mean me. I'm the only "mister" in the vicinity.

It's the man in the ridiculous hat! He's holding a wooden kid's musical instrument; I think it's called a recorder, painted bright yellow with blue curly-cues and such. Or maybe it has fresh strands of ivy wound around it. You can't be afraid of a guy carrying one of those. I feel a bit less apprehensive, though up close he's bigger than I had imagined when I saw him from above. Wide and muscular, he's one of those people who have never been young and lean, and who never ages beyond a certain point. Dirty toes grip a pair of well-worn sandals way too big for his feet. He notices I'm staring at them and looks down.

"Hand-me-downs," he says.

"Are you supposed to grow into them?"

He laughs a pleasant laughter. "Maybe someday they'll grow wings and I will fly away."

He looks vaguely familiar, though I can't imagine where I could've ever seen him before. His skin's like burnished bronze, his cheek bones high and prominent, and he has black hair, straight as an Arizona road. His neck is thick and scruffy. A red bandana blazes around it like the band about a captured bird. He paces back and forth in front of me. I'm reminded once again of the way a bear lumbers. Everything about him seems to match his rough-hewn, bear-like physiognomy. Except his eyes. They're moist and brown as a rabbit's.

"I saw you down below," I say

He nods and laughs.

"The hat," I say and point. "It gave you away."

"It was made especially for me out of virgin rabbit felt by my second– no, no, wait, my third mother-in-law. I tell you now, it is sacred."

"I'm not so sure there's such a thing as a sacred hat. But I do know for certain there's no such thing as a virgin rabbit."

"I am Wakjunkaga of the Winnebagos. But you may call me Abis."

"Pleased to meet you. I'm Manuel of the Markovitzs. You can call me Manny. I don't think I've had any other nickname."

"No?"

"Well, maybe the one my dad used to call me when I was a little boy."

"Which is?"

"Well, it's kind of embarrassing…."

"Ehhh?"

"No, you'll laugh."

"Tell me."

"Well, all right. Man-man. He used to call me Man-man."

Abis frowns. "Well, maybe we will think of another."

"Maybe."

We shake hands.

"Sister! Come meet my new best friend Manny Man-Man Markovitz!"

His skinny dog trots out from behind the rocks, sits down, and offers me her paw. I kneel and shake it with fully extended thumb and forefinger, turning my head to avoid the pungent odor.

"You are U.S. American citizen, no?"

"Yes.'

"I will tell you what–a secret about this hat. You see this wilted feather? Once it graced the heiny of U.S. America's noblest and proudest symbol."

"I'm sorry, I don't know much about birds and nature and all, but I'm pretty sure that's not an eagle feather."

"No, no, not eagle, blue jay! See this band that holds this great and noble feather in place?"

"Some kind of snake skin?"

"Snake skin? Ha! You are joking Abis now? It is genuine uktena hide! No, no really, I am not fooling you. It is true! I captured him myself when I was only three years old!"

"I don't even know what an uktena is."

"It is good you have come, Man-man. You have so much to learn."
He slaps his forehead.

That gesture is the give-away. Now I know where I have seen him
before. The Atlanta airport. He wasn't wearing the hat then. Two security
guards and a ticket agent were all talking to him at once, trying to explain
why his little dog couldn't ride on his lap in the plane. He uttered oaths,
gestured impolitely, and kept slapping himself like that in the forehead.
Later I saw him board ahead of me, without the dog. I was in the last row
of the plane. He was way in the front.

I remembered thinking then, God, what a clown. He sure doesn't look
like first class. But there you are. Must be Greek. Going home. His
immigrant son has made it big in America and now he's bought Papa a
first-class round-trip ticket to visit him in the United States. The stay's
over, and peasant Papa's going back home to his village and his goats.

"Soooo, what do you think?" he asks, putting his flute into his pocket.
Out of another pocket he pulls out a good-sized piece of wormy-looking
wood and a paring knife. He begins whittling furiously.

"I think that was a very nice song you were playing before. Very
unusual."

He bows and smiles. "Cusabo."

I reach into my pocket and offer him some coins. This seems to offend
him deeply. He nearly snarls. His little skinny dog looks at her master,
turns and snarls at me, too, and snaps her little jaw as if she were a
mastiff. Then she runs away as Abis kicks savagely at her and nearly
misses. He screams something in a language definitely not Greek and
makes figs with his fists. The dog whimpers, tail beneath her legs, and
keeps ten feet distance.

"Hey!" I yell, "Please don't do that!"

Abis looks genuinely puzzled. "Why not?"

"Because, because it's inhumane."

His brows gather into low fogs. "Huh? I always kick my little sister."

As if she knows I'm defending her, the little hound of compound
ancestry comes trotting up to me. She rubs her head against my pants leg
as if she were a cat.

"Peeeew!," I say, "Don't you ever bathe that thing? Damn. What has
she been rolling in?"

He shrugs. "Mostly dog shit."

"Obviously. God, there's nothing worse than the smell of a damp,
dirty dog in the sun."

"Yes there is."

"I don't want to hear about it."

"Hey, Rabbit, this guy's okay, n'est-ce pooch? He takes good care of
you when you don't need to be taken care of, huh? Maybe we could teach

two old dogs new tricks. What do you say, little sister? Is this not the very man we have been looking for?"

With those words, I become quite wary. "So, what are you selling?"

"What makes you think I am selling anything?"

I point to the wormy wood, which has mostly transformed into an elaborate little mask as we have been talking.

"This? No, no, this is for William Love. You like it? It is made from the wood of an old church he bought. Plenty of worm holes. Makes the carving an instant antique. Most of the flat boards he has local artists use to paint instant ancient icons. Mostly St. George and the Dragon. Very popular with the sucker tourists."

"Besides looking very old, your little mask there looks very North American Indian. I've seen ones just like it in the American Museum of Natural History in New York City."

Abis grins mischievously. "Hey, you catch on fast."

But I don't catch on at all.

"Do I look Greek to you?" he asks.

"Well, no, maybe. I don't know. I guess."

"Uh, uh, teach, no jumping to conclusions."

"Wait a minute, how'd you know I was a teacher?"

"What do you think we get here, bartenders from Brooklyn? Observe, Manny-man. Learn. Ninety-five percent of the visitors we get here are teachers. They dream about this place, then they save plenty of euros and dollars and yen and what such and they come to see if the shoe fits. Other five percent, could be anything. You bring lunch?"

"Are you selling sandwiches?"

"No, I'm panhandling, Pilgrim."

"Pretty good John Wayne."

"I watch all those old movies on DVD. Re-mastered. Colorized. Big screen television. High definition. Almost better than life, huh?"

He stares at me intently.

"Wait a minute, you've got a big screen H.D. T.V. and a DVD and you're out here in the middle of nowhere bumming lunch? And didn't I see you in the first class section of the plane?"

"No, Manny-man. *He* has the big screen television. William Love. He just lets me watch it. You know. On the yacht. He gets plenty of movies flown in from his pals in the States. He's probably on his way back already. Or pretty soon. First he's got to pick up the goods. How do you say, 'stash the swag and get.' Got his gold mine to salt back home. Know what I mean?"

"Not one word."

"Sooo, what you got for lunch?"

I hold out my brown bag. He snatches it and sticks his nose in. "Okaaay. Protestant white bread. Could turn that into God. Looks fresh. Ooooh, and ultra pasteurized American soft-serve processed cheese. What have you done, Manny-man, brought this stuff from home?"

"My friends weren't sure I would like the food here. I packed a loaf of bread and a jar of cheese spread, just in case."

He shakes his head the way my dad did when he disapproved of something. Then he grins. "Ahh, bottled water. At least that's local. Oooh, and what's this? Candy bar. I used to know a stripper by that name in Salt Lake City."

"Salt Lake City? Try again."

"Oh, no, it was in Cairo."

"You're Egyptian?"

"No, no, Cairo, Georgia, USA. Pronounced KAY-Row. I make the mis-pronouncement on purpose. Oh, and fruit. Lots of fiber for the bowls."

"Sometimes I get constipated when I travel."

"Now you got fruit. Take care of everything. Good boy. Real regular fellow. Come, follow me to the eating place."

He walks back to the navel stone. I follow. He takes off his handkerchief, spreads it out and sets my lunch on it. "Please," he says, "I insist. You must join me."

"Abis, we can't use an ancient monument for a picnic table!"

His brow wrinkles. "Why not? We're hungry."

"We might damage it."

"It's made of stone, Manny-man. It has been here out in the elementals for, what? Two, three thousand years? How can we damage it? This is not a hammer in my hand. It is an apple. Formerly *your* apple!"

I shrug. "Well, I guess it'll be all right."

As he begins to divide the food with his dirty hands, I stand next to him. The dog curls up and falls fast asleep with her damp butt on my left shoe.

"Here, Rabbit," he says, tossing her a bit of apple. She doesn't move.

"Why'd you name your dog, 'Rabbit'?"

He waves his hand. "No, no, Manny-man, that is not her name. That is just what I call her sometimes."

"I don't get it."

"She is a special breed dog. A, um, rabbit hound. Like me. You know what you have forgotten to bring?"

"Catsup?"

"WINE!!" he shouts so loudly my neck stiffens. The ladies and gentlemen of the Putney-Porter Unitarian Church of Wilmington, Delaware all look over at us. Abis grins at them and waves. Some wave back. Eventually they all move on with the guide. Abis turns to me. "No wine?"

"Sorry, just water."

"Nothing but a temporary problem," he says and lumbers off through some bushes, then behind the ruins. I have this odd sensation I'm in the middle of a movie set. Everything seems so unreal in this shimmering heat.

The dog continues to sleep, fitfully, on my shoe, transferring bits of dung from her fur to my sock every time she squirms. Once or twice I try to slide my foot out from under her. Each time she growls deeply and I keep still.

Five minutes later, Abis trots back into view, carrying a large English-style wicker picnic basket with the handle in his mouth, and, one in each hand, two enormous, dark green bottles of what turns out to be fine white Cretian wine. His ugly dog–I suppose the right word for this beast would be homely–rises and trots to him, sort of grinning as dogs do. I think of Circe and wonder if this is some of her handiwork.

When he gets closer, I can see the bottles are dripping with condensation as if they had just been plucked from a bucket of cold water and shaved ice. They seem to have come from the other side of civilization.

He climbs up on the navel stone, sits down in the lotus position, and opens the picnic basket. The lid squeaks and hinges back toward me, so I can't see in. He pulls out a fluffy, bright yellow cotton towel and wraps one of the bottles in it for insulation. Next, he conjures up a round, fragrant, loaf of bread. With his bare, unwashed hands, God knows what they've scratched, to say nothing of those bird guts I think I saw him pull apart, he breaks off a piece and hands it to me.

"Thank you," I say as calmly as I can, and sort of rub the crust on my shirt, pick away the pieces I think he's actually touched, and taste for the first time in years real bread, with hard, thin crust and a soft, warm center. I bite off a second hunk lustily and chew like my new savage friend. Then I stop in mid-chew, suddenly aware that spectators are surrounding us.

As they stand about and gawk, I feel guilty and as exposed as if I'm performing a sex act in public. Then this horrible thought slams into my head like a brick: what if this basket belongs to one of them? What if they call a cop?

I grin.

The blue-haired lady from Delaware City says, "Mr. Markovitz, do you realize you are possibly making grease stains on a foreign temple? We must accept and respect the sacred shrines off all peoples, even the savage pagans."

I'm about to stammer out a feeble explanation when Abis leaps to my defense. "Ha, this is what I ask you, blue-haired lady from Des Moines, who died and made you Oracle, huh? This is my shrine and I say off with you, beat it, go away, scram. This is the libation part of my sacred holy rites, and also a delicious part of lunch. Again I say unto thee with this sacred word: scrambola!"

"That is very rude, young man. I don't care who you are, I am an American citizen and I have just as much right to be here as you do. How would you like it if I called the security guards?"

"Ha, guess what, blue-haired lady, from Des Moines, this is not America. Here there is no security!" He lumbers down from the rock, puts his forehead to the ground, and blows her a kiss from the wrong end.

I cover my face with my hands. The dog growls and yaps. The woman steps back and puts hers hands to her chest. My cheeks feel like two charcoal briquettes. But for the first time since Sara died, I am suppressing real laughter, too.

I press my lips together, but pretty soon, I'm trumpeting, and Abis and I are holding onto each other's shoulders for support. By the time I look around again, the ladies and gentlemen from the Delaware Unitarian Church are gone, and Abis is offering me more bread. "Fresh baked," he says, "still hot from the oven, and here is Greek cheese. A meal in itself."

I take a hunk of the cheese. The bread he had given me I seem to have squeezed into a thin wafer. But in my mouth it still has a lovely, fragrant texture. Meanwhile Abis is scrounging about in the picnic basket again. He hauls out hunks and wheels of more cheese, a napkin full of black olives, fresh apricots wrapped in mauve tissue, a small crumpled bag of fresh pistachios, two plump, fragrant brown pears, and four perfect pieces of baklava in a small tan bag with grease stains halfway up its sides.

"For later, on the back of a donkey," he says and winks. "And if you do not like baklava, two perfect, ripe, American Milky Ways all the way from the United States of Atlanta. Hey, how come I did not see you get off the plane, huh? You took a different bus into town than Abis? You take a taxi?"

"I, uh, walked."

"Good for you! Taxi drivers here are ignorant. One third do not even speak English!"

He pulls two squat, thick-stemmed glasses from the picnic basket, opens a bottle of wine and pours. "Usually," he says, "I drink retsina for lunch. Right from the bottle. You know, in my village. But for you, Manny-man, I have stolen the best!"

I look around wildly. "Oh, jeeze, you *did* steal this basket."

"Hey, hey, relax, don't toss out your cookies, n'est-ce puke? I did not steal this basket, okay?"

"You swear?"

"Absolutely. It is only the wine that I stole."

I swallow hard, remembering that movie where the guy's toes are beaten as flat as Florida with a ball-peen hammer in, I'm pretty sure it was a Greek prison. Or was it somewhere in the Far East?

"Hey, hey, not to worry. I stole the wine from William Love, so you see, it is okay. No, really. He lets me steal what I need. It is all right if I only take what I need, not what I want, okay? I am only borrowing what I can't give back. Love forgives our trespasses."

Abis pours more wine into our glasses, climbs up on the navel stone, and sits.

"Must be quite a guy, this William Love. You sure he really exists?"

Immediately Abis stands up, nearly falling off the navel stone. He whips his hat from his head and holds it over his heart. "To me he is a god! A god among men! A god even among Greeks! Even among my people! I say he is of my people. To us, our greatest crime is stinginess. Huh? Huh? And William Love is no criminal. Not that way, anyway."

Abis winks, sits down, nearly toppling again, and smiles. Then he puffs out his silly hat and puts it back on his head.

"Well, then, to William Love," I say, and raise a glass.

Abis does the same, then takes his small carving knife in one hand, picks up a wheel of cheese in the other, then stabs instead of the cheese, his own right hand. The blood begins to flow profusely as he screams out what is no doubt a vile curse in that same foreign language he had used on his dog. Then he begins to howl.

His dog howls with him. "Rabbit," he says calmly, "why do you get so upset? This wound is nothing, a wad of doggie spittle. I am such a fool. I tell you, I would carry dog shit in my hands if you gave some to me. Here, sweetheart, I will prove it to you; defecate into your brother's hands; I will carry it."

Abis rips off a piece of the towel he's wrapped around the second wine bottle and bandages his wound. Then he says to the dog, "Such a fool the Great Earthmaker has chosen for your master. Ah, well, people are always telling me this. My right hand is always fighting with my left and I am such a fool I am powerless to stop them." He holds up both his hands in front of his face. "Stop it, you two! Stop it!" he screams. "Or you will both have to stand in the corner!"

I'm just sitting there with my mouth wide open. But I'm too tipsy to move about and I figure the wine is the reason Abis is acting silly, too.

He turns back to me and holds up his glass. "To William Love, wherever he is today."

I lurch forward, uneasily. We touch glasses then I drink down all the wine in my glass. "You say you usually drink retsina with lunch?"

"Amen."

"But for me you bring the good stuffing?"

"Amen."

"Okay, okay, that dodin't make sense, seeing as you obviously already had this wine in your pissesson when we met. Unless you-"

"What?"He leans forward, a suspicious look on his face.

"You did steal this swine."

"Okay, okay, no. I did not steal it at all. William gave it to me. Especially for you."

"How did you know I would show? Hey, that rhymes! Know, show, glow, flow. See? It doesn't make sense."

"Not you, you. Just someone you. You know what I mean?"

"No."

"Okay, okay, look. A whole bunch of someones, they come along to Delphi, right? And the right someone is going to offer his lunch to share with me, right? That is how I will know it's the right someone. 'You will know him by the lunch he offers.' These are the very words William Love said unto me."

"So he sent you?"

"William, he doesn't send anyone anywhere. He suggests. Yes? No?"

"To find me?"

"To find someone."

"To share lunch wit?"

"And two bottles of good wine." He pulls the cork from the second one.

"No more for me, tanks." I put my hand over the rim of my glass. "I'm too dizzy from the first 'en."

"Then this one will clear the head, no?"

I can't argue with logic like that. Not in my condition. My hand lifts off the rim and Abis fills the glass again.

"Where do you come from?"

Abis stands, nearly toppling off the navel stone again. "Up above." He points vaguely toward the mountains. "No, no, wait, from down below." He whirls and points, I assume, to a place beyond the valley and the hills, toward the sea. "In a village by the bay. The ship is in the harbor. The yacht. William Love's. We must go to it. And the great villa in the hills above town on the other side. Come, come, drink up. Then we journey down. I will take you there. Through the valley and the hills."

"When I first saw you and Rabbit down below, what were you doing? I swear it looked like, like you were tearing apart a small animal."

"Ha, ha, no. I was, um, was chasing down my old shoe. Yes, my old shoe. This one."

He takes off one of his sandals and sticks it in his mouth. When he goes to pull it out again, his mouth is growling at his fingers and his teeth grip hard while his hand fights to work his sandal loose. Finally, the hand wins. He throws the sandal as far as he can. Rabbit yips and dashes after it as if it were made of sirloin. "I was teaching stupid dog how to stalk rabbits for me to read. Soo, you bring your luggage? It is in the bus? Good. I will take it. I will bring three donkeys and we will go to see the sights and William Love."

Now it is decision time for me. I'm like Hamlet, debating whether to follow his father's ghost. Does my usual, probably instinctive, reluctance overcome my would-be sense of adventure? Like Hamlet, I don't set my life at a pin's fee. Unlike Hamlet, I'm a damn coward. Adventure calls. Exciting, life-changing adventure. I came to Greece to change my life. So here is opportunity knocking, and as usual, where am I? Cowering behind the door.

"No," I say quietly, "I think not."

"Exactly what you need, Manny-man. You! You think! All the time you think! Where has your thinking gotten you so far, huh? Now you *do*! You do not think, you *do*! Come, I say, on the back of a donkey. Riding on an ass. Asses to asses. You remember? Don't look so sad, I make a joke. Adventure with me. Learn a few new tricks. You are still not such an old puppy. Come. Eat strange food. Meet strange women. Big breasted women. Learn what it is like away from pure reason. Come. You meet William Love. He is much funnier than Abis."

"I don't know."

"Look over there. You want to get back on the bus with them?"

"Well, no. I guess you got me there. Oh, what the hell."

Before I can say another word, he lumbers up the path, motioning all the time for me to follow. His dog sneaks up behind me and growls. Then she runs up ahead to her master. I rise and follow, toward the tourist busses, past the ancient shrines.

## TWO

All this time, I'm mumbling, "Am I really going to follow this guy to God-knows-where just to meet this pal, or boss of his, or God-knows-what? What if William Love doesn't even exist? What if he's just luring me away to rob me or something? What if he's planning to slit my throat and leave me dying, gasping for air like a carp out of water in the hemlock bushes? What does he really want? What does it matter?

Abis ambles over to the long line of tourist busses. Somehow he goes directly to mine. How does he know? He raps gently on the glass door. The driver, perched on his seat like a cormorant in a rusty cage, is reading a newspaper, actively ignoring Abis, who now begins slamming the glass door with his open palm. He screams, "You know I am here! I cannot be ignored!" The driver dismisses him with a wave of the hand.

His dog, I guess I'll have to continue calling her Rabbit since he never will tell me her real name, capers about on her hind legs in front of the bus. Spectators gather. Some applaud. Rabbit yelps and turns somersaults. More spectators congregate. I can see by his body language that the bus driver is really, really pissed. In an entirely different sense, I'm pissed. Otherwise, why would I even contemplate going with Abis?

Rabbit barks twice, then leaps onto the hood of the bus. How can such a little dog jump that high? She squashes her nose against the windshield. It's really got to look grotesque from the driver's side of the glass, to say nothing of the smudges of snot. Just as I'm wondering how much longer the driver will stand it, he jerks open the door violently and hops out. Not two inches from Abis's face, he screams something in Greek. I don't understand, of course, but just from the tone you can tell it's impolite. He and Abis exchange many words, punctuated by lively hand gestures.

"I tinkhepiss," I shout.

The driver screams something else in Greek. Abis clutches at his own chest in a mock heart attack. He takes off his hat and holds it toward the heavens, like he's expecting someone to drop him a tip. His dark brown eyes remain unblinking, but his mouth is wide open and gulping. The driver's face is purple-red. With his fingers, he imitates a low bodily function. Abis grins and points to me. The driver, a little, bald-headed guy, stretches his chin up and stands on his toes trying to peer above the crowd. Repeatedly, he jumps in the air to get a glimpse of me.

"Is sokay!" I shout and give the driver what I hope is the universal "okay" sign with my raised right hand. I smile. The driver spits. I push though the crowd to get to him, grovel in my pocket for my wad of Euros, peel off a chunk, and hold them out. The driver shrugs as if to say,

"You want to leave my protection and go off with a madman, it's your funeral, pal."

As I continue to hold out the bills, the driver hesitates one last time, maybe hoping I'll come to my senses. Then he shuffles to the luggage compartment, opens it and plops my brand-new leather suitcase rather deliberately into a mound of muddy dirt where a motor home has recently discharged some liquid which I sincerely hope is just plain water. I hand him the money.

Abis screams, "Too much! You will ruin him! You will ruin all of Greece! You will ruin the whole world! Americans! I spit upon your economic dominance!" He bends over. His spittle lands on his own crotch.

"Oh, hell, Abis, i's snot even ten bucks."

"Ten bucks?" His forehead wrinkles.

"Don't play dumb. You know what I mean. Don' tell me you've forgotten th'strange rate. You're not stoopid."

"No, Manny-man. I must offend myself against your charges; I *am* stupid. Very, very stupid. How much is ten bucks in American dollars?"

I throw up my hands. Abis laughs and grabs the handle of my suitcase. While I stare, open mouthed, he scuffs my new leather bag over two hundred yards of sharp marble rock and course sand to three donkeys who happen to waiting for us up the road toward Delphi. Why he doesn't bring donkey to luggage is beyond me. The reigns of the asses are held by a small boy.

As I trot to catch up, Abis shoos the little boy away and hoists my bag onto the back of the smallest donkey, a grey-brown beast with long, dark eyelashes and what seems like a wistful smile. She already has a small, bruised and stained brown leather satchel on one loin. Abis lashes my bag to the other. Bits of silica dribble from its abrasions.

The remaining two donkeys are equipped with saddles, thick padded blankets and rope bridles with faded red tassels. They stand about, shifting their weight from foot to foot, grinding their teeth. The sound makes my hair stand on end.

"These beasts, they, they do belong to you, right?"

He shrugs.

"They William Love's?"

No answer.

"Abis?"

Abis rubs his chin for a moment. Then he grins. "Sure, sure. Love's beasts. I take care of them for him. Gives me stable employment!" He laughs his infectious laugh at his own stupid pun and I laugh, too. "I take care of all his animal needs. I am his angel!" He laughs again and points to the beasts. "We ride now. To him."

I gulp hard and try to mount. It's no use. I have never ridden an animal before in my life. Not even a birthday-party pony. I'm scared of them. But I'm still tipsy enough to try. With Abis's help I'm soon aboard, or rather half on, half off. Swaying. We move forward. Gesturing wildly with my hands, I begin my farewell address to the Delaware crones, who have gathered about us. I don't want them to worry about me, I explain. I want them to know that I am fully sober now, and fully and soberly in control of my life and the whole damn universe. But my words don't seem to be coming out too clearly.

One of them says he is going to call the American Embassy on my behalf. Another will write her congresswoman. My friend with the arthritic cats says, "Oh, Professor Markovitz, I will call your family immediately on this cellular telephone no matter what the roaming charges if you do not stop this tom-foolish nonsense at once!"

"You can't call my family, ma'am. No telephone service in Paradise, yet." I imagine the headlines in next week's *National Inquirer*: "Direct Dialing to Heaven Established. Area Code 403 Reassigned Soon."

I attempt to explain all this, but my lips are still not moving very well. As I try, Abis laughs so heartily he nearly loses his mount. I shut up and hold onto the handle thingie on the saddle. We begin our trek down the narrow, white gravel footpath toward the parking lot. I look about. This is such a beautiful, magical place. The green wilds and groves, the marble ruins of a civilization that still means so much to me. But, Dear God, if it could only seem real to me again. If only I could wake up and come alive again. Reality lies all about, but it is not substantial to me anymore. Only Sara is actual to me. And she's dead. I see her presence everywhere, in the dying flowers and the withering, wasting leaves. I'm going down and down in the undertow, and trusting a madman, or trying to, a fool, to pull me out.

We pass the line of tourist busses. My ex-driver sits and reads his paper. It's as thin as he. Why doesn't he bring a good thick book? I shout, "G'bye, g'bye, an' tank you!"

Without lifting his head to look, he holds up a few fingers and jabs with them toward the sky. It could be friendly. He *is* smiling. Mediterranean ways are so hard to understand.

But Abis understands. He laughs. "Been many years since I have tried doing *that* on the back of a moving donkey!"

We leave behind the paved tourist road and travel down and down and down again for hours on a narrow mountain path that winds between the pines and cypresses and rocks. Above us are the blue-grey cliffs, beneath our feet, the yellow-ivory stones and grey-white gravel. All the world here seems to be made of weathered stuff. Time-worn boulders jut from rocky soil. We pass though fields of yellow-green planted vegetation. Every bit of it seems to be withering into shades of brown in the late summer sun. Abis sees that I am seeing it, and he says, "Soon the harvest will begin."

Every planted field is turning toward its harvest. I think of the dried-out, browning leaves of the books in the university library. What are they turning to? I was with them when I should have been somewhere else. And now it rents my soul. "Abis," I say, "I'm a son of a bitch! No offense to my mama."

But he doesn't hear. The hot, dry air chafes my skin and makes it seem to flake away and settle on the dry, hot stones. The stones themselves vibrate in the heat as if alive. Everywhere life extrudes from the stones. Half-dead vegetation grows from every pore, every fissure, every minute crack, clinging and clinging, trying to stay alive. Trying to grow and flourish. Flowers sprout from stalks that otherwise seem dead. Patches of lush green verdure intersperse the planted fields of dry, burnt umber. Where and how do they summon up the nectar to grow? I envy them.

# THREE

At the lower depths of the valley we pass a few deciduous trees. Tall and broad, their leaves are limp but healthy. We travel on, sweating hard, replacing the water we lose with long drafts of warm, white Cretan wine. I keep peering down through the blue-white haze of shaded valley of the olive groves and beyond the trees to the blue Aegean Sea. Miles in the distance, great ships ride the azure water, tankers, and freighters and pleasure yachts, and two-masted schooners. Which, if any, belong to this fabled William Love that Abis says he must take me to?

Soon my view of the water becomes blocked as we enter a low, dipping plateau filled with fragrant pines. The ground is littered with their rusty needles. The wind picks up. More needles fall from the trees. The sky turns darker blue, then steely-grey. I see it now as the ancient Greeks perhaps had seen it, dark storm clouds from the gatherer Zeus, drifting in from the Aegean, a gift from his brother Poseidon, the sea. I'm so intoxicated I can believe in them.

Rain falls lightly, more like mist at first, then becomes a shower of silver, then a virtual waterfall. We are inundated. What can we do? We're utterly exposed. The downpour doesn't last too long, but when it ends there is nothing dry on ass, man, dog, or luggage. I am happy, though. The air smells sweet and new.

As I start to recite a little silent prayer to God for the flowers and fragrant air, the wind comes about and my nose is slammed with the fetid stench of wet dog and donkey. I must hold my sleeve to my nose to avoid dying. I'm about to curse when the sun comes out again and the smell begins to moderate as the animals dry out or I get used to their pungent stench.

Rabbit sniffs and yips about the donkey's hooves, running ahead, falling behind, sniffing here and there, panting, rolling in the sand or any pile of sheep manure she happens upon. My poor donkey's feet shift jerkily from side to side and back and forth as he tries to keep his balance under the limp, unsteady fish that rides his back to no avail. I tumble forward into the mud. Abis pulls up. "At this rate to get there, we won't get there. Ah well, it is good for you, then it must be good for me, *ne, ne?*"

He slips off his donkey like a boneless bear and reaches out a hand to pull me up. I reach for him and try to stand, but slip in the mud again and flip onto my stomach. I try to get out of the mud by doing the breast stroke. It's impossible. The water is only eight inches deep. I flip over and sit with my legs sprawled in front of me. Abis lights a cigarette.

"Watch this," he says. With the lit cigarette still dangling, he slam-dunks his face into the water. His mouth and nose remain submerged so long I begin to fear he's drowning. I reach over to raise him up by the hair. Just as my outreached hand gets near, he lifts his head out of the water with as much force as he'd slammed it in. The cigarette's still lit!

"How do you did that?"

"Hee, hee, a great trick, huh?"

"But how?"

"Watch, I'll show you." He sticks the filtered end of the cigarette to the top of his tongue, then he curls his tongue up a bit and slowly takes the entire cigarette into his mouth without letting the lit end touch any part of him. With the cigarette entirely inside his mouth, he closes it, grins, and raises both palms to the sky. Then he opens his mouth again and the cigarette folds out neatly as he rolls out his tongue. "This I do quickly like a conjurer as I am ducking my head into the water and nobody ever sees me tuck it inside my mouth. They think like you that I have defied the powers of the waters. Watch, I will do it again, this time at regular speed."

He begins, then lets out a horrible scream, spits out the cigarette and splashes muddy water onto his tongue. "Why do I do this? Manny-man, I am a fool! A fool!"

I'm dumbfounded.

"Rabbit," he says, "Oh, my dog, do you know your older brother is a fool? Don't answer me now, sweetness. But you must think about this and when we are alone you can tell me in your own voice."

He sits down beside me in the mud puddle then turns over on his stomach. "What a good place to pee."

I shift over a bit. He hums. Then he turns on his back, sits up, draws his heels to his buttocks, wraps his arms about his knees and says, "Manny-man, there are overhanging rocks below. Like little caves. There tonight we shall find shelter from the harsh glare of the stars. All Americans love to camp out, right?"

I sit up and shout, "Nay, negative, *au contraire, nein, nyet, boo,* and no!," gesturing wildly with my right hand. I would gesture with both hands but firmly believe just then that my left hand has gone on with the luggage. Then I discover I am sitting on it. "Ah," I say, pulling it out from under me. "Abis, this is an anniversary."

"It is?"

"Yes, indeedly. Two million years ago today my ancestor Og Markovitz and his wife, Sadie Berkowitz-Markovitz with their whole and entire reform congregation came down from the trees and into caves. Then it was a mikey, mikey, no, mighty, mighty struggle to get my people out of the caves and into air-condidoned condominimums."

"Why do you tell me this story?"

"Don't you see? To stay here in the woods, to camp out, would betray two million years of evolution."

"But, Manny, we have no choice. We must stay. Necessity is the mother of detention."

He puts his hands behind his head and stretches out supine in the mud. Rabbit hops onto his chest and licks his muddy face.

"No motels around here?"

He laughs.

"How about a peasant's cottage?"

He stands up quickly. Rabbit yowls as she slides off his chest and splashes into the mud. "Be reasonable, Manny-man. Look at us. Even the poorest peasant would not take in drunks covered in slime." He stiffens his back and puts his hand to his heart. "*I* would not take me in. And I, sir, am a peasant, or my name is not Abos of Euboea!"

He totters, then falls back on his buttocks, creating great splashes that nearly engulf me and do engulf the dog. In a moment, she rises, sputtering.

"Hmmm," I say, standing up. "Then we shall become clean again. Aren't there streams? Surely a country as advanced as Greece has clear streams."

"Yes, but what good will it do? Then we would be clean, wet drunks."

"Hmmm." I sit back down, then lie on my back, letting my head down into the mud. My index finger points to the sky. "I've got it! We could sober up!"

"I would rather camp out."

"Yes. You're right. Well, so beat it, then. To hell with two million years of progress. Where has it gotten me? Depressed! Great granddaddy Og, we are here!"

"Have more wine," Abis suggests. "And let us ride. We make camp in just six hours."

"I'm so dizzy I don't think I can get out of this mud."

"Ah. This is why Abis is with you. To lift his pal out of the great morass he is in."

He stands, gives me his hand, slips back down in the mud and begins to scream wildly. "Help! Help! A beast is pulling me under! Help!"

He flaps one arm frantically, spraying us both with muck. His other arm is hidden below the water.

"Hmmm?" I say.

"The tie snake! He has me by the balls! Oh, Gods above, below and sideways, I shall have to cut them off or be pulled under and drowned!" He looks around. "Oh, say, Manny-man, you are a professor, tell me, will they grow back? Hand me a knife. I shall cut them off and throw them away and cut off half my penis; then it will only be twice the size of any morbid man's. I shall chop it up and from each little piece delicate and lightly-scented flowers will grow. These I shall fertilize with my doggie's dung personally, as many of my tribe have said I would."

"What's a tie snake?"

He stops floundering about and looks hard at me. At the same time he pats Rabbit's head, depositing mounds of slime on her skull until it is piled up like a cap as ridiculous as his own, which, by the way, has remained somehow on his head, though his feather is now a bit more limp. He says, "Don't they have tie snakes in this nation?"

"Hell, I don't know. I'm a tourist here. You're the native."

He wrinkles his brow. "No, Manny-man, this is not my country. It is yours! No, no, wait, it has all come back to me now. You are right. It is back home that the tie snakes live. In the swamp lands of Abis Ababa. Or wherever home is. So, what has me by the balls?"

He looks down, trying to peer into the muddy water that now barely covers his groin. He reaches into the water with his right hand. "Ahh, it is me. I have me by the balls with my left hand. I am severely hurting myself. What shall I do, Manny-man?"

"Let go."

He nods. "This is more comfortable."

Rabbit barks. She's so thoroughly caked with mud she looks like a giant grey slug, a decided improvement.

"Come, we must go," Abis says, waving me on.

We get out of the mud and begin chasing the donkeys. But they will not let us mount. We have to stagger three steps behind them until they lead us to a stream of clear mountain water. When we strip to the skin to get in, I see that Abis has a curious tattoo above his left breast. It's a small circle divided into four pie parts, with a smaller circle in the center, sort of like what you see when you look through the telescopic sights of a rifle.

The water is bone-chilling cold. We wade in anyway, with our dirty clothes in our hands. The mud turns to silt. We become clean again, and pseudo-sober. I come out of the water with my wad of wet things as soon as I can. My lips are cold as clams. I stick the bottom lip out and try to see if it is blue. I can't tell. "Know what, Abis? Forests should be equipped with mirrors."

"They are," he says.

The sun is out again. Unsteadily, I begin spreading my shirt and shorts on a pine tree limb.

"Manny-man, you must come back into the water!"

I turn to look, but he's out of sight. From the sound of his voice, I figure he's beyond the bend in the stream.

"Come and help me catch this terrapin for our dinner, Manny-man. It is a great delicacy which any peasant, or nobleman, too, even William Love, would give many beads and gorgets for."

I wade back into the stream. "Abis? Where are you?"

No answer.

I wade upstream and down, turning around and around until I am dizzy. He is nowhere to be found. "Abis!"

I wade back to shore. He's not there, either. The shoreline looks different. The donkeys are gone! Everything I have is gone, even my clothes! "Heeelp!" I scream. The only thing he has left me is a large turtle, lying on its back, struggling atop the pine needles. What the hell am I going to do? I have no money and no identification! I don't even know where the hell I am! And I'm stark raving naked!

# FOUR

In my whole life, I've never been naked in public. Now what? The turtle's still struggling on its back. I bend down and turn it over. As it pokes its head out and looks at me, I ask the ugly little beast, "Any suggestions?" It doesn't seem to venture any. My clothes, my baggage, my passport, and my money have just been stolen by a liar, a trickster and a thief. I can't say he stole my dignity. I gave that away. Well, what the hell did I expect? He *told* me he was a liar, a trickster and a thief. Did I figure he was lying when he said he was lying? What's that oxymoronic sentence they use in freshman philosophy classes? "This sentence is a lie." I'm caught in the middle of that sentence. I wanted to believe in him. I believed I could believe him. But that's me, the world's most naive human being over the age of six, always taking everyone at his word.

The turtle looks to the right and the left, then up at me. "Okay," I say aloud, "let's go over this calmly and rationally." Of course, I'm well aware I'm saying this to a turtle. "What the hell, you seem to be a reasonable enough reptile. How did we both get into this mess? I'm as helpless as the day I was born, and you might possibly be eaten. By me, if I can't find anything else real soon. We've both got to make our way naked among strangers. Only for you, it's your natural condition."

I try to pick up the beast. "Whoa!" I yell as the damn thing starts to put up a fight, kicking and clawing and scratching and snapping. Trying to turn it is like trying to shift a spinning gyroscope. It falls from my hands and plops into the sand. My hands are scratched and bleeding. Are turtles poisonous? I check for fang marks on my hands and fingers, see none, take a deep breath and try to scoop the beast up again. How can something just twelve inches around put up such a struggle? Damn.

Five times I try. Five times he plops to the ground. But the sixth time he withdraws into his shell and locks himself in. Has he given up? Warily, just in case he tries to come out again and sting, I lift him by the edges. He stays in. Holding him straight out in front of me with both arms stiff, I start walking through the brush, looking for a road, a house, or a scrap of cloth to gird my loins. Mostly I'm trying to think of a plausible explanation for anyone I run into. I decide on one word: *mugged*. That's my story and I'm sticking to it.

After about twenty minutes of following the stream, I smell a wood fire. In the distance a thin slip of smoke is rising. It's got to be a chimney. Moving toward it more quickly I come to a clearing and spy though the bushes a small, neat, one-story cottage with a red tile roof. Under a pine tree, rocking slowly in a rustic chair, is an old woman in a black widow's dress. Holding the beast in front of my crotch, praying silently it's not a snapping turtle, I move forward. As soon as the old woman sees me I'll start looking pathetic.

But what will I say? I know just two words in Greek, "Yes," and "socks." Neither seems appropriate. I had ditched my Greek dictionary as so much excess baggage before leaving Athens when I discovered more street and shop signs in my own language than theirs. Almost everyone in the city loved to entertain Americans in English, or be indifferent in Greek. But what about here in the provinces?

I'm beginning to panic and try to get as tight a grip on myself as I have on the turtle."One, two, three, "I say to myself, then barge out of the bushes, making a hand gesture like someone clunking me over the head, nearly losing my grip on the reptile in the process, yelling, "Tourist! Mugged! Tourist! Mugged!" Fumbling to keep my private parts hidden, I say, "Uh, me American tourist. Me mugged. Look. Got it? Mugged!," then involuntarily in Greek, scream "Yes," and "socks."

The old woman's mouth is wide open. She points and grins. She's toothless. Then she starts laughing so hard I'm afraid she'll have an embolism. I stand still. My face flushes. She rises, turns her back to me and goes into her little cottage. Now what? I'm dumbfounded. More dumb than founded. She returns surprisingly fast, considering her age and weight, with one of her black dresses and holds it out to me. It doesn't look clean. She gestures for me to put it on.

I come forward, bow my head to her, and take the dress with my un-turtled hand, back away into the bushes and dress. The hem comes to my shins. It feels surprisingly cool, but very, very strange. The damn thing buttons from the wrong side, too, and smells as if it had been worn for two weeks straight during hand to hand combat with a fetid goat.

I return to the old woman, carrying the turtle as an offering. She takes it and yells something. A small boy appears from behind the house. Good God, I'm thinking, that looks like the kid that held the donkeys in Delphi!

The boy takes the turtle in his small hands, struggling with it as the ferocious reptile starts to come out of its shell. He runs with it into the house.

"Was mugged," I continue. She doesn't move. I say it louder, then add, "Thank you for your help so far, by the way. May I use your telephone? Umm, *el telephono? La telephone?*" I make a gesture like someone dialing. Do they have touch tone service here? I switch to a gesture like someone punching in some numbers and holding a phone to his ear.

The old woman says, "You talk so strange. Are you a nudist from California?"

I'm startled by her sudden admission of English. More startled by her throaty accent. It's not quite native English but certainly not English spoken by a Greek. Nor, come to think of it, does she look Greek. More Asian. Perhaps Mongolian. She has high cheekbones and a wide, handsome face and straight white hair pulled back into a bun.

"You speak English. Thank God."

"Funny thing to thank God for."

"Please, ma'am may I use your phone?" Again I cock my ear over and make a gesture like someone dialing.

She imitates my dialing gesture, except she mistakenly dials around her ear. Then she shakes her head. "No, phone here, mister nudist. Why are we using sign language? Is that how it is done in California? I have never been to the West Coast. Do people out there really wear beads and fringes?"

"Not since the nineteen sixties," I say."Where's the nearest phone?"

"In town. Take you two, three days by foot."

"I don't think I can very well travel in this. Do you know where I might be able to get men's clothing?"

"Not unless my son-in-law returns."

"When will that be?"

"Next year. He is out hunting. On assignment. With him, you never know."

"Is the boy your grandson? Could I send him for some men's clothes somewhere? I'll gladly pay."

"Where you keep your money? You got pockets in your skin?"

"I, I mean, when I get someone to wire me some, or something."

"Come in. Rest. Have some delicious soup. Terrapin. With bread. Raisons. And hominy."

"You have hominy in Greece?"

"I bring it with me. The bread I bake here. On location. The raisons are local, naturally. Who takes raisons on so long a trip? Come into the house and eat. I'll send my grandson to bring back my son-in-law. He can't have gone far yet. The boy will find word of him by the grace of the gods above and below. My son-in-law will know what to do with you. He has three donkeys. Sometimes he is a clever man."

"Wait a minute! What's your son-in-law's name?"

"We call him Chufee."

I let out my breath in a long sigh."I am called Manny Markovitz."

"Is that your name?"

"Yes, of course."

"Your true name?"

"Yes."

"I am called Icki. Here and abroad. Some call me Selu, naturally."

I nod, but I have no idea what she's talking about.

She says, "You eat now. Bread. Turtle soup, later. And later, too, you will tell me who your people are. Where you are really from. It is okay. I am not afraid if you are from down below."

We go into the house and eat the bread and raisons. Then I lie down on her bed and sleep the sleep of the utterly befuddled.

I have no idea how long I'm out, but when I wake it's dark. My head is aching. My sinuses must be the size of Greenland, Mercator projection. I feel woozy. My eyes won't focus right. I sit up. The old woman is weaving on a loom by the light of a kerosene lamp. She sees that I'm awake and brings me terrapin soup, thickened with hominy. It smells terrible. It tastes worse. I eat it gratefully, sitting at her little pine table. Despite the way my stomach churns, I get it all into me and soon feel less nauseated.

All the time I'm eating, she sits on the floor next to me, her legs folded under her the way Japanese women used to do. We are joined by the little boy and a beautiful young woman. "Hello," I say.

She nods.

"This is my aunt," the little boy says in English, without a trace of accent.

Someone knocks on the door. "Love," the old woman says, and shuffles to open it. As she reaches for the doorknob, the door springs open. Matter-of-factly she says, "My son-in-law is home," and steps aside to let him in. He bounds into the room.

It is Abis, of course. Fully clothed, clean and dry. Grinning. Holding up my clothes, dripping wet and covered in slimy, stinky mud, worse than when I saw them last. "He, he," he says, pointing to my dress, "now you have really gone a-broad, huh? I am making a little joke on you, Manny-man. So this is where you went!"

"Where I went? Where the hell did you go?"

"To catch turtles for soup. As I told you I would. I walked upstream. Why did you not follow in the water after me? I put turtles on the opposite bank for us to take here to my second, no, no, third? No, no, wait. It is my first and third mother-in-law to cook for us. Ah, Mother-in-law, you have an unexpected house guest, huh? But you, Manny-man, you never show up. You leave your clothes on a bush and steal my terrapin and off you go! Thief! I should be very mad at you! Here. Sorry I got them wet again. I did it crossing and re-crossing the stream looking for you to bring you many good things. No, no, please do not thank me by fawning all over and kissing my feet. You will crack the leather of my sandals with your wet kisses. You are my best friend, and I have risked life and best limb."

He grabs his genitals and shakes them like a low Shakespearean actor. "For you I have rounded up the donkeys. Two of them. But do you care? No! Come outside. I must talk to you like a man. Like a human being. Away from the presence of these women. Come, I say. Up. Up."

He walks outside, still carrying my dripping clothes. We stand under the moon. He says, "Now look what you have made me do. You have made me return to the place of the mother of my two or three first wives. This is something you should have to do only once or twice a year. Like having your teeth cleaned. Now I have to say goodbye to them when I have already said goodbye so that I may leave with you for America."

"Whaaaat?"

"No, no, I am crazy. I mean *from* America. To here. To visit William Love and his vast, vast empire."

Abis whips his hat off his head and holds it to his heart. "To take you to Love's Island. As is foretold. To get your slice of life, *n'est-ce pie*? Here, put these things on. You look like a fool in that dress. I am telling you this very privately, Manny-man, black is not your best color."

"They're sopping wet!"

"Oh, so now that is my fault?"

"Yes!"

"No! It is your fault for making me drag them through the mud again and again looking for you. Everything, it is all your fault. You must take responsibility for our actions. All of them. I am sorry but I have somehow lost your underwear. No, that is a lie. I am a fool. I have left it behind. On a bush somewhere. Because there are some things even Abis will not do. Carrying shit-stained underwear is one of them."

"It was not...."

"Please, stop. Do not apologize to me. It is all right. But hurry now. We must go this very night or we will miss the party. We will miss the yacht."

"You mean, 'miss the boat?'"

"A yacht is a boat. Come. We must go."

The young woman comes out of the house. We see her slim silhouette in the moonlight as she lights a cigarette.

"That one," Abis says, "she will change my tobacco yet."

"What does that mean?"

"She is the last of the old woman's children and my last sister-in-law that I have not yet married. Now because of her we must stay here until morning. There is a corn crib behind that shed. I am sure I can dingle her many, many ways if we stay the night."

"You were once married to two of her sisters?"

"One after the other as the first died. Or was there one wife in between? I forget. I am a stupid man."

"And now you want to marry this sister?"

"Not marry. I know how to be careful now. Rubber dickie glove. Ha, ha, is this not what do you call it, 'rubber dickie?'"

"Are you also saying that little boy in there is your son?"

"Of course he is my son. One of twelve or so. That I know of. Who can keep track?"

"Don't you think that's a little irresponsible of you?"

His brow wrinkles. "Huh? Why?"

"You're driving me crazy, Abis, if that's your real name."

"Not a long drive, huh, Manny-man? That is a joke, huh?"

I say nothing. I'm thinking about Abis and his children. Why doesn't he care? I mean, he's more concerned about *my* welfare, hell, his *donkeys'* welfare than his own children. I would have given anything for a son, for a living part of Sara. No, I can't be that way. I can't be jealous. And maybe he knows what he's doing.

Abis is silent, too, for a moment. Then he says, "It had been provided in advance that I should marry the first woman I encountered. This the priests and conjurers told me when I was just a very little boy of eight or nine with a penis only eleven inches long. As they predicted, so it came to be. Oh, oh, look, she is going into the stream to bathe. Come. I must go to her and erect my penis. 'Come, dick, up!'"

He slaps at it. "Wake, boy, wake!"

He turns to me, "These kids nowadays, you can never get them to do what you want. They have a mind of their own. Like the anus. These are the names of my two worst children, Dick and Anus."

He begins to walk off toward the stream. I remain leaning against a pine, holding my wet, dirty clothes. "Come, Manny-man, come!" he says and I follow after him. Maybe I can protect that innocent girl.

We see her silhouette again as she undresses and slips into the water. Abis takes his clothes off, too, and motions for me to do likewise. He spreads out his things on a bush. I remove the borrowed dress but carry my own clothes to the stream. We enter the water. He has a long stick in his hand. "Watch this," he says and, submerging to the nose, wades after her. I follow. We get close to the young woman.

She screams, whirls about, and says in perfect English, "Who did that?"

Abis rises, holds the stick in the air and grins. She slaps him hard. He says, "Ah, I am a fool," then submerges completely. She screams again, then giggles. Now I lose them completely in the dim light of the falling moon. After a few feeble, futile searches, I wade back to shore. I have my clothes at last, and now they are clean again, but nothing else.

Maybe I should hide his clothes to teach him a lesson. And what lesson would that be? Besides, he still has my luggage, my money and my passport. No, better to go back into the house, wait until morning, get my things, and part company with him forever.

As I walk, I hear giggling in the woods. It stops. So do I. Soon I hear the unmistakable sounds of vigorous and highly enthusiastic sexual intercourse. I make my way back to Abis's two-time, and perhaps soon-to-be three-time mother-in-law. I don't think he carried into the water, as he called it, a rubber dicky-glove.

# FIVE

Near dawn, Abis taps me on the top of the head. "No more," I tell him. "I'm going home."

"How? You got no money, no passport, what? Everything is on the third donkey, Manny-man, remember? You must help me catch her now. Before someone else takes her in. She is an ungrateful slut and will go with any man that gives her a handful of hay and a promise of oats."

I sit up. My eyes are wide open. "Are you saying someone else might be getting my money and my things while we sit here?"

"Sure, sure, you bet. That's the way of the world."

I leap to my feet. If this is a ploy to cover his stealing my belongings, he won't get away with it. "Come on! Let's go!" I shout.

He grins and nods. "Oh boy, this is great. Action. I love that stuff. Come on, let us bathe in the cool stream. Then we will have some of the mushy swill the old bat who is my mother-in-law calls breakfast. I think old Selu pulls off scabs from her skin and cooks them. Believe me, Manny, she taught all her daughters everything they know about cooking." He looks around. "I say this quietly unless their spirits are listening."

"You mean your dead wives?"

"You bet."

"Look, Abis, let's just go, okay? We can take a bath and eat later. I've got to get my luggage back. I'm lost without it."

"*Da nada*, pal, *da nada*." He brushes the thought aside with his hand. "We must bathe in the cold stream as my people always do. Then we will eat my dear, dear sweet mother-in-law's delicious, good, hearty, tasty gourmet hominy breakfast. Nine out of thirteen nutritionists will tell you it is the most important meal of the day. And maybe we will find my sister-in-law and do nookie sixteen other ways. Believe me, she is plenty sore today already."

I'm a fool. I go along with him. We hang our clothes on a bush and enter the stream to bathe. The water is numbing cold. Abis tries to entice Rabbit into the water but she is not so dumb as we humans. My teeth chatter as I say, "I g-got them mostly clean last n-night, b-but Abis, h-how d-did you get m-my clothes s-so m-muddy? Did you really d-drag them all t-the way here?"

He looks terribly offended. Then at once he brightens. "I'll fix it!" he shouts and makes a mad dash for the shoreline.

Before I can scream out, "no!" he grabs my clothes, including one of my shoes and dashes back into the water. He dunks them vigorously over and over into the cold water.

For some reason, I think, well, at least one of my shoes is still dry. His damn dog, Rabbit, must be tuned to my thought waves. She seizes the dry shoe in her mouth, dives into the water and swims up to Abis. He reaches for the shoe. She lets go. It floats away. He reaches out to grab it. In doing so, he loses his grip on my other shoe. They both float downstream for twenty yards or so, way too fast for us to catch up to them. Then they sink into the murky depths.

Abis turns to me, shrugs and grins.

"They were the only shoes I had left."

"Do not worry so much, Manny-man. *My* feet will be fine! I still have my sandals. This way you will not have to lend me your smelly old canvas shoes for me to walk comfortably!"

"Yeah, well, that takes a great load off my mind. Did it ever occur to you that now *my* feet will be bare?"

"Do not worry so much, Manny-man. Two out of four feet will be covered. That is over sixty-two percent! That is a good batting average in American baseball, no? Even if they do add a hundred points when they figure it. Even Jim Thorpe could not do better than a 620 batting average, huh?"

As he stands on the shore shouting encouragement, I continue looking for them. But finally I have to give up. My sneaks are well and truly gone. I get out of the water. The dog shakes herself vigorously all over me. Abis hands over my dripping clothes. "Good thing your wallet is on the third donkey, Manny-man. Otherwise it would be plenty sopping now. You are one lucky man. Here, put your magnificent and fashionable wardrobe back on. Naked here, you will be arrested. Explain that to your Board of Regents of the University System when the newspapers run that story back home. I see it now. Headlines this big. 'Local Professor Naked in Woods of Delphi. Thinks he is Greek God. Not God. Jailbird. Doing Hard Time.' Let me tell you, Manny-man, Greek prisons are not pleasant. No wine. No ouzo. Few girls."

He picks up a bowl that has been hidden under his clothes, scoops out a handful of mush with his hand, and passes me the bowl. I scoop out a bit and taste. It is cold, hard, hominy, god awful stuff. But I am so hungry I swallow it down, anyway. As I chew I think to ask Abis how he knew I was not just a teacher but a professor. How did he know we were governed by a board of regents? But I let it go for now. Instead I dress, shuddering as I struggle to draw those cold, wet things onto my body.

Abis's son is holding the reigns of the two riding donkeys. I ask, "Any idea where the third one might be, the one with my things?"

Abis grins and shrugs. The boy does, too. Obviously a nut off the old tree.

"Take me down to the coast where I can contact the American embassy or my credit card company and maybe catch a bus or a boat out of here. I'm reduced to nothing but my word, but I'll give you that if you will loan me twenty bucks."

He shakes his head.

I hobble up to him. What do you mean, "No?"

"William Love provides."

I sigh.

"Oh, Manny-man, this land is not your land. It is his land. You must trust me. I will show you. I have promised to take you to his very yacht and home. I have promised to take you to the little picnic he has provided for you and the select few. It is okay. My son is all grown up. He does not need me here anymore. It is better I wander the earth with you than stay here and give my two or three time mother-in-law so much trouble. I have promised to take you personally to William Love. Do not worry. Trust in me. You will not die on the island. You will come awake again, come back to life. He knows you are coming. I have called him myself. He is waiting. This is his place."

"What do you mean this is 'his place.'"

"His olive groves. His farm. His winepress and vineyards." He laughs. "And here is where suckers are pruned."

He motions with his head and arm for me to follow him. I do. He begins to walk through the pine trees. The boy and donkeys remain. Rabbit runs ahead of him. I follow as best I can, considering I have no shoes. Hidden under the pine needles are rocks sharp as fangs and twigs like honed needles; my feet discover every thorn. When I catch up to them, Abis and Rabbit are standing over a boggy-looking, stagnant pool of water. It could be man-made. The stench of rot and urea is overwhelming. I have to hide my nose in my wet sleeve.

"Come closer, Manny-man, look in."

I go to the edge and peer into water so full of tannin it's the color of strong tea. But here and there I can make out anchored in the fetid shallows what look like wooden statues.

"Aging," Abis says. "He has marble ones off the coast. In the salt water. Getting a little worm treatment. 'Different worms for different media.' That is how he explains it. To each its own. Someday worms for you as well, Manny-man, but not so soon."

Rabbit runs off the path and into the woods. Abis lumbers after her. I follow, slowly, until we arrive at a clearing. The dog begins to dig frantically in the wet, bubbly loam. Abis picks up a shovel and helps her, uncovering the top of a large bronze statue.

Rabbit squats down and urinates on the statue. "Good dog," Abis says. He drops his pants and showers the bronze with an enormous quantity of his own pee. "Now you," he says.

"What?"

"For the patina."

"Are you serious?"

"From all things, beauty, Manny-man."

"All this stuff is stolen, isn't it?"

"It is not real, Manny-man. All made. Some cast from originals, but all unreal." I have borrowed personally from the great museums, monuments and private collections. Borrowed, Manny-man, only borrowed."

"For what?"

"For museums, for people willing to suspend disbelief." He gives me a sly smile. "Other uses, too. On the island."

"What island? What other uses?"

"That is for me to know if you don't know. For you to find out. Soon. The old woman, why do you think she is here? She and the boy are the guardians. Caretakers. They come for the seasoning season. They guard this place of the make-believe good. She is very, very clever with the shotgun. I know. They will go home soon. You know what I mean."

"No. I don't know."

He winks. "You know."

I think about the old lady's primitive cabin. Is it all a sham? If this is really William Love's land, his art farm, so to speak, what kind of set-up does he have? And where's his palace if he's so rich? At Versailles the queen had a little artificial peasant's village in the back lot where she could go every afternoon with her friends to play at being a poor shepherdess. Maybe this William Love–and I'm beginning to believe in him more and more–is doing the same thing with this old lady's shack. Maybe his mansion is hidden on the other side of these woods.

"Abis, let's go that way."

Rabbit growls as I start to bear off to the left. I take one more step. She snarls, baring her little yellowish fangs. Abis takes me by the shoulders and turns me the other way. "That way is a private way, Manny-man. Private harvest. You do not want to know."

"Oh yes I do. I mean art forgery is one thing. But if he's growing anything illegal, I don't want anything to do with it, or him."

"No, no, Manny-man. Umm, it is okay. I will tell you the story now. That way does not lead to Love's land. It leads to the other. If you go that way you will be lost and miss him whatsoever and finally."

"You're sure?"

"Oh, sure."

"You're not lying to me?"

"I do not lie to you unless I tell you I do. Not about anything important to you. Come."

He leads me through a little wood to a pathway. The child is waiting for us with the two donkeys, holding their bridles. Without so much as a word or a pat for boy or beast, Abis mounts. I mount, too, and soon we are on a wider path, not paved, of course, but a lot wider than yesterday's, and showing signs of much use.

In fact, the road is so wide I figure surely it gets plenty of traffic and we will run into someone else soon. In the olive trees, birds trill splendorously. Abis listens more intently than I do. Almost as if he knows what they are singing.

"Abis?"

"Yes?"

"When do you think we'll catch up to the third donkey?"

"Soon, Manny-man. Soon."

"Do you know what kind of birds those are?"

"If I give them a name you will not hear or see them anymore."

"Why do you suppose they scatter so quickly when we approach?"

He shrugs.

"When I was a boy I used to hunt with a BB gun. Somehow the birds would sense the danger and fly out of harm's way. When my friends and I were unarmed they would stay."

He shrugs again. "One of us puts them in danger."

"Why don't I have the sense of a crow? Could we stop for a while?"

"Why?"

"My stomach is very, very queasy."

"You must make the smelly brown rainbow?"

"Not yet."

"Let's go on, then."

"All right. Do you really think back then when we were naked we could have been arrested for indecent exposure?"

He shrugs.

"I mean, we were on private property, right?"

"Maybe we are in a hurry to stay on schedule."

"I'm feeling a lot better now. Do we have anything to eat? Maybe that baklava we saved from your lunch basket?"

"We shall ask that donkey if we ever catch up. Ungrateful, sorry, prejudiced, overweight, lazy, rotten-tooth, scabby, stubborn, slobbering slob of a beast."

He looks about as if to find more adjectives in the olive trees that line the road.

"Abis?"

"Yes?"

"What do you mean, '*if* we ever catch up with him'?"

"Her."

"All right, her. All my belongings are on her back, remember?"

"This was always an independent beast. Even as a puppy. Believe me, we are better off without her. Let some other man put up with her tantrums." He spits forcefully between his fingers.

"But we have to get her back! Dammit, my *things* are on her back!"

"And my donkey was under your things. We can always find you more jockey brand undershorts, Manny-man. But a magnificent donkey such as her, not such an easy thing to steal."

"You were just lambasting her."

"I forgive her. I am a forgiving man. Did I not forgive you for getting me wet? Already I miss her soft brown eyes. Despite she is the daughter of Circe and a pig. She can drink like a man. And she understands me. As a puppy I brought her here all the way from Love's Island from the other world where my people once flourished. Can you say anything like that for this stupid beast upon whose back I now ride? Forgive me, stupid beast, but you are a stupid beast. Also you do not drink retsina wine and stagger as she does. You are a Baptist beast."

"You know your things were on her back, too. Doesn't that make you want to get her back?"

"I had nothing. I have nothing. It is all the same. What do I need that a donkey could carry on his back, er?"

"How about some clean clothes and something to eat?"

"Look here, Manny-man, I have wine. Good wine. Wine of the Gods! Such a thing does not grow in the backyards along the road. But food and clothes do."

"Yeah, well, we can't live on wine alone. And I forbid you to steal anything from anyone."

Abis knits his brows. Then he grins. "Property is theft. That is written in somebody's bible. We live by crime. We kill to live. To believe anything else is sentiment. Rejoice in what you steal, from Mother Earth, from the gods, from the beasts and plants we enslave and eat. Communists and Capitalists, Gurus, Gardeners, Ag-nostics, Pro-nostics, all know the same, except they won't admit it, we live by the death of other things, moral is what moralists say. And nothing, none of it is permanent anyway. Come, donkey, forward."

"You still haven't answered my question."

"To you, what is the question?"

"Will we catch up to the donkey?"

"Where is my crystal ball, Manny-man?"

"On the other donkey," we say in unison.

"If we don't resort to stealing food out of gardens and clothes off lines, what will we live on?"

He taps the top of his head with his left hand."

"What if I *have* no wit? Which obviously I don't since I'm here, God knows where, doing this!"

He shrugs. "If you weren't having such a bad time, Manny-man, you would be having such a good time. Nothing good or bad but thinking makes it so."

I prod my donkey to catch up to him. My damp clothes cling to me. "Listen to me, I'm starving!"

"Maybe William Love will provide. Move over, here comes a wide load."

"I sit up straight to see better. But I still see nothing. Then finally, off in the distance comes a man walking beside a donkey burdened with two enormous, old-fashioned baskets roped onto each of the animal's sides. The baskets are filled to over-flowing with cantaloupes.

Abis says, "This one scares me, Manny-man. He is my brother, but he can be evil."

Attached to one of the cantaloupe baskets and swinging from the end of a rope is a horrible sight, some kind of inflated animal part, an internal organ, perhaps. The top is closed off with a string. But it's moving as if it's still alive. Like it's writing in pain. Twisting and kicking to get off the rope from which it hangs. A terrible noise punctuates the contortions, like chickens being strangled.

"Oh, God, Abis," I say, pointing, "what is that?"

"An ox bladder, Manny-man. You act like you never saw one before."

"I haven't. Why is it wriggling like that?"

"He has captured something inside. Kanati, he uses that to carry his little children."

"His *children*? What the hell are you talking about?"

"He carries his little brothers in that thing. What do you think? It is live small game he keeps in there. It is a bladder pouch. Do you not carry a briefcase to work with lunch inside?"

Tied to the donkey's harness with rope are three small piglets. They trot behind the donkey to certain slaughter as happily as if they were following their mother. What do they know? Pigs are not existentialists. Abis smiles, points to them and says, "Umm, little brothers. They look good to eat. See that one with the spot on his head? Does he not look plump?"

Abis rides on ahead until he reaches the man and his beast of overburden. Then he dismounts and takes off his ridiculous hat. Holding it humbly with both hands to his chest, he converses. Every now and then, one or the other looks toward me. Sometimes one of them grins.

Melon man is toothless. The breeze brings me wafts of Greek, and the wonderful musk scent of ripe melons.

The heal of the melon man's left hand rests lightly on the flank of his donkey. His right hand waves incessantly at the gathering horse flies. The donkey's tail flickers and the skin under his brushed grey hair shudders here and there in an effort to keep the flies from alighting. But the musk of the melons is too attractive. Man and donkey are losing.

Abis waves his hand in a slow absolution as if he were giving his blessing on the flies and beasts and us all rather than shooing anything away. In fact, the flies seem to be leaving him alone, deliberately. As if he's their boss.

"Manny-man, this is Odysseus. Back home he is called Kanati. We are good friends since we are this big. My father, he stole his father's goats. I tell you this in English. We think maybe he might be my stupid half-brother. William Love, he took us both in as orphans long ago to come back and forth across the shining big sea water into the two lands to work for him."

The melon man nods and raises both hands in greeting. His hair is cropped short, about the same length as his stubby beard. Both are grizzled black. Both eyes and cheeks are hollow. The skull beneath the skin. Sara.

His skin is antique bronze, tanned into leather. Abused by seventy, perhaps, hard years in the sun. Crows' feet? Eagle's toes. His face is one mass of deeply etched, hard lines. Yet the eyes are gay and laughing. Moist, and light blue, like the Aegean close to shore, just beyond the breakers, where the white sand reflects through.

I am guessing now: most of his ancestors were Greek. They intermarried with the ancient Alpine warriors who came to conquer and ended their days settled on the plains. All that ambition and terror and subjugation come to this: high, prominent cheekbones on a melon man, light blue eyes and a Celtic nose.

"Odysseus or Kanati?" I ask. "Which name do you prefer?"

Abis translates. But it isn't Greek they are speaking. It is more like that language Indians use in the old cowboy movies.

Abis turns to me. "Here he is called Odysseus. We call him Melon Man everywhere."

He steps into the road. "Rabbit! Here, girl!"

As Abis turns his back to us, the old man slips me my lost wallet! Then he hands me my lost sneakers! They are dry and cleaner than they have been in years!

"What the hell!" I say, then "thank you, sir," and put them on.

He motions for me to follow him. Abis trails behind, leading the three donkeys, stopping now and then to take a squeeze from his wine skin.

We go through a small wooded area and to a paved highway. On one shoulder of the road is a shrine, a square marble pillar, three feet high, with a glass case perched on top. Inside the glass is a faded icon. It could just as easily be Apollo as Joseph. Maybe it is both. Odysseus leads us across the road back into the forest. It becomes dense and gloomy. The farther down we go into the ravine, the more plentiful and larger the hardwood trees. Odysseus is ahead of me and Abis is behind. They keep looking about as if making sure we are completely alone. What are they up to? My heart beats hard. I feel my wallet over it, in my breast pocket. What a stupid thing to die for. Yet in a strange way, my fear comforts me, for I realize now for the first time since Sara died, I want to live.

We come to a stream. Abis says, "Spit, Manny-man, spit."

"What?"

"Unto thee I say verily, 'spit.' Hawk thee up one big juicy muckle."

"Okay, sure." I say and spit.

The old man squats down and dabs the end of a small stick in my wad. Then he digs a little hole and places the moistened wood on the bottom. He takes a small yellowish leather drawstring purse from around his neck, opens it, and removes a small pinch of reddish-yellow powder.

Abis says, "It is dried wild parsnips from back home. And seven well-beaten earthworms, local. He is mixing it with splinters that have come from a tree hit by lightening."

The old man plucks from his pocket seven yellow pebbles. He fills the rest of the little hole with them. I remember the significance of seven to the ancient Greeks, but damned if I know what's going on here.

He builds a small fire over the hole. Then he leaps to his feet and unsheathes a long, horrible looking, brightly burnished, wooden handled sword of some sort. It's "U" shaped blade seems designed specifically to slice off heads. He brandishes it with extraordinary skill, like a samurai warrior. I feel awe for the sinewy, muscular vigor of the old man and the captivating power of his deep, rolling, voice that rolls like thunder. Though I don't understand a word he is saying, the tone and timber ravish me. My arms goose bump.

He stops his chant, goes to his donkey, plucks a ripe, fragrant melon from the basket, and holds it out in his left palm like an offering to the gods. Suddenly he raises the blade above his head and with the other hand swings it down with such controlled force the blade cuts the melon in two without touching his palm. I would have sliced my own fingers off.

Odysseus hands me both halves of the cantaloupe and grins.

I turn to Abis. "He does understand Greek, doesn't he?"

Abis nods.

"Thank you," I say in Greek. I had learned that, and two other words from the old woman, "pot," and "outhouse."

Odysseus nods and mumbles something.

I pull out my own little pocket knife, unfold the largest blade, neatly quarter the fruit and pare it from the rind. Then I stick one piece to the end of the blade and hold it out for Odysseus. He takes it and eats.

I do the same for Abis. "If God Himself were come to lunch, we could feed him these melons. No shame. And some of my fourth wife's baked breadfruit." He laughs and winks as Odysseus opens three other melons with considerably less flourish.

And so we have cantaloupe and wine for lunch. And some pistachios the melon man has stashed away in a sack.

"Is this not as I have foretold? William Love provides."

"He does?"

"*Si, si, señor.*" Abis takes off his cap, bows low to Odysseus and his donkey, and mumbles something in Greek. He tosses pieces of melon to Rabbit, who devours them as if they were beef steak.

The old melon man winks. By now the little fire is out. We walk back to the miniature pit.

Abis says, "We must turn our backs to him."

"Why?"

He motions with his hand and we both turn around and sit. The old man chants in that Indian sounding lingo. Then he comes around to face us and speaks to Abis, who translates what he says this way: "Okay. This one, meaning me, shall have the sun for his brother long before he moves to the other land. No diseases fill the body. Only sorrow fills the mind. You, meaning Abis, shall be the cloud-breaker before the cloud breaks upon you. Then perhaps this one, meaning me, will come to come to understand some of it, and more, should he learn to embrace, though now he keeps the rain dancers and the sun dancers at arm's length. Soon he will dance with the empty moon. The dreadful mother. He shall do you, meaning Abis, much more, himself less evil in the coming great storm."

I shrug. Odysseus takes his donkey's reigns in his hand and begins to walk. When they have gotten ten or so feet toward the road, the old man turns and looks back at us. He waves. Then he is gone from sight. We rise to our feet and, leading our own beasts, follow in the old man's footsteps toward the road.

## SIX

"Abis, what was all that mumbo jumbo with the old man about?"

He smiles. "He is Red."

"A Communist?"

"Thunder. He is father to the two boys. That is why his voice is heavy and rolling like thunder. But I must warn you now; if we ever meet him again, you must never, never call him 'Red,' or he will cause terrible weather on both of us. You may call him by his true name, which is Kanati."

"I have no idea what you're talking about."

"So."

"Is any of this going to make sense anytime soon?"

"You bet. Anytime soon."

"Can you at least explain that stuff about digging a hole and burying my spit?"

"Of course I can."

"Well?"

"Oh, you mean, now? It is simple, Manny-man. He has foretold your future."

"And?"

"You heard him. I translated his exact words to you. He said you would figure out some of it without me. Such is your destiny. Of course you will never figure it all out. Not enough time, though he says you will live long and prosper."

"And what was all that you were saying about 'William Love provides?'"

"Whose melons, oh, oh, excuse me; I forgot you are a professor. I must speak properly. *Whom's* melons do you think you ate? And whom's pistachios?"

"William Love's, I presume?"

Abis makes an awkward bow and nearly falls off his donkey. "My brother is his man. It is his donkey. His melons. His farm. Ranch?"

"Farm," I say. "But assuming that they were William Love's melons..."

"Were."

"Fine. I know that now. But it doesn't necessarily follow that he sent them for us. He was simply sending them to market. We just happened to be in the way."

Abis smiles and shakes his head. "You are such a fool, Mr. Big-deal Professor Manny-man. I will tell you a story now. Back home, where I lived with my first wife. No, no, third. Second. Under the grape vine and paper birch trees. Back home in the high, wind-swept, frozen mountains of the Persian Gulf, when my name was still Abdul, I first met William Love on the mountaintop. Stern and vigorous and forgiving. Before that time, I, too, thought like you. But now all is different. All is changed. Utterly changed. Now I know. William Love provides. He knows what I need and what I only think I need, and how to give me what I need. He lets me steal what is necessary. Yes? No? Yes?"

"How can anyone argue with a true believer? Your logic is, how shall I say, 'peccable.'"

Abis grins and nods his head. His hand comes from behind his donkey's flank and reveals the writhing animal's bladder that had been hanging from the melon man's donkey. He unties the drawstring and, carefully reaching in, pulls out by the feet two wildly thrashing, harshly screeching Guinea fowl!

"Hee, hee. I stole his two children. We will eat plenty good tonight."

"You are incorrigible."

His brows furrow. "That is good, no? I take it for a great compliment."

"No. It is not good. Have you never heard the phrase, 'Thou shalt not steal'?"

"Sure, sure. Only in my translation, I leave one word out. Fine, go on and shake your head and be Mr. Moral Stick in the Muddy Water, Manny-man. But you will eat very well tonight, sitting next to me at the campfire. So be it, Mr. Big Deal Morality Beyond Mine Knee Jerk Liberal Imperialist Oinky Pig Fascist Communist. We make camp in, what, six hours? Yes, exactly. Then see what happens when your bodily need function arises and you are transformed into one hungry animal who prefers permanently borrowed Guinea fowls with sage and other spices to thou shalt not steal."

## SEVEN

"We are here, Manny-man. Tonight, we cannot go any further. It is in this place we make camp and eat well."

I pull up on the reigns. My donkey stops and pees profusely, so close to Rabbit that the dog would get wetter than she does if she weren't so nimble. I try to dismount, but my legs are so sore from riding they won't lift by themselves.

Abis sits up straight on his mount and peers ahead, one hand shading his eyes like one of those Neoclassical North American Indians in a Benjamin West Painting.

"What are you looking for?"

"I will show you when I see it, Manny-man."

"I'm starving. Aren't you?"

"Oh, ho, did I not tell you this would happen, Manny-man?"

"You're right. I admit it. Let's cook the guinea fowl."

"See, see, Mr. Hungrier Than Moral Imperialist Labour Party Running Dog Lackey of Big Business Standard Oil Military Industrial Condominium? Is it not exactly as I have foretold? Now you are ready to commit felony theft and crimes against nature? Now you are ready willing and able to eat someone else's tough and stringy children?

"Okay."

"NO! This I will not permit. All your life you have led such an upright life and now you want Abis to lead you astray to the path of damp nation? NO!"

He dismounts, takes the two fowl out again by their legs and flings them high into the air as he sings "Born Free" with his hand over his heart. The two little birds flap their wings, squawk, plummet straight to the ground, and hit with a solid "thunk."

"Hmmm. They must have had their wings clipped."

The birds run off into the woods, commenting.

Once they are well and truly gone, Abis turns to me. "This idea of yours to eat someone else's children, it sucked mud though a straw, Manny-man. We stole someone else's property."

"You're the one who said property is theft."

"Oh, Manny-man, Abis was a great liar then. Property is not theft. Theft is theft. Have I forgotten what I was put on Earth for? I have been a fool. I have almost gotten my best friend into trouble with his god. I am no good. Now I must find a special supper that I have prepared for you. Great, huh? In Abis we trust. All others pay cash. This is what you should put on your American money."

"I've got to be nuts following you. You should be following me."

"What? You know the way?"

"Abis, what am I doing here? It's, it's like the left side of my brain has gone on a separate vacation. This is just not me. "

"It is your stupid brother? Sometimes mine does many things I get blamed for. He is my evil twin. Like Prometheus and Epimethieus. These are friends of mine from down below. I do not think they smell very good anymore. Both have been in the ground too long. Hey, Manny-man, you believe in the Great Spirits?"

"Great Spirits?"

"You know, Lord of the Sky, Maker of Thunderbolts, Great Immortal Head Honcho. Supreme Big Boss?"

"You mean God? What's that got to do with anything? I guess maybe I still believe in God. It's hard, very hard."

"Just one?"

"What do you mean, 'just one.' There's only one God, isn't there?"

"Abis knows there is only one and only God, the True God. Which God is this?"

"Which one? *God*, God. The one who created the whole universe."

"How did he do that?"

"I don't know. Just brought it forth, I guess."

"Ah. 'Bring forth.' Like pregnancy?"

"Well, yes, I suppose, metaphorically."

"Ah. Soo, your God, she is a female God. Pregnant. Knocked up. Blimped out, er?"

"No! He's, he's .... "

"Come, Manny-man. We will travel while we talk. I will take you to supper. Your God, he is married?"

"No! Of course not. How could God be married?"

"What? No one good enough for him? I have a maiden aunt like this. How does he give birth without a womb? No wife? Does he .... ?" Abis gives a little pantomime of masturbation.

"Abis, that's disgusting!"

"Why?"

"Well, because we think of God as *spiritual*. Ourselves as spiritual."

"Was not you who told Abis you believe you are made in your god's image?"

"True."

"Then why are you not pure spirit?"

"We are, or are supposed to be spiritual, in the sense that we believe this world is not important. It's the next one that's important. And the soul."

"Then how come you are always building big houses to live in here in this world? I will tell you a great secret now. Many years ago I swallowed my god."

"You mean 'swallowed your pride'?"

"No, no, I mean I took God into my mouth and swallowed."

"Oh. You mean like the Eucharist?"

"I do not know this Hugh Caress. What I am telling you in private is that I swallowed my god whole. Seriously. This is true. My god is inside here. This is what you must learn to do, too, Manny-man. It will make you bigger. It is true you live in a big American mansion back home?"

"I wouldn't call it a mansion. Four bedroom, two bath brick veneer ranch. In a nice neighborhood."

"Plenty of room for friends, huh? You are married?"

"I was. She's dead now."

"What is her name? Was?"

"Was. Her name was Sara."

"So, how come you do not take up with a new woman? She is dead. You are not dead. Abis has had to restock many, many times in his life. Wife dies, I replace her. Wife leaves, same thing. I replace, wife leaves."

"It's funny my being lost out here in a foreign nowhere with a madman. My friends back home told me not to do anything silly. 'Don't make any major decisions about your life or anything else for at least three years. You're not seeing reality now. Not clearly. You might do things you'll regret later on,' they said. So what do I do? Pack up my whole life, go to Greece and wind up on some dirt road with a looney-tune."

He grins. "Great, huh?"

"I don't even know."

"You *are* in bad shape. But tell you what, Manny-man, you trust Abis. This is on your dollar bill. You stick with me and I will make you whole again. You will make me whole again. Like a corporeal merger, okay? Do not two halves make a whole?"

"The world should come with a user's manual. As soon as you're old enough to read, your parents should be required by law to give you a card that has these four words printed on it: Life Doesn't Make Sense. That's really what they should teach you in school instead of math and civics. Then you wouldn't spend half your existence on earth trying to figure it out and the other half bitter and disappointed because you haven't."

"Whoa, Manny-man, you are over twelve and are still thinking there is a meaning to life?"

"You're saying there isn't?"

49

"Life has no meaning, Manny-man, it is nothing to do with meaning; Life is an experience , something to be enjoyed, not looking backwards or forwards, but seeing and smelling and tasting and hearing and feeling now."

"So here I am, taking Nietzsche's advice instead of my friends'."

"This Ned Cha is a man you know back home?"

"In a way. He's the one who insisted I hitch a ride with a madman. Not someone who thinks he is mad, but a true, if not certified looney-bin. I like to read Nietzsche. Not that he always makes sense. But I'm not at all certain I would have liked to travel down a mountainside in Greece with him."

"Hey, Manny-man, do not worry, huh? I am not this guy! I am his fool of a brother. I don't write anything down. I don't even read! We are having fun?"

"Yes. I guess we are. So why do I feel so guilty?"

"This is a quiz, Manny-man?"

"No. I'll tell you why. Because Americans, even Jewish ones, all of us, are Puritans. And Puritans are such assholes. Nathaniel Hawthorne tried to tell me that, but I didn't understand. All my life I have never wallowed in the mud the way we did back there. Not even as a kid. My mom would have killed me if I ever had that kind of fun. I never even participated in any semi-dangerous sports as a kid. Not that I would have been any good at them. But I never even tried. I'm not the Hamlet type, Abis. Maybe I would have made him a good sidekick. 'Here you are, Hammie, here's your cloak and sword, pal, go get 'em'."

"Look, Manny-man, dinner!"

"What? Where?"

"In the road. Way over there. See it? I think it is little brother in the road! But I'm not sure. Hard to identify anything that far away when the sun is going to sleep."

"Listen to that horrible squeal it's making! Is it a pig?"

"Yes! It *is*. It *is* little brother! I know his voice! Come, we must hurry to supper."

He spurs his donkey and they shoot on ahead. I almost lose sight of them in the gathering dark.

"Can you see it?" I shout.

"I do see it. And smell it, too."

"Oh, yeah. I do, too," I say, catching up to him. "Hey, look, it's one of the melon man's piglets. The plump one you pointed out, remember? I recognize that spot on the top of its head."

"It is the only clean spot on him."

"I think he's stuck in that mud puddle."

Abis lumbers off his donkey and pulls the slime covered, wriggling piglet out. He holds it up to me. The rope about his neck is three quarters clean cut, one quarter frayed. "He, he, Rabbit, look! Our trick has worked again! We shall eat smelly little brother tonight. William Love provides!"

"I thought those pigs belonged to your pal, Red."

Abis puts his hand to his lips so quickly he nearly fumbles the piglet. "Shooosh! Now we must watch out for bad weather."

"Maybe it would be more correct to say the melon man provides, not William Love?"

"Ultimately, these oinkers, they are William Love's."

"Look, I will gladly pay for the pig."

"Never mind your cash, Manny-man. Take the cash and let the credit go, uh? Let us dig a pit and have roast pork. This will be our camp."

"Okaaay! I'm starving."

"No! NO! This we cannot do. I have forgotten. Abis is such a fool! Why have I been sent here? To do what? We cannot stop now. We will miss William Love's Great Feast."

"Tonight we will make our own."

"Okay-donkey. I am a very flexible kind of guy. One day I take communion at the table of one god, next day at another. Same plate. Come, we must work quickly now. Night is falling faster than a shotgunned squirrel. No, wait, faster than a greased snail. I almost forgot what side of the sky I am on!"

Abis drops the reigns of his donkey. I pick them up and lead both animals as we leave the path and return to the wood. We follow again the flowing stream of bright water. Abis slits the little animal's throat. Blood gushes out. The squeals are horrendous. They seem to echo into eternity. Watching and listening I can understand why hunters have so many rituals to appease the souls of their prey. And yet, this act of killing and butchering seems here in these woods as clean and as natural as picking out a pork chop wrapped in plastic in my hometown supermarket. He skins the animal and hangs the carcass from a limb. I dig a pit. He builds the fire. I gather fallen wood. He cuts the flesh into strips and washes each strip in the fast flowing stream of bright water. Traces of blood mingle with the water of the stream and wash away. The stream becomes clear again, and pure. In a sing-song chant, he says "This I give freely to the Long Man, who is my brother."

The fire now is raging within its borders. Abis cuts off chunks of uncooked fat and muscle. Tossing them into the flames, he chants, "This I give freely to the Sacred Fire, who is my brother."

He prepares the meat, and himself, for eating with a fastidiousness I wouldn't have believed he had in him, and eats with a reverence I find quite touching. We have salad, too, made of wild greens and garnished with a dressing of wild herbs and a bit of the leftover wine. As we eat this magnificent feast, he says, "We are opposed to the animals, who are our brothers. Always fighting them for their flesh. But the plants are friends of the people."

We eat and eat until our stomachs are round as melons, and drink the last of the wine. It has cooled in the waters of the stream. As we sit leaning against a tree and burping, Abis says, "Now I will tell you a secret."

"What's that."

"Dog's name. She is not called Rabbit. Only over here. Over there she is sometimes called Hare."

"What are you babbling about now?"

"Okay, okay, I will tell you the truth."

"That would be nice."

"Her true name is Idomene. Secretly she is part wolf."

"Must be a well-kept secret. Which part?"

"Umm, the tail, I think. She has one ear of coyote, one of fox. And a mind like a small, spoiled child. Sometimes they call her here Cerbera."

"You mean, 'Cerberus,' the hound of hell?"

"No! That is wrong. She is a girl. Cerbera. Female. She has no peanuts and testaments."

"Ahh."

"Manny-man, both of us are not from here. So why did *you* come? Unlike me, you had to pay your own way, no?"

"When Sara died, I didn't know what to do. How to handle my whole life again on my own."

"In this way, you are brother to the snake. This is how they feel when they are living in the old skin."

"Really? I don't know much about snakes."

"They shed, Manny-man."

I nod, and burp.

"But here is the thing, they are still the same old snakes in new skin. This is what snakes are like. But who knows. Maybe with humans it is different sometimes. So how come you did not break away and go out to look for new rocks to rub against? Have you no libretto any more?"

He tosses bits of roasted meat to Rabbit, who leaps high up, catches each piece in the air, and gulps it down before she falls back to the ground on her side, making a sound like "oof."

"Manny-man, when your dick is up, what do you do?'

"I try not to think about it. I concentrate on my research."

"When my dick is up, it pulls me out the door. I have no choice. I am attached to it."

"That's nutso. Of course you're attached to it. It's part of you. But you're in charge of your own body, Abis. All of it."

"No! You are the one who is not so, Manny-man. Whatever that means. Tell him, Rabbit, Dick is like the snake. A big, fat, long snake. It has a mind of its own. When he gets up, he leads. Abis can only be pulled along where ever *he* wants to go."

"Look at me; I'm not ruled by my gonads."

"What a shame."

"No. We're rational animals who can sublimate our sexual drive to our life's work. We can be disciplined to scholarly pursuits. That is what civilization is. The ancient Greeks knew this. Everything in moderation. Exercise, thought, and useful work. We can't do what we want all the time; that's what vacations are for. Otherwise, nothing in this world would ever get done. You can sublimate just as well as I can. That's the core of Judeo-Christianity. What we call the Protestant Ethic. It rules the world."

"Oh, Manny-man, you must beware of what you know. Have sex in moderation? Get exercise? This is crazy-speak. If done right, sex *is* exercise. Here is a fact: chasing and catching women is the only exercise your best friend gets. These women, they *like* being caught. No matter what you say. This is what you must believe. Do you not see? Here is an old saying among my people in Israel, 'you do not know how the bones of the infant grows in the womb of its mother.' This is not an exact quote, because Abis is very, very stupid. Okay, so what will you do? You will spend all your nights at your desk in your university hall and then one day you will be in your clean university elevator and some infant held by his mama will sneeze and spray mumps spit all over your face in this elevator. You know what will happen next? The next day you will be sitting there in your clean room in your clean university hall alone with your pen in your clean hand while this mumps worm crawls down from your face into your balls. Then you know what? Pretty soon your balls will swell up to the size of a small European village and your dick will fall off and you will be dead. No dick, dead."

"Abis, you will never, ever be civilized."

"Please Gods of here and there, never, ever make me civilized."

"The soul is a blank page, Abis, to be written on by experience. That is how the soul learns and prepares for the next world. Under normal circumstances, the individual is in perfect order. Given a sabbatical from work, with pay, and a decent government or private grant, a man can take the time out to see the order of the universe and write it down for others to see."

"Huh?"

"That's what I'm doing in my book. Though I call it *Revelations: Finding Love and God in Literature* let me make this clear, I am a Sociologist, and this is a sociological study, *not* a literary one. And right from the start it's been funded. That *means* something, Abis! I'm very proud of that. I've devoted eight years of my life to it, just gathering the material from libraries all over America. Even when Sara was sick. And you know what? Now it's nearly ready. Notes sorted, files ordered. All I have to do now is the actual writing. My great moment is at hand. How's that for exciting, huh? Think of it, Abis, the supreme act of creation!"

"Manny-man, you are one crazy white guy. This cream act of creation, it has a chin like yours? Does it climb into your lap and put its warm arms about your neck and hug?"

Rabbit is circling about, making a nest for herself in the leaves.

"For some of us that way is cut off."

"Oh, Manny-man, that is not what I have been telling you. You must put down your pen and chase many, many women until you catch one. You are not the one who died."

"No. I must devote my life to Seneca and Plato, not climbing rotten boughs. Not to love. To understanding."

"But that is the very point of love. Manny-man. It is what you don't understand that will help you. You need to climb rotten boughs and fall now and then. Let go. Fall a little. It is painful, yes, but you heal. Look at me. I don't understand nothing! And I don't need help understanding because I understand. Understand?

"There's a lot I don't understand. And it's not helping me at all. Not that I want to forget what's happened to me. I'm not forgetting a damned thing. The enemy you don't see is the most dangerous. He might be sneaking up from behind."

"Make your enemies your friends, Manny-man. Okay, okay, you say these things, so how come you are here with Abis and not home creaming creation?"

"I don't know."

"Good."

"I just couldn't work. I'd go to my desk every day and wind up just sitting in front of my notes. See, you don't know this Abis, but it's not so easy to create and make it real. I just took my pen, threw it against the wall and walked out. God, you should've seen it. Made an ink stain on the wall this big. Looked like someone had ray-gunned a cat."

Rabbit has curled into a ball. She is asleep. Her breath comes easily and slow. Abis shifts his bedroll closer to her. Folding his hands behind his head, he looks up at the stars. "So, why did you come here, Manny-man, I mean to Greece?"

"To see the old statues I've seen in books all my life but have never gotten to meet in person. It was a toss-up for me between Athens and Rome.

"Rome is no good, Manny-man. Too many stone horses spitting into stone fountains."

"I used to gaze at the photos of the ancient statues in my college freshman, *Art is for All of Us* as if they were mail order brides. I mean I really loved them and expected them to be as young and as beautiful as their pictures. But in the Athens Museum, when I saw them in person, it was like their very souls were gone. Like bumping into your favorite move starlet from your youth and suddenly realizing, my God, the woman's seventy now. And the worst part for me was the basement, where they store all the worm-eaten marbles they've salvaged from the ocean floor. God, Abis, have you ever seen those things? You look down from a railing and all you see are these lifeless lumps of stone, barely recognizable as the Gods they used to be."

"You know what I am thinking, Manny-man? I am thinking you have put your passions in the wrong place. Here is some more truth: all this, it doesn't matter. This art stuff it is beautiful and beauty warms the soul. But art is not flesh. These souls you talk about in the marble had not left. They were never there. Statues do not have any souls. They only reflect the souls in us. They are rock. Chiseled rock. So they fooled you, huh. Looked like real? Like Tramps of Veal?"

"So maybe that's why I went to Delphi. To find the real word made flesh."

"You rest now, Manny-man. Tomorrow we will go to the banquet. Only we are a day late and a drachma short. Only drachma do not exist anymore, either. The whole universe is changing. Day by day. Like the moving stream. At least we will feast on the dregs of the feast, huh?

"Abis, as usual, I have no idea what you are talking about."

"It is much the same for me about you, Manny-man. But we learn from each other. For now we will rest. Tomorrow perhaps we meet up with William Love."

# EIGHT

I can't sleep. The stars are too bright. My nose itches. The dog snores. I try counting various barnyard and domestic animals, game and commercially caught fish, even dead Slavic novelists.

The dog begins to howl.

"Chufee, darling," Abis says, "do not sing so loudly as this. Instead, my sweetness, you must go and read a book or something until noon, eh?

"How about *Call of the Wild*?" I suggest without opening my eyes.

"No!" Abis shouts. "She has too much of that in her already. Besides, this book you suggest is maybe filled to brim with doggie sex scenes. She is too young for that."

I open one eye. "Oh, Jeeze, it's already light out."

"Of course; it is nearly ten o'clock Greek Daylight Savings Time."

"How nearly?"

"Within three hours, Manny-man."

"It is?"

"Of course. I do not make the sun and stars stand still; it would scare you. And I do not ever lie. About time."

"You're sure? How do you know?"

"Have I not told you my true name? Truly, I am Arno of Trieste. Among my own people, there is an old Latin trick we have learned from our ancient Roman ancestors. You push a stick into the ground like this. Then you draw a great circle about it, thus. Then look at Rolex watch."

"You're not wearing a watch."

"It is in my pocket, Manny-man. The metal wrist band was bit in half many years ago by the great tie snake."

"Then how .... oh, never mind. Can you get her to shut up?"

He winks, opens up what looks like a folded handkerchief, and tosses her some food. She stands on her hind legs and begins bolting and gobbling, frequently falling back on all fours. Abis, too, is bolting and gobbling the remainder of whatever he gave her. They could be twins.

"Uhh, what's for breakfast, Abis?"

"She is eating your half, Manny-man. This is how Abis makes her silent."

Then why in hell didn't you save me some of *your* so-called half?"

"Ahh, this is because it is my so-called half. This is what you have said yourself. Thank you."

"Wait a minute, where's the rest of the piglet?"

"I have fed the sacred fire while you were asleep. That was one hungry Great Spirit, I tell you."

"You *burned* all that meat?"

He grins.

"Well, what am I supposed to do, starve? I know, I know, 'William Love Provides.'"

"Come. We find him now. Wickedly split."

"That's 'lickety-split.'"

"Right. Makes much more sense your way, Manny-man. Come on, up on donkey."

"No."

"It is good for you. Otherwise you will starve here. Ferocious carnivorous mountain goats will come down from on high and eat you like American hamburger, no sesame seed bun, hold the pickle, no fries with that."

"No."

"Ally-Oop."

He gives me a boost. I am back on the donkey again.

***

"We've been on the road eight hours today, Abis. We must have covered forty-five miles. My butt is so sore I ...."

"No, Manny-many-men. We have only gone one mile today."

"That's nuts, Abis."

"We have been on road only ten minutes."

"Impossible."

"Did we not leave our camp at ten in the morning, Greek Daylight Savings Time? Here, look at my watch."

He pulls his watch out of his pocket and holds it out to me. The hands, indeed, do point to ten past ten. "Hey, wait a minute. That thing isn't even running."

"It isn't? Oh, I forgot, never wind it. Chufee, she never winds it, either." He points to Rabbit. "The donkey cannot. She has no opposable thumbs."

"Then why the hell do you carry it?"

"Look at your own watch, then."

"Mine died in the mud puddle. What was that, six years ago?"

He grins. "Then why do you wear it?"

"Because some day I can get it fixed."

He grins.

"All right, all right." I rip it off my wrist and fling it away with all my might. "There, happy?"

He grins even more broadly. "Perhaps we could have it fixed in the village? There is a great watch fixer there."

"Fuck the son of a bitch!"

"Manny-man, it is still only ten minutes past ten, Abis Daylight Savings Time."

He points to the sun. "Get back on the donkey."

"I'll walk a bit. My butt's too sore."

"Ha, ha, this is great. You waddle like a duckling with a load in its diaper."

"Best I can do under the circumstances."

"Okay-ducky. Abis will jump down, walk, too."

"Fine."

"We're high-stepping now, huh, Manny-man?"

"I'm starving."

"You're cranky."

"That's because I'm starving."

"Not far now. Maybe a ten minute walk. You will eat plenty, soon. If he is still there."

I stop short. The donkey wants to keep going. She almost yanks the reigns from my hand.

"What do you mean? What's not very far?"

"William Love's Feast, Manny-man. Not very far. How do you reckon? Maybe 200 yards, maybe half. Beyond that ridge. Big table. Big. Lots of meat for you and Chufee."

"You mean William Love's house is just over that hill?"

"You bet."

"Then why in hell didn't we go there yesterday?"

"Search my fleas. You are the one who wanted to stop and eat someone else's piglet. Did not Abis tell you it was not kosher?"

"No."

"Ahh. Abis meant to do this. That counts."

I scramble up the little ridge and peer down. Abis is right behind me.

"Good Lord, what is that?"

"Ha, ha, did I not say? But no, you must eat stolen pig when we could have stolen from this!"

Abis spreads out his hands and turns one hundred eighty degrees. Before us is a grassy, level field and an enormous, brightly colored, striped tent. From the peaks of each tent pole, banners flap about in the breeze. Their colors, red, black and yellow, match the stripes of the tent.

Abis nudges me. "Plenty of picnic tables under that big top."

"What is going on here?"

"Party!"

"Who has this kind of money to blow on a picnic in the middle of, of, hell, I don't even know where we are. I mean, who *is* this guy, Abis?

"I have told you many, many times. It is William Love."

"So what is he, an olive oil baron or a drug tsar?"

"Ha, ha, you are one crazy person, Manny-man. Come, now I can reveal everything."

"This is a guy with dreams, Abis. I mean, look at this place. It's like something King Arthur might have owned."

"Come."

"This is a movie set, right?"

"Come. We remount. We shall ride through this olive ranch there and into Love's Plains to feast."

We descend though a grove of olive trees. Their thick boles are gnarled and nearly black, with fleshy, mildewed leaves that nearly devour the sun. I don't think then to look up through the gloom to see the fruit. We cannot see the tent now, or the plane.

The road becomes little more than a donkey path. Branches slap our faces. No Indian path is worn in the soil underneath. No marks are visible on the trees to guide our way. But Abis is unwavering in our voyage through the gloom. Soon we reach the end of the grove. The sun is shining again. The tent looms before us. We are on a level with it. Now it seems even larger, and higher-peaked then it did from above.

Abis spurs his donkey, who trots off toward the tent. He seems to fit the scene before me perfectly, as if this were his true element. He approaches the tent, dismounts, and goes to one knee. His back is toward me. He could be making the sign of the cross. He could be scratching his crotch.

He rises and turns to me. I catch up to him, dismount by his side, and look about, slowly, trying to seem nonchalant. "Very nice," I say. "What's inside?"

Abis shrugs.

"What's that supposed to mean? You don't know?"

"Sire, this to me is an enormous surprise. It is great, huh? All Abis expectorated was a little camp and tiny puppy tent, maybe. But this! This is big! Unto thee, verily, I say wheee!"

With his left hand, Abis raises the door slit, bows low from the waist, and with his right hand, gestures grandly for me to enter.

I do.

Abis follows right after me, his nose actually pushing on my back, nearly tripping me with his foot, which I deftly avoid. In doing so, I stumble over a rock and fall flat on my face. Abis trips over my leg and tumbles on top of me, squishing my face against the dirt floor. He rolls off and I roll onto my back and stare up. A long line of servants, in livery, no less, is staring back, solemn faced. Abis laughs and winks. Two servants come forward and help us to our feet. Another gestures toward one of the long banquet tables. Two more pull out chairs for us, one on each side of the table.

It is only then that I realize we are the only guests. Though the tables are still covered in white linen, they are soiled here and there where food or wine has been spilled. The huge ice sculptured center pieces, mostly melted, remind me of the sea worn marbles in the basement of the Athens Museum. The few plates remaining on the tables are dirty. Most of the place settings at our table have been cleared away. Other servants continue clearing the tables we are not sitting at. The two who had helped us to our feet are now bringing us clean napkins, silverware and china. Another relights the chafing dishes on the sideboards. We are served.

The air is oppressively warm. The odors of hot canvas, stale spices and too many flowers confined too long almost choke me. But the leftovers are unbelievable: caviar and stuffed mussels with pine nuts and almonds. As the chafing dishes catch fire and warm the food, allspice and cinnamon perfume the air. Fragrant fruits are brought to us, soups and spinach pies, roasted lamb and shish kabobs, cakes and Cretan wine, Peloponnesian brandy and ouzo from the hills.

Abis sits beside me, sometimes using forks and sometimes the flexible utensils God provided him on the ends of his hands.

"God, what a meal," I say.

"Just a little picnic, William style."

"More like one of the great feasts of history."

Abis shrugs. "Willy does this all the time."

"Where is he?"

Abis shrugs. "All have left, *n'est-ce depart*? I think the feast was yesterday. We messed the boat eating stolen pig. It will make Kanati very angry, I think, when I have told him what you did."

"You mean, William Love is gone, too? Then why was all this food still out?"

"Maybe for us, huh?"

"Look at this place, Abis. Oriental rugs strewn on the dirt floor, tapestries hung on the canvas walls, gilt mahogany sideboards, cut flower arrangements taller than we are, ice sculptures, banquet tables the size of Bayonne, New Jersey, God!"

Abis shrugs. "What a dump, huh? Let's drink some more." He holds up his wine glass and a servant rushes to refill it. Mine, too.

Near the base of the tent, the canvas begins to shake. The vibrations move along a line until they reach the door flap. Through it, Rabbit marches in, leading the donkeys with the reigns in her mouth. She stops just shy of the Persian rugs, drops the reigns, bolts forward and leaps into Abis's arms.

He laughs and shouts, "Hume, I say, Hume! A bottle of hay for the asses!"

One of the servants makes a gesture to two others, who come forward and lead the donkeys off. Meanwhile, Abis stuffs his dog with roasted lamb and milk. He laughs again, takes a long, long draft of the wine bottle, and claps his hands three times. "William!" he shouts, "can you hear me? This is great! Just great! Bring on the dancing girls!"

Immediately jugglers enter the tent. Boys and girls. Maybe students from some circus school. Several balance balls as they dance. A few toss hoops.

"Guess what, Abis?"

"What?"

"I think I'm getting drinka-drinka-drunk again!"

"Good for you!"

"It's a first for me. Getting intoxicanted twice in three days. What happened to the dancing girls?"

"The waaah?"

"You mean they aren't here? Maybe I just read about them in *The Odyssey*, you know, and thought they're here. What about the musicians? Those are musicioans, are they note? On the pipe and castanets? What would be the Greek urn for that?"

"Beats hell out of me, plenty, Manny-man."

"Whom's food are we eating? Is this really William Love?"

"Who looks a gift's whores in the mound? When life takes you out of the wet and gives you dancing girls, you just enjoy where you are, *n'est-ce place*?"

"Ooooh, no, you don't, Amiss, I can't exempt that. Excuse me, does anyone here speak my language?"

The servant who had ordered the others to take the donkeys from the tent steps forward.

"Hume, sir," he says with the refined English pronunciation of the Royal Family and old time BBC announcers. "May I be of assistance?"

Abis points to him and laughs. "Great! This is great! Ha, ha, what a disguise. You would never know!"

Hume puts his right index finger to his lips, looking across the expanse at Abis as if through imaginary bifocals.

Abis roars with laughter. "Sure, sure, I get it. Wheeee!"

Hume turns back to me and smiles benevolently. I look up to him in a haze. As if I'd taken a large dose of laughing gas. But still, Hume's face seems 'wrong.' Like it's not a face but a latex mask. *Turn around, man, let me see if there's a string holding it on.* In my best English imitation accent I say, "Recuse me, my good man, but you inform me, please, if it is the wine I happen to be seeing, or is it really you?"

"I'm afraid I cannot answer that one, sir, as it is quite impossible for me to see through your eyes."

"Well, could you tell me what the bloody hell is going on, then?"
"Dinner, sir."
"Yes, yes, of course, but whose?"
"Yours, sir. And Mr. Abis's."
"What's Mr. Abis's last name, by the wade?"
"Mr. Abis, sir? Your guess is as good as mine, or his, for that matter."
"And his status?"
Hume glances over at him, then back to me. "Peasant, sir."
Abis winks and makes the universal "okay" sign. The one made by astronauts and cosmonauts and politicians from Boston to Bangkok. The one you see on statues of Christ, Parvati and Buddha.
"Hume, this is Mr. Love's feast, right?"
"It was, sir."
Abis tries to suppresses a giggle with both hands, but can't. He nearly chokes on pistachios until he projectile coughs the nut-phlegm halfway across the table.
"Well, whaziz Mr. Abis's status with Mr. Love?"
"Once again, strictly hazard, sir."
"Messenger? Gofer? Omic relief?"
"Sometimes it would seem he's in charge."
Abis laughs so hard he falls off his chair.
"Bus he's not?"
"If you say so, sir."
"Well, my god man, do pour me a another beaker full of this blissful Hippocrene and beedled buddles winking to the brim."
"Here you are, sir."
"Tell me abou' this feast."
"Held yesterday evening, sir, for, uh, shall we say, the, uh, main guests, that is. A sort of English-Greek medieval fest. But to my mind with rather anachronistic elements, though I'm sure it would not seem so to Mr. Love."
"Why is blazes not?"
"Time does not seem to be the same with him, sir. Or place. For him they are fused in the *Corpus Amori,* so to speak. Everything and all is one. Hence the rather incongruous gaggle of medieval Majorca ware, Etruscan gold servers, 21st century plates and 19th century silver service. Not at all the thing we would do in England, sir. But for Mr. Love it all seems to work out perfectly in the end."
"Ohhh, an do you really tink so?" I say rather too loudly.
"I believe so."
"Hey, Manny-man, whad I tell you, hey?"
Abis stands up, pushing his seat back with his legs. It topples over backwards. Then, I can't believe it, he climbs up on the table and walks

across it. Uneasily, to be sure. I figure he's going to topple off any second. He knocks plates and bowls about as he wobbles toward me. Though he arrives more or less intact himself, he destroys a lot of china in the process. He sits on the edge of the table next to my chair, dangling his feet off the side like a kid with his feet in the water. With both hands he motions for me to come closer.

"I must tell you a great, great secret, Manny-man."

He leans forward. "If you think this table's something," he says, "you should see his house."

He looks around. "More than any one sect will admit, it is very, very eclectic!"

"Eclectic, Abis, where the hell'd ja learn a word like tha?"

He laughs and stretches out supine on the tablecloth, scattering and smashing more dishes, plates and serving ware. As china hits the floor and cracks, he lies on his back on the tablecloth. Using an overturned faience bowl as a pillow, he holds his right hand above his head and drops red olives into his mouth.

"Rather true," Hume affirms, quite unruffled. "The food before you is, of course, a concession to time and place. To Greece, I mean. To here and now. And to the majority of guests, who, being Greek, are accustomed to it. But the vessels that contain, contained, this sumptuous feast, are, indeed of other times and other places, now, alas some lost."

"You mean all this crickery Abis is knocking to th' floor is real?"

"Everything is real, sir. Even reproductions."

"Ah, ah, Holmes, them you are saying is all of this is real, but it isn't really real?"

"You have it nearly perfectly, sir. The dishes Mr. Abis is now tossing to the floor are real. Only a philosopher with long training in the art of ontology could possibly think otherwise. But if I may venture a hazard, Sir is confusing reality with authenticity."

"All righty, then Holmes."

"Hume, sir."

"Uh, Humesur, then. As we Americans are want to say, 'what's the poop here?' Iz this Majorica medienvel ware here medi-evil or what?"

Abis finishes off the last of the red olives, picks up the bowl they had been in, and pushes it to me. "Inspect it for yourself, Many-man. It is if you say it is."

"That is hardly a satisfictory answer, Abis. I, sir, am hardly an expert in midlegal magic-oral ware."

"Hey, you are more expert than me, Manny-man. Tell him Humey-love."

"Everyone his own expert, or so it would seem nowadays, sir. As for a satisfactory answer, that is the heart of the matter. Take the British

Museum. Or the Louvre, if you prefer, though, being French, it has its own problems. Or your own National Gallery."

"Whatever do you mean, mine good sire?"

"As you know, it is a secret poorly kept by the high priests, that is, the museum curators of the international art world and their attendant art experts, that many of the paintings attributed to the great masters are not by them at all. What is that old saw? 'Of the twenty-seven authentic paintings by Vermeer, thirty-five are in America?' Ironically, some of the paintings that make this or that great master's reputation were not painted by them at all."

"What? You saying they're fakes? Forgerereries?"

"Neither fakes not forgeries, sir. Not even copies. They are the original masterpieces. But they have simply been attributed to the wrong artists. And over the years they have become what we take them for, so to speak. Gierdo paints the 'Madonna of the Fish.' Fifty years later it becomes, who knows how–through an honest mistake, perhaps, or a rapacious lie–a Raphael. Accepted by the experts, the high priests of art, who are paid by the museum curators to uphold the sacred icon."

"But damn their hides, it is mos' defiantly *not* a Raphael!" I shout, spilling a half glass of wine on my shirt and sucking on the material.

Calmly, Hume refills my glass. "Even in pure science truth is rarely Truth, sir. Only perception. Everything is flux."

"Drink up!" Abis says.

"Flux," I say. "Flux and wine. When did Mr. Love abscone?"

"It has been a while. Really, you should have been here earlier, sir."

"Abis and I were delayered."

"An old story with *him*, I'm afraid."

Abis laughs.

"Wait a minute! Wha'chew mean, I shoulda been here? How could I be espected? How ja even know abou' me?"

"Ah. We did not, of course. What we meant, sir, is that if you were coming, you should have had to have been here earlier to meet Mr. Love and his guests. Really, you did miss quite a bash."

"Ahh, well, do tell him I'm awfully sorry I mesh 'is bash. Three's a good chap. Pinkies up and all that."

"If you are with Mr. Abis, sir, I am sure you will have ample opportunity to tell him so yourself."

"Ya really tink so?

"More wine?" Abis asks.

"In dutitably," I say. "Well at leas' it was a neat and orderly soiree, humm? That counts for so mush. Don't you think so, Doom?"

"Hume, sir."

"I was taught on my mother's knee. Every think in its place. A place for every think. God's in 'is heaven an' all's right with the whole fucking world. An orderly fucking life reflects an orderly fucking universe. No kidding. Though I mus' admit I've found a few thinks out of place in God's closet over the pass few years. And I can't seem to figgur out where I should put them. God, I'm not going to cry, am I?"

"Perhaps sir should stay out of God's closet."

"Yeah, well, He's th' one that shoved me in there in the first damn place. Oh, well, gotta be philosoical about all this. We see what we can see. At lest Mr. Love and his host were orderly, uh? One does so hate rickous, drinken pipple, does not one?"

Hume looks about. "I fear Sir is jumping to conclusions, again. Things are hardly as they were back then. We've done much tidying up ourselves. Things as you see 'em are as we, not he, arranged. Is Sir ready to sober up with some coffee? Sobering up those that so need it is my speciality."

"Oh, Hume," Abis shouts, "poffee your coffee! Bring more wine! Bring on the dancing! Bring on me!"

"I thought you were asleep, Albee," I say.

He claps. The dancers and musicians re-enter the tent. Abis slithers down from the table, staggers to the middle of the floor, and, with one hand in the air, dances. His other hand is on his groin. He dances with the young dancers, making lewder and lewder gestures. Stripping off his clothes.

"Go Hecate!" he shouts. "Go Persephone! Go Moon!"

He moons. The jugglers, the musicians and dancers howl with laughter. He dances with his dog. She whirls about on her hind legs. I point at her and scream, "Socrates's defininition of a man!

Nobody hears me, though, as Rabbit and Abis dance faster and faster. She seems to be following every move he makes, though, of course, it has to be Abis who is actually doing the following. I stand up, whether to protest the growing obscenity or join in, I'm not sure. But as soon as I get to my feet, I fall on my face. My head is too heavy for my neck. Like a water balloon. It splatters on the floor when I hit. I can feel Rabbit licking the ooze that is my brains.

# NINE

It is morning now. My head is being drop-forged into the shape of a Belgian waffle. Wine fumes well up from my stomach and fill my sinuses. Still, I am glad to have survived.

The eastern sky is washed with red. It fades to orange, and then pale bluish-green. "The sky? Abis! Wake up! Where's the tent?"

Abis is ten feet away, in a brand-new sleeping bag. So am I, come to think of it. I try to sit upright. My stomach heaves up to where my heart should be. My heart is in my throat. If I had one hundred million dollars, I would give it all if I could just puke. My tongue is a hair ball any cat would admire. Finally, I get to my unsteady feet and explore. Fresh holes show where the tent poles had been. So Abis and I, the dog and the two donkeys are basically in the same place we were, only the environment has changed. Rabbit is on her back, fast asleep beside Abis, her front paws dangling in the air. Fifteen yards away, the two donkeys stand about in the lifting fog, untethered, shuddering and snorting and munching on hay. The vapor of their breaths rises and dissipates in the still, moist air. When the one farthest away lifts her head and shakes it, I realize a third beast is standing behind her. The one with the luggage! My suitcase and Abis's saddlebags are unloaded neatly on the ground beside her.

Abis is snorting and blubbering in his sleep so peacefully I haven't the heart to try to wake him again. I just retrieve my passport from my luggage and sit down again, straddle-legged with my back against a weathered marble boulder, scratching lichens with my fingertips and wondering. The morning light is gathering quickly now. The rim of the sun has completely cleared the lip of the eastern ridge. Until it burns away the fog, why not let Abis sleep? I think about Sara.

I must have a new life now. I must send my remaining days and nights without her. I must convince myself of that. And accept this fact and try to put away the pain and the longing. I have no choice. Only memories. And you cannot live on memories. The old life has fallen away. I must let go. This is hard.

This is hard.

I open my wallet, take out her last little note to me, and remove it from its little plastic pouch. I know should crumple it up and throw it away. But I can't. It is my purgatory:

"Darling," it says, "I do not regret having to die and leave this earth. I only regret leaving you."

Abis snorts and stirs into life. Both his eyelids lift together.

"Ahh, you're awake!" I say, brightly.

Abis rolls over on his side. "Have the servants bring Abis strong Greek coffee, Manny-man. With cream. No sugar. Aspirin. Toast. Butter. Tell them it must be Swiss butter. The bread must be from France. Tell them it must be fresh. Less than four days old."

"They're gone!"

He sits up. "Huh? What do you mean?"

I shrug. "But the third donkey's back. You suppose she returned on her own?"

"Oh, Manny-man, who knows what an animal's motives may be? I do not even know my own. Why is it not hot? It should be, what, two hundred Greek degrees by noon."

"The sun isn't high enough."

He looks around. "Why are we up and staring at each other, Manny-man, when the sun is no higher in the sky than the length of a land snail's penis?"

"Because I've made a great decision. I'm going to try to put my old life aside as best I can and go on. I mean, I've always known I would have to do that, but, I don't know, this morning, despite the hangover, or maybe because of it, being out here with you on this great adventure, full of life, I've really begun to wake up."

"It is true?"

"Yes!"

"I mean, no coffee?"

"Nothing."

"Humm. Hey, Manny-man, you got any kids?"

"Sara was pregnant once. But we lost her."

"Lose? How do you lose a kid?"

"She was stillborn."

"Oh. I was thinking maybe you just forgot where she is."

"I know where she is. With her mother."

"Ah, that, too. So why did you not have more?"

"We were afraid to try."

"Ah ha! So you did not become a fool overnight. You have been working on it!"

"Diligently. All my life."

"So is this not a good morning to wise up, Manny-many-man? If you do not do it now, you will do it later, huh?"

I nod.

"Your god, Manny-man, do you think he damns people for being fools? This is wrong. Hell could not be that big. My head feels as if it has been kicked by a large, hoofed animal. Here, let me sit up. No, that is worse. I shall lie down again and tell you something small. Abis buried his first wife, too. And third. I was very sad for number three but sadder still for number one. You know why? When you are young, you are not looking for death. He sneaks up behind you and grabs you hard by the ass. It hurts. You get older, you start to peep behind corners. 'Hey, Mr. Death, are you back there?' You want to make sure Mr. Death is not waiting to put a big plastic shopping bag over your head. Wife number two, she left me. Number four, I left. She put the nag in managomy."

"Abis, if you could spell, you'd still be married to her."

He shrugs. "Now I am looking for number five. No, wait! Number nine! I do plenty of interviews. With this."

He unzips his pants and unleashes a gallon and a half of urine into the whitish, sandy soil.

"Any other kids besides the one back there with his grandmother?"

"One. Two. Three. Eight. Five back home in Addis Ababa. One on Sapolo island. She is married with two children of her own. By same man. What a woman! Two back home in Spain. Three back home in Waycross. Others back home in Japan all grown up. Need some on Love's Island. And more in Greece. That is what you need, Manny-man. A Greek woman with strong back and good thighs. Carry you some of the way on her belly." He makes a sweeping gesture with his open palm toward the whole of the Aegean. "Live on the island. Eat octopus. Breed. No more books."

"Books are life."

"Ptwah." He spits. "Life is life. Ptwah for being a liar to yourself. For being a liar to life."

"At any rate, I shall never marry again."

"I have said this, too. Then two, three weeks later, Abis is hitched to a new star."

"No. Once was enough. Now I shall devote myself to learning. To work. No more rotten boughs to climb. No more love."

"Poor Manny-man. Still afraid."

"Work. And books."

"Books are very, very nice, Manny-man. And it is true a man's work is good to have. But these books, do they put their little arms around you and say, 'I love you, Daddy? Does your work put flowers on your grave and have your weak chin to pass on to your grandchildren? Do your books or job grow up and send you naughty postcards from Brazil?"

"Can we just sit here a while, Abis? I don't feel so good."

"Abis does not feel so good, either, Manny-man. But he knows the remedy."

"Where did you really grow up, Abis? I mean for real?"

"In an ugly, stinking place. In a swamp. It was called by white men, 'the reservation.' It is called by my people, 'hell.' I was raised by my ugly grandmother. Abis gets all his looks from her, because she had none left for herself. Every day I would get up from my corn cob crib bed and look out toward the hills beyond the valley and then down again to my ugly village. And then one day my grandmother, she catches me grazing out at them. She tells Abis this: she says, 'Grandson, you must promise me you will never, never, ever go to visit those hills beyond the village. The air there is freezing cold. It is the place of the people of the mountain. We are the people of the bear. You see, once my family was bears. This is why Abis is sometimes called Yanu, 'bear.'"

"Yanu is your last name?"

"No, no, that is my family name. This is true, Manny-man. My ancestors were hairy bears. This is why your friend Abis sometimes acts like a bear. Sometimes I go on two legs. Sometimes on four."

"Yes. I saw that act last night, as I recall."

"You were there with me?"

"I think so."

"The bear and the Abis, they eat the same foods. Abis sometimes likes to have sex like a bear."

"I'm not even going to ask."

"This is why, even though Grandmother said to me it is bad, Abis always as a child looked to the hills and mountains with great longing in his heart. Abis had to see the beautiful mountain meadows. To taste the mountain springs and wild blueberries. Then one morning, when I am beginning to grow hair under arms and around my penis, I disobey my grandmother and leave. That very morning I climb and climb the mountains toward the sun and the stars. I go so high that almost I can see the silver cords that hold the inverted stone bowl that is the sky above. When I am thirsty I drink the water of the cold mountain streams. I breathe the cold mountain air. And eat mountain fruits and nuts and animals on my voyage."

"Despite the fact that your grandmother told you not to go?"

He winks. "Sometimes Abis is very, very naughty. But wait. For it is there on the high mountain plateau I met Selu. This is the same Selu that you have met who is my mother-in-law now in Greece for William Love. Only then she is young and tantalizing. And she has sightly young daughters, too. Some are still in swaddling, beautiful, beautiful babies. But one daughter, oh, but one, she is fully grown, a beautiful, beautiful young virgin, Manny-man. She is made in her mother's image. High cheekbones. Handsome figure. It is impossible to choose between the mother and the daughter, so this I do not do. I have plenty of sex with both. In the corn crib and the barn."

"Both?"

"Ha, ha, oh, Manny-man, this is how I manage it. Every day we are out at the same time walking the same path to the flowing stream. Near this place Abis spies a hollow tree with many holes in it. For many days afterward I see a racoon family out walking from their home in this tree. I hide in a bush and learn they are looking for a new place to live. So I take off all my clothes and become a racoon."

"Okay. So now you're a racoon. Gotcha."

"Oh, Manny-man, you must take this lie for a truth. This is what we call 'faith.'"

"Let's just say metaphor."

"Okay. So now Abis says unto them, 'Little brothers, please accept my gift, for I and my younger brothers must go to the low ground and kill brother badger. You must move in here to our home and make it your home.' And this they do. Then the clothes I have shed I take and stuff up some of the holes in the tree. I call for help in the Indian way, like the song of a bird. Selu and her eldest daughter come running. They find me naked. I say unto them, 'Sisters, please, you must help me plug these holes in the trees. We will smoke out this whole family of my brother raccoons and feast this very night. You must take off all your clothes and stuff them into the other holes in this tree so they can't escape.' But even then there are not enough clothes to plug up all the holes. So I say to Selu, 'Sister, you must stay here and this daughter of my sister will come with me back to your settlement and find more clothes to stuff. Also we will bring back with us fire.' And so together hand-in-hand we go back to the corn crib and do it many times in many ways. Then at dusk we go back and find Selu still guarding the tree."

"She stayed there all that time?"

"Selu is not the brightest firefly in the forest, Manny-man. You have seen this already. We say unto her, 'We have found fire, but we cannot find any clothes to stuff in the holes,' and Selu says, 'My fool of a daughter, you must stay here and keep the fire going. Abis, you must come with me to find more clothes to stuff.' Then Selu and Abis return to the house to make the two backed beast many, many times and finally return to the hollow tree and smoke out my brother raccoons and feast upon them all night. Mother and daughter as well. After this I stayed many, many days with them. I made great friends with the other daughters as well. Then when the sun comes up, it dawns on Abis that it is time to return to my grandmother. I take with me Selu's eldest daughter as my first wife. Ha, ha, this is only what I call her, then."

"But you stayed married to her, right?"

He nods. "I will tell you this, young married life with her is bliss. We had a house with pretty rooms in it. And the smell of baby shit. Then, when this my first wife died, I returned to the hills. I had plenty more sex with Selu then, and with her second-oldest daughter, who soon becomes

Abis's second wife. Selu soon remarries herself. To a lawyer. He becomes my attorney-in-law. Manny-man, do you have a sister?"

"NO!"

"Too bad. *Set damage*. That is French."

I nod. "So this old woman, Selu, she actually is your two-time mother-in-law?"

"Yes. She is the ripened corn. And my grandmother, do you know who she is? Have you figured it out?"

"Figured what out?"

"That she is Mother Earth!"

"Oh, yes, of course. I should have known. So what shall we have for breakfast?"

"William Love provides."

I look around. "Not this time. Looks like we'll have to pick up the tab."

"This is because he does not have to. We can take care of ourselves and do not need this minor miracle from him. Or, maybe he *does* provide. As he sees fit. In his own way. For verily as you have said, Manny-man, he has brought back to us the third donkey. She is a sorry pig for leaving me. Lysimache!," he shouts.

The third donkey comes to him and nuzzles her nose under his armpit. He puts his other arm about her neck. "I love you now for coming back to me. Later I shall spit on you for leaving. Give me wine, my fourth daughter."

He takes his *bota* from about her neck, uncorks it, and squeezes out a considerable stream of red wine to fill his belly. Then he tosses it to me. "Here, Manny-man. The breakfast of the gods!"

"I couldn't."

"The gods won't mind!"

"No, really."

"It is pretty much all we have."

I take a hard squeeze.

"We must be up and moving, Manny-man. We do not want to miss the boat. I will tell you what, it is some great boat that William has!"

He rummages about in his satchel and comes up with some stale, hard bread. I hand him his *bota* to put away. Instead, he soaks the bread with its dregs. "So William Love is not around to help us, huh? Tent gone, too? It is in the past. In the past."

"Does that make it no longer real?" I sigh. "Maybe so. I guess we'd be fools to live as though the past *were* real."

"Sure, Manny-man. The past is where the dead ones live. You cannot live with them. You would get to smell pretty bad yourself plenty quick, *n'est-ce phew*? Hey, look around you, pal. The world is God's pocket.

Made for picking. While you still have the touch. Then it is someone else's turn. This is the truest gift of the Great Spirit."

"Same as He gave to Job," I say. "With no more justification, and this time, without a word."

"So what do you expect from this god of yours, huh? He is going to write? Send you a post card? Pick up the phone? Email? Text message? Tap you on the shoulder and grin? No, Manny-man, you must figure it all out for yourself. Ignore the contradictions. Look in your heart. Not in your brain. All will be okay. You will see. Love provides. But we must make tracks in the sand. By the time the sun goes to sleep again, we shall be at William Love's door. He will take us in with open arms. Then you will see. Have I ever lied to you?"

"Abis, you are a pack of lies held together with sinew and string."

"Ha, ha, then you are the other one, huh?"

"Who isn't?"

"There has only been one perfect person in this world, Manny-man, and he is leading this expedition."

"Let's catch up with Mr. Love."

"To William Love. Then you will see what a lie is and what is not. Has not Kanati always said this? You shall sort it out all by yourself."

"I've as good a chance as any."

"Manny-man, you are one crazy son of a snail. But this is good, huh? Please God. This is good, I tell you."

He wacks his donkey. I wack mine. We are off. Lysimache, the third donkey, follows close behind. Rabbit rides on Abis's lap.

# TEN

The sun is setting now. We climb a rocky hill and look down at a small harbor. A few anchored sailboats dance about in the middle of the inlet. The water is clear and blue. Three small, wooden fishing boats are tied to pilings on the quay. One is bright yellow, one black, the other red. Their nets are strung up, drying in the wind. A small, round, whitish, rocky island protects the u-shaped inlet. From our vantage point, it looks like a dried apple about to enter a mouth.

Like tiny, untended flowers, houses crowd the hills that surround the u-shaped harbor and the apple-island. Most are painted white. Scattered here and there, a few are terra-cotta. One halfway up the hill is the color of an orange dreamsicle.

The sun settles deeper into the water. Now just a rim resides on this side of the horizon. Its last long, orange rays tint the tile roofs and the stucco walls a vivid orange-red. As the shadows deepen farther into night, the tall, slim, green cypress trees become more black and tenebrous and imposing as their silhouettes punctuate the low, squat forms of the houses like the tall, slim shades of the underworld that gathered before Odysseus at the garden of Proserpine. Like a *trompe l'oeil* canvas by Cezanne.

In reality, I think, it is Love's Island. Finally.

And yet, none of the houses seems large enough to be his. By no stretch of the imagination could any of them be considered a mansion.

"Which is William Love's?"

He points to a huge ocean-going yacht steaming out into open water.

"I mean, which house?"

Abis doesn't answer.

"He doesn't live here, does he?"

"Live here? Ptewie. Oh, Manny-man would you live here?"

"Why not? If I were Greek. It's gorgeous. Wouldn't you live here?"

"He doesn't."

"All right, Abis, then where the hell does this William Love of yours live?"

"I have told you before. Over shining big sea waters."

"Oh, well, excuse me, where the hell does he live, Hiawatha? Try to be specific."

"You mean where does he live now?"

"Right."

"Umm. On yacht. Ha, ha, the joke is on us. We have missed the boat. Again." He sits down on a boulder. "So, Manny-man, what do we do now?"

"What do you mean?"

"I mean, how in hell do we get home?"

"Not we, Abis, you. I have a ticket. And that's it. I quit. I'm gone. You're on your own."

"Huh?"

"I'm serious. I'm gone, Abis. Finished. Finito. Finis. I really mean it this time, too. I'm going back to Athens, even if I have to hitchhike. Then I'm catching the next plane back to America, locking myself up in my study and never coming out again until my work is through."

Abis shrugs. "Okay, sure. But how will Abis get to meet William Love?"

"I don't give a fuck!"

"Oh."

"Don't look at me like that. I'm sorry, but dammit, that's the way it is, okay? I don't care anymore. You've been leading me on for God knows what reason. You know it and I know it. And I quit. You either lost, or tried to lose, everything I brought with me. And you have lied to me over and over and I'm through."

"No, Manny-man. I have not lied. Hardly."

"Yes. You promised to take me to William Love and every time we supposedly get close you say we've just missed the boat."

"We have just missed the boat, Manny-man."

"So why should I stay with you? It's not doing either of us any good."

"What you are saying is a lie, Manny-man. It is an, an untruth. A prefabrication."

"All right, all right, I'll admit it has been, well, interesting. But damn, Abis, I've got to get on with things. I can't dawdle my life away with you, for God's sake."

"Why not?"

"Because I've got to get on with things!"

"You are getting on with things, Manny-man."

"I mean, real things!"

"So you are really going to go?"

"I'm sorry. But yes."

He unties my battered piece of luggage from the third donkey and hands it to me. I back away a few feet as he stands, watching. I turn and start to walk away.

"Manny-man," he says.

I turn back.

"What about some money?"

"No. I'm sorry. I can't help you."

He runs up to me. "Here. You must take this." He shoves a crumpled piece of paper into my hand. I unfold it. It's an American hundred dollar bill.

"No, Abis. You keep it. I lied. I have one of my own in my sock."

"I know. But maybe perhaps you need this one, too, because you say you must hitchhike all across America where it is very expensive to eat and get laid."

"I'll be all right."

I hold out my hand to shake his.

"No. Among my people, we do not shake hands. You must simply say, 'I go now.' Then I say, 'go then.' This is all."

"That's it? I mean that's all?"

"Yes. That is all."

"Well, then, um, I guess I, I go now."

"Go then."

We remain facing each other for a long time. Then I turn and start to walk away toward the village. After a few steps, I look back. Damn it, I want to shake his hand. I want to say, 'thank you,' though I'm not sure for what. Maybe exchange addresses. Something. But he and his donkeys and the dog have already vanished.

Something occurs to me. I check to make sure the hundred dollar bill he offered me was not my own. It isn't. Not that the money is so vital. I do still have my credit card in my wallet, and my ticket. But it would make my next few days a lot easier to have some cash.

I stay that night in a small tourist hotel in the village. In the morning, I catch the bus to Athens. The next day I board the plane to Hartsfield-Jackson Atlanta International Airport. I'm so confused. I feel awful. Throughout the flight, I stare out the window, thinking.

I should have stayed. For what? What purpose would it have served?

No. In the end, I'm better off without him around. So what if the mystery of William Love is never solved. I'm better off without him.

So now what? I mean, what will I do now? I'm not ready to go back. I'm not ready to go forward, either. For a while there, I thought I was. But I'm not.

# PART II: THE RAIN

Two halves make a whole.
-Mrs. Denton,
my third grade teacher

# ELEVEN

The terminal at the Atlanta airport is charmless and robotic. Passé modern art without craftsmanship. Disembodied, mechanical voices. The modern lifeless world. Tedious corridors of insidious intent. I can just imagine what Abis would say.

In fact, it's gotten to the point that anytime I think of something ironic or funny or wrong my thoughts seem to come out of his mouth and in his voice.

On the other hand, getting rid of him has its compensations, too. At least I'll keep dry unless I'm in the shower. I'll remain fully clothed in public, eat no more turtles and above all, stay clean and sober and above all, rational. Besides, he's out of my life anyway so I might as well get used to it again. Let him drive the Greeks crazy. He was fun to a point. But now it's time to get back to my books and my study. Back to reality.

On the other hand, I don't feel quite ready to do that, yet. Maybe I should've stayed in Greece. Why did I really leave?

Because I was afraid.

No, no, I shouldn't be so hard on myself. I was being prudent. I could have gotten in real trouble. If some of the stuff he got me into became known back at my university, I could have been fired. The kind of crap he got me into is better enjoyed in recollection. Like the stunts you pull in high school. I'm way too old for that now.

Luggage slides out of a chute and onto the luggage conveyor, which hums and squeaks. I grab my bag, place it between my knees and start to retrieve the claim check from my wallet. A dog barks close to me. I look around. Suddenly, a hand grabs for my luggage! It's the old bait-and-switch, or whatever you call it. Someone or something distracts your attention, another grabs your stuff. I'm being robbed right there in the Atlanta airport! I grip my bag and yell for help.

"It's all right, Manny-man. I will lug your luggage. No, this is great! It is very, very fortunate Abis has come in time. Look, Chufee-dog, it is Manny Marknowits, our third oldest pal from the nether lands. Is this not great? We can take him off to meet William Love for realsises now!"

"How in hell did you get here faster than I did in my jet? And how in hell did you get that mangy mutt through quarantine?"

"Shuuush, now, Manny-man. These are the two easiest things to apply to truth. First, I have sold William Love, his donkeys. Then we took a limitsine to the small airport. Next we flew on his private wings to Athens airport and then on a Concorde out from there to this very spot you are in! *N'est-ce place?*"

"Concordes don't even fly anymore, Abis. Not in years."

"What, so now I am a liar?"

"And how'd you smuggle that dog back in?"

"Easy as pine. Put this harness on doggie, put these dark glasses on Abis. Poof. Dog becomes invisible to border guards because owner is one blind son of a bitch. Ha, ha, they do not know whom is the owner of whom. They do not even realize she is a bitch. Manny-man, they do not even check to see which way her gonads are pointing. Come, kimoslobie, we go to William Love now. White man want Indian talk like movie Indian now?"

"Just, just, just."

"Come we go now quick. You are picking up a bad stammer here in the freezing wind by the open door."

"It's eighty-five degrees."

"If we stay here long enough, it will get cold. Come. Our plane is waiting."

"What plane? What are you talking about?"

"It is a small private parts type of plane, Manny-man. A charter flight waiting on the little bitty end of the airport deserved for important executives like us."

"William Love has arranged a private plane?"

"Come, Manny-man. We go to Love's Island right away. Wickedly split. We will have a great big time. Make love with the moon. You will get plenty of stuff to put in this book you are writing. Come. Abis will lug the luggage."

He lifts my suitcase. The lock flips up. The lid pops open. My stuff tumbles out. He jerks up on the handle. The rest of my stuff spills out on the floor. It looks like the guts from a sacrificial goat. Abis gives the bag a final shake and the last pair of undershorts flutters to the floor.

"No worry, Manny-man. It was a cheap suitcase. You are a rich man. You must buy one worthy of you."

"I paid a small fortune for that thing!"

"Umm. You got taken, pal. Good thing you have me, Eduardo d'Espagnolia, to save and protect you from the unscrupulous and strange people we encounter in this strange country. No, no, wait, I have forgotten where we are now. It is I, Bubba, of Southeast Georgia, USA to save you, good ole buddy. Ha, ha, we are back in Dixie. We will eat hush puppies and grits, and say funny things like 'ya'll' and get us one dem pick-me-up trucks painted primer red and get us somedem purdy southern bell bottom wemmin. What you say, Manny-man, want to call Abis 'Bubba' from now on, an' be good ole boys?"

"No," I say casually as I continue my frantic endeavor to gather all my belongings off the floor. People are staring. Abis bends down to help me and accidently boots a roll of my socks out the door.

"Wow! Look at this! That is some funny-looking underwear, Manny-man."

He holds a pair of my shorts up to the light. "What is that, hearts on there? Please tell me these were a gift from some woman who did not like you because all honkie white men have tiny penises."

He tosses the boxer shorts into the bag. I retrieve the socks and toss them in, too. From around his waist he unwinds the rope he's been using as a belt, ties it round my bag, picks it up and jogs off. I follow him, his dog and my stuff through the airport. We take a steep, two story escalator down to a train that talks in a mechanical voice like robots out of George Orwell's worst nightmare, then a tram and finally a taxi cab.

"There!" Abis shouts. The taxi screeches to a halt in front of a small terminal building. The field is littered with small airplanes of every vintage and shape, like some sort of museum of aviation. Abis gets out, slams the taxi door so hard the driver and I both wince, and shouts at me through the open window, "You wait here, Manny-man. I will arrange everything. Trust me. Take good care of Chufee."

"Chufee?"

"Dog. Whom you called something else over there, remember? Chufee is her name here." He puts his finger to his lips. "Shuush. Do not call her by that other name on this side."

I can tell by the slouch of the cabdriver's shoulders he's getting a bit edgy. Who can blame him? I guess Abis notices, too, because he says, "Pay taxi guy, Manny-man. Do not give him a big tip. He is half-drunk already."

With that the driver gets out, flings my door open, and jerks with his thumb for me to get the hell out. He looks like he's about to hit me. I give him a big tip. He boots my bag out of his trunk so hard it breaks open again as it slams the pavement. The cab squeals off like a pig out of hell. I stand next to the curb with spilled luggage, and a panting, drooling, smelly dog.

Abis comes running back. The dog jumps up then settles down, content to sniff at Abis's crotch for a few minutes before turning to bark and snarl at me.

"Are you sure that's the same dog? She looks bigger to me now."

"She ate lots of junkets food on the plane. Come we must hurry now."

He snatches up a handful of my clothes and runs off. I scoop the rest into my bag and run after him. It's getting pretty dark, but I can make out that he's getting into a waiting airplane. The engine is already running. I climb aboard. Abis seals the door. We're on our way.

The plane is crowded with huge, canvas bales of unmarked cargo. There is this pervading sweet smell that I think might be marijuana. I sit next to the pilot, a thin, sullen-looking man who is taking into his nostrils what I hope is snuff.

"Excuse me, sir, what are those things? Army duffle bags? Would it be all right if I sorta moved this one over a bit? God, they're heavy. What have you got in them?"

"Don't you never touch nothin' in here again, fuck-face!"

"Yes sir. I mean, 'no, sir,' I won't. I'll, I'll just sit here and be really, really quiet and sort of lean over them like this, if that's okay."

"An' keep your fucking mouth fucking shut. Got that?"

I nod and sit without moving a muscle, listening to the drone and occasional miss of the engine, to Abis's snoring, to Chufee's snoring, and the pilot's frequent snorts.

"Hey, you."

"Me?"

"No, your brother. Yeah, you, genius. Th' asshole snoring in the back there said you was the one with the cash."

"The cash, sir?"

"Cash, shit-belly. No checks, no cards, no trade units, no loans. U.S. American currency. Fork it over, now!"

"What?" I shout. This wakes up Abis and Rabbit, I mean Chufee. Also, it seems to disturb the pilot deeply.

"Hey, Einstein, you understand what I'm saying to you? Pay up now, mother-humper, or I fucking drop both of youse right now."

"How much do we owe you, sir?"

"Like I told your pal back there, three hunnerd twenty-five bucks."

"But I don't have it."

"Do not pay him that much, Manny-man. This is an outrageous overcharge. Negotiate him downward. Do this instantly. Tell him there is no worry. William Love will pay him the very nanosecond we land."

The muscles of the pilot's jaws jut out, then disappear as he grinds his teeth. He makes the plane veer sharply toward the left, then level out again. We fly for a while in silence. Then he presses a button and like magic the lights of an airport come on below us. He circles once, then sets down. As soon as we come to a halt on the asphalt, he shouts above the roar of the engine, "Out!"

Abis says, "No, no, my good man, dreadfully sorry, but this is not Love's Island."

"Out!"

"No. First you must take us where we want to go. Did you not shake my hand on this bargain?"

The pilot pulls out a small pistol. This encourages us to disembark. My second foot no sooner hits the pavement than the plane taxis off again. The lights in the little rural airport, wherever it is, go out. We are completely in the dark. No moon.

I hear a woof, and Abis's disembodied voice out of the dark say, "You should have paid him, Many-man. Now what will we do?"

"Abis, I can't see a damn thing!"

"Do not panic, Manny-man. You are not blind. It is night."

"I know that."

"People and small dogs, they cannot see at night."

"Obviously."

"Wild animals, they can see in the dark. This is why they are over there, hunting now."

"Over where? What kind of wild animals?"

"Ferocious ones, Manny-man. Mountain lions, cougars, panthers–I am not sure the difference between these three–plus bears, wolves, coyotes, badgers, wolverines and many, many, many kinds of poisonous snakes. All of these hunt at night and the moon is sleeping."

"Well, it's not very likely they would be hunting on the middle of a paved air strip somewhere in God knows what part of, I'm guessing Georgia, would they? I mean there's got to be a town nearby, don't you think?"

"This is the very place they would be hunting, Manny-man. Especially Mr. Poisonous Snake. There are nineteen varieties of highly poisonous kinds in this territory, plus many exotic imports that have escaped from zoos and airports. Do you have matches or a flashlight in your suitcase?"

"Shit!"

"What kind of shit, Manny-man?"

"Deep."

"Do you have a good, strong flashlight in suitcase, with lots of beam power, Manny-man?"

"Sure do. Matches, too."

"Can you light one of these for us now Manny-man?"

"No. That is why I said, 'shit,' Abis. My luggage is still on the airplane. I've lost my stuff for good this time."

"Oh, those darn airlines, Manny-man. Always losing luggage. This is not a major problem. We will just sit here on the tarp and wait until the rosy fingers of Dawn thrust up like a happy lark at daybreak. Probably another plane will not land here tonight, do you think? We must hope that lions and bears do not eat us before the rosy dawn arrives. Then we will find this small town, USA that this air field belongs to. We will call for help. We will take a cab and ride in great style. You have a quarter to use the pay telephone if we find one?"

"When's the last time you ever saw a pay phone. Abis?"

"Do you not have a cell phone?"

"If I did, which I don't, it would be packed in my luggage."

"This is very bad planning, Manny-man."

"Why did you negotiate a plane ride with a criminal, Abis?"

"Abis did not know he was a criminal. He did not tell me this."

"You think Al Capone would've told you he was a criminal?"

"I do not know this Al K. Pony, Manny-man. This is a criminal liar friend of yours from your university?"

"No. If he were he'd be a dean. Didn't it even occur to you that that pilot might have been a criminal?"

"Abis thought he was a pilot. I do not hang out with the criminal element as you do, Manny-man. Chufee, come here, darling. Make a little 'woof' if you have not been eaten by wolves, swallowed whole by the Uktena, or possessed by evil spirits, honey."

She woofs. I hear Abis move toward the dog and shuffle and grope toward them. "Whhaaaa!" I scream as something comes down hard on my shoulder.

"Do not shout like that, Manny-man. What hit you is probably the hand of me, Abis of the Choctaw Nation. I mean, Enea of the Creek People. Formerly Abo of the Ainu. Manny-man, it is you who are Abis of the Chickasaw. For you are my twin brother, no? The head to my body? It is either me who is touching your shoulder or my crazy brother, William. Either it is this, or I am touching the evil shoulder of a spirit. Please tell me it is you, Manny-man. I am making myself very scared. Here, Chufee. Please come to Daddy."

Abis whines and moves off, presumably to find the animal.

"Abis? ABIS? WHERE ARE YOU?"

"Does white eyes want the good news or the awful?"

"Better give me the good."

"This will take some time, Manny-man. I must think of something."

"Okay, then, what's the bad news?"

"We are not exactly on a paved air strip."

"What exactly are we on?"

"Umm, it seems to be part of an old, abandoned road now going to nowhere. With new landing lights attached. Now that my eyes have adjusted to the dark light I can still see nothing out there but trees. There is no airport terminal, Manny-man. No terminal at all. No planes. Not even a crop duster. Soon we will be eaten by spotted bears and mountain lions."

"What do you suggest we do, then?"

"You must come over here to Abis. Shuffle your feet as you walk. There are many, many big snakes in the area who like to warm themselves at night on old blacktops. Do not step on them. This may piss them off."

"I'm not moving until daylight."

"Suit yourself, Manny-man."

"What was that noise?"

"What noise?"

"Sort of like a slither."

"That is what it was, Manny-man. A slither."

"Do you think it was a big slither or a little slither?"

"You mean like a poisonous kind of slither, Manny-man?"

"Oh, God, Abis, that's exactly what it was. A definite poisonous slither!"

"Look over there, Manny-man. In shadow. Do you see it?"

"Yes. What is that?"

"A bear. Do you not smell it, yet?"

"That musky odor? I thought that was just us, needing a bath."

"Bear."

"Is it sleeping?"

"No."

"Do they feed at night?"

"Yes."

"Why isn't it moving?"

"It is staring."

"At what?"

"You, Manny-man."

"Why?"

"To him you are like Puppy Chow to Chufee."

"I'm going to run, Abis."

"Then the snakes will get you."

"So what should I do?"

"Come to Abis. Slow. Shuffle your feet when you walk."

"Oh, God, this place is swarming with mosquitoes!"

"There are no mosquitoes in Georgia, Manny-man. You must trust me on this. I have read this truth in the Chamber of Commerce Magazine. In the bathroom once. When I had diarrhea. I got to read the whole article. Twice. Besides, I, personally, Yanu, the great warrior of his people, have not been eaten once by even one tiny mosquito."

"Abis?"

"Yes, oh, my friend."

"Are you really an Indian? I mean, no joke?"

"This is no joke, Manny-man. This I am!"

"Abis?"

"What?"

"Why isn't your dog barking at the bear?"

"She is not so stupid as you think."

"Where is she?"

"Perhaps she is not so loyal as you think. Perhaps she has been possessed by spirits. Come. We will go to that tree over there. Slowly. We will climb it and sleep. It will be like a Hilton Hotel of the Forest. It will have plenty of Spanish moss to wrap ourselves in to protect us from the red bugs."

"Abis, I can't climb a tree!"

"Okay. No problem. I will bury what parts of you I find on the ground in the morning."

"Look! I think the bear has moved closer! Can you smell it?"

"It may not be a bear."

"What else could it be?"

"A spirit. This is the very shape they take, Manny-man."

"No, God damn it! There is no such things as spirits! It's a goddamned bear! Now give me a boost.

He does.

I reach the highest bough I can and straddle it as if I were back on the donkey, which it sort of feels like, a donkey with a very, very bad skin disease.

"Wrap your legs in plenty of Spanish moss, Manny-man. That way the snakes perhaps may not get you."

"What kind of snakes do you think they were down there? They were *huge!*"

"Uktena. The horned snake. Very, very, very poisonous. You can rest now. Abis is almost sure they usually do not climb this high, I think. Try to sleep. I will keep guard. I will stare down the bear. Look her straight in the eye. That is the best way to handle her. Unless she has cubs in this tree. Look around. If you see baby bears, you must hand them down to her, gently. Use a soothing voice. Then you must put your anus hard on the limb of the tree so your soul does not leave your body and go north to dream of snakes. Otherwise you will be bitten."

"If I tried to sleep I'd fall. No thanks. I plan to stay awake the rest of the night."

# TWELVE

My eyes bang open as if they were spring loaded. The sun has been up a few hours already. The dog is asleep next to me, her feet dangling from either side of the limb. We are nearly two feet off the ground. Abis is on the leaf mold directly beneath us, his back against the trunk. His feet are splayed out in front of him and he seems to be carving on that Indian mask he was working on in Greece.

I groan. He looks up. "Ah, ha," he says. "Hand Chufee down by the scruff of the neck"

As I do so, she hangs completely limp "Abis," I say, "she's dead."

He takes her limp body and places it in his lap. Immediately she opens her eyes and begins to lick her crotch.

"Do you know why a dog licks its crotch, Manny-man?"

"Why?"

"Because it can."

I get down from the tree as best I can, considering how stiff and sore I am. The insides of my legs, my buttocks, and my thighs are itching so badly I have to pull down my pants instantly to see what's going on.

I'm covered with horrible red welts. "Oh, God, Abis, what is it?"

"Umm. Chiggers."

"Will it spread?"

"Only if you sit on the bark again. Ha, ha, they are tiny red bugs. This is what the people here call them, 'red bugs.' Abis should have warned his pal about them last night, huh?"

"Can't you do something? I mean, if you really are an Indian, don't your people have some kind of special sacred remedy for this sort of thing?"

"Rubbing alcohol and sand, Manny-man. First you rub on alcohol, then you spread sand. The tiny bugs will come out of your pores to drink. Then they will get into a bar-room brawl, throw big rocks at each other, die."

"Very funny. Hey, how come you didn't get bitten? You don't even have one mosquito bite!"

He shows me some kind of bark. "I have this. I rub it on my skin."

"Why didn't you give me some?"

"Too late now, Manny-man. You should have asked for some last night. He, he, look over there. A fat tree stump. That is what Abis mistook for a brown bear in the dark. Ha, ha, I am a fool. Would you believe it, people have told me this before? Benedict, Hume, even William Love. All of us. We have said to our own ears, 'Abis, you are one grade-A number one fool.' And fool that I am, I believed them! But Manny-man, you are not a fool, are you? You are a college professor. Are all people liars? I must tell you this: your good buddy Abis would carry dog stools to Texas. Look what I have done to you. You have ended up, where? In the middle of nowhere. You are all bitten up. Lucky for you I am never lost."

"Wonderful. So where the hell are we?"

"Exactly smack dab in the middle of nowhere. Georgia, USA, I think. The coast is maybe that way. No, really. Stop wringing your hands, Manny-man. We are not far from Love's Island, I can tell you that. It is great. Abis can feel it in his shin bones. Come. We will ask the Long Man how we go. Just as we asked the missionary of Delphi."

He walks off. I follow, scratching. What else can I do? He stops and sniffs the air several times. I do, too. It has a sticky sweetness to it. Like wild honeysuckle, or tea olive. Only much, much stronger.

Abis looks about and grins. He begins trotting down the wooded hillside. The dog and I trot after him until we get to a large stream. "We follow this to the sea."

"Makes sense."

"Hmm. This is good. If it makes sense to you, Manny-man, then we must do it. We will follow Long Man. Ha, ha, unless we get bored. Then we follow our hearts."

"Why don't we just plan to do this sensibly?"

"That is the very thing Abis likes about you, Many-man."

He gets down on his hands and knees, scratching under leaves, peering behind tree trunks, bushes and stones.

"What are you looking for?"

"My war bundle."

"Ah, of course. I should have known. What's a war bundle?"

"I will show you when I find it. Umm. It is somewhere here. Abis is sure this is where he hid it."

"When?"

"Last night. No, no, wait! Three months ago last January! HA! Look! It is here!"

He reaches down under a mat of leaves and pulls out a sort of leather wrapping.

"Are you saying you've been here before?"

"Umm, umm, uh, no. Ha, ha, Abis put his war bundle here last night, Manny-moon. See, it is made of deerskin."

He places it on the ground and unwinds it, taking out the oddest assortment of objects I have ever seen outside of a museum, naming each one for me as he lays it out on the leaf mold.

"Manny-man, this is the mummy of an eagle. This is a mummified snake. Also here we have a weasel and a black hawk, two eagle's feathers, one deer tail, two wolves' tails, one war club, very old, three flutes, and paint medicine. Very, very valuable. We must guard this war bundle very carefully or we cannot go on. Come, let us ask the river what to do."

He puts one ear close to the water, nodding periodically, humming, and saying, "yes," or "no" now and then, as if he were talking on the telephone. Then he stands up.

"Hey, Manny-man. It is great! Long Man says to follow him to the sea. Let's go. We will find William Love at the end of the river."

\*\*\*

After we've followed the bank for an hour, Abis says, "We cross over Long Man here, where he is wide and shallow. Come. He is only ankle deep in this spot."

"But why cross if we're gonna follow it to the sea?"

"*Him*. Follow *him*."

"Okay, follow *him*." I slap my neck. "God, these mosquitoes."

"Soon we will come to a big bend. If we cross here we can meet Long Man again in two miles, where he straightens out his back again. If we follow the bank on this side it will take two days to get to the same place. Come. It is only ankle deep. Trust Abis, remember?" He picks up his dog, then almost drops her trying to juggle the little beast and the war bundle.

"Want me to carry that?"

"NO! It is very bad for paleface honkie-puss to do this thing! The war bundle is an Indian good luck charm. Like the rabbit's foot is to Irish people. Heh, it was not so lucky for the rabbit, huh?"

"But what if we get lost?"

"Not even possible. We are so close now to William Love's Plantation that Abis knows this land like the back of his head. Like the back of his own fanny. Come. We will cross the river now. This way we will avoid the horrible waterfall ahead and the nests of uktenas!"

He wallows into the river. I wade in after him. Up to my knees. Then my thighs.

"I thought you said it was shallow?"

"Not to worry."

"Ahhhhhhhhh!" I scream as my feet slip out from under me. I'm being carried rapidly downstream.

"Manny-man, do not go swimming now. No time for this nonsense."

"Help me, you bastard!"

He shouts after me, making a megaphone with his hands, "How did you know? Chufee told you? Well, she is a bi ...."

But I can't make out anything else. The current has taken me too far away. I flounder about, trying to gain a foothold on the bottom or grab something to stop my backward progress. The water is too deep. I'm going to drown. Snakes are trying to grab my legs and pull me under. I hear the roaring sound of rushing water and remember Abis's idle chatter about a deadly waterfall nearby. I grab for branches. I grab for the bank. I grab for rocks. My hands are raw and bleeding. I'm going under! My head dunks into the stream, then out, then in again, then out. Rush of water. My bottom hits bottom. My head is in the air. I'm not moving anymore. The water swirls about me. "Oh!" I cry, then "hmm. Gosh. Not deep at all, here."

I stand up and wade to the bank. Then this horrible wet dog stench hits me like two tons of manure. I hear barking, and whimpering as well. Sure enough, Abis's wonder dog is floating downstream toward me. I wade back out, grab Chufee, or Rabbit, or whatever he's calling her today, by the scruff of the neck just as she's going by, and take her to shore.

In gratitude, the bitch growls and snaps at the hand that just saved her. I drop her on the sand. She shakes evil smelling river slime all over my pants, shirt, shoes and face. Abis floats into view. He's holding his carved mask in one hand and his ridiculous war bundle in the other. His hat somehow has remained tightly on his head. He bumps bottom, stands up, and says, "Manny-man, this is a very foolish thing you have done, running away like that. But fool that I am, I forgive you."

"Thank you."

"You are most welcome."

"Where are we?"

He cups his hand to my ear. "Hear that noise? We are close to the dangerous rabids. Hip to haunch with the horrible waterfall. Very steep. Like Angel Falls, near Abis's home in the swamps of Venezuela. It is plenty lucky for you that you have decided not to swim anymore today, Manny-man. You would go over to the other side. Well, at least we have had our morning bath, *n'est-ce plunge*?"

"*Oui*," I say as I reenter the stream and splash the slime off.

"Now we must be careful of the tie snakes."

"Now we must find fast food restaurant."

"Oh, Manny-man, food? Is that all you ever think about?"

"Yes, when I'm starving."

"It is lucky for you that finding food in the woods is what Indians do best. You must wait here. It may be dangerous for you."

I sit down under a tree while Abis and his dog go off to hunt nuts and berries, or whatever you find in the forest.

***

He returns in about a half hour with a bag of burgers, some camping equipment, and a tent.

"Where'd you get 'em?" I ask as we eat.

"Over hill, over dale, Abis bit the rusty nail."

I walk to the top of the little rise. An unpaved road leads to a little trading post kind of store. "Why didn't you tell me?"

"Too dangerous."

"Did you have enough money?"

"This is why it was dangerous."

"You *stole* this stuff?"

"He, he. Come. We must go."

"No. I'm going down the road and hitch a ride back."

"Back where? With who?"

"I don't know."

"With strangers who will beat and rob you for your pathetic canvas shoes and that gold filled molar of yours. One half ounce, twenty-seven karat. No. You must stick with Abis like gluons. He will protect you. Only he can lead you to William Love. Do you not want to go to his mansion?"

"Does he really have a mansion? Aren't you making that all up? I mean, does he even exist?"

"Oh, so now Manny-man is a prognostic? Did not even Hume tell you of his existence?"

I say nothing. I just scratch.

"Okay, okay, Manny-man, I will now tell you the whole truth. You deserve this."

"Great."

"Do you ever wonder why I know so much about this land we are in?

"Frankly I just assumed you'd been here a time or two before, despite what you've said."

"Many, many times before, Manage-man. This is my land for William Love."

"Wait a minute, now you're saying this is his land, and you're some kind of manager of it?"

"We will go soon to his house. Very soon from here. Once all this was Indian land. Now only the name of it is. Really, it all belongs to Someone Else."

"To William Love?"

"This is the ancient land that we speak of. The island of the lake between the two rivers. Here live a species of woman of great beauty. Here they will feed you oranges, figs, bananas, and hothouse grapes and none shall be unafraid. Oh, Manny-man, it is to Love's Island that we journey. He is rich beyond compare. He has the things of this world, too, and he expects his servant Abis to bring you unto him. Oh, that Willy! He knows everything! I tell you, he is rich! And now, Many-moon, we have a tent, and the stuff of survival. You would regret all the rest of your pathetic life if you did not complete with me this last of my great adventures on this land, Manny-man. Come. We go East now. East is West at last. But in the beginning, East is not West, *n'est-ce place*? Come, Manny-man, we go East. We shall find Love."

"Did you steal this stuff?"

"William Love provides."

"All right, fine, we'll do it. But first, let's walk downstream a bit."

"Why?"

"I wanna see the waterfall."

"Too dangerous. Uktena."

Ignoring him, I walk along the bank, following the shallow rapids. He remains for a minute, then shrugs and catches up. He walks beside me some of the time, but lags behind now and then to sniff at something before trotting on ahead. I don't know where Chufee is until we hear her growling and barking in the woods. Immediately Abis runs to find her. I run to find Abis.

The little animal is snarling and snapping as she crouches low and circles a bush. I back away. This time for sure there's got to be a snake in there. I hear the rattle. Abis picks up a forked stick and goes forward. "Hush, little sister," he says, "Abis is right here, Chufee, darling."

Carefully, he probes with his wooden weapon. Then he thrusts his forked tip into the bush and drags something out. "Come here, Manny-man," he says, cheerfully.

I shuffle forward a bit. "What is it?"

"Look."

I peer over his shoulder. On the ground lies a miniature bow and a quiver full of small, stone tipped arrows. Not toys, mind you, but scaled-down miniatures like something elves would use. I go around Abis to pick it up.

"NO!" he shouts.

My hand recoils as if I were about to touch a spitting cobra.

"This belongs to the Little People."

"Midgets? Are you saying William Love keeps a colony of Indian midgets on this land? Should I say Native Americans?"

"No, Manny-man, this belongs to the Little Men. And soon there will be thunder." He bends over. "Little Men, I want to take this," he says and picks up the little bow and arrows. "This is good. Later we will use them to hunt."

"What are you talking about?"

"Perhaps they are the Thunder Boys. We have been chosen by them, *n'est-ce pick*? This makes Abis very afraid. Oh, Manny, what if they have returned from the Darkening Land?"

"Beats me."

"What if it turns out that Abis is one of them?"

"Could be."

He squats down. "You do not believe me, do you?"

"Frankly, I don't know what in hell you're talking about."

"The Thunder Boys. These are the two sons of Selu and Kanati. One is wild. One is tame. When they talk it is like rolling thunder. This is why my people call them the Thunder Boys."

"Thank you. That explains everything."

"No, no, wait, I am a fool, Manny-man, a fool! If this bow belongs to the Little People, this is good. They will help us. If they are not mad because we have taken their bow and quiver. Then they will drive us crazy."

"As you say, for some of us, it's not a long drive."

"Okay, Manny-man, you have convinced me. We will use this gift and not put it under the bush again. They will lead us straight to William Love. For we are like lost children. And that is what they do, help lost children."

"I think I have more faith in the dusty road back there than in your little people leading us out of here. In the meantime, I want to see this great waterfall we almost went over."

"You are sure?"

"Yep."

"Okaaay. But we must cross back over the Long Man and approach from the other side. Big rocks block our view from here."

We wade across. In a few minutes we come upon the mighty falls.

"You're right," I say. "This is dangerous."

"You bet."

"Must drop, what? Nearly eighteen inches?"

"Straight down, Manny-man."

"Would have killed us, for sure. "

"It is not so much the drop that kills, Manny-man. It is the great horned snakes that come to drink of these waters. Even their spit is poisonous."

"Uh huh."

He points to the opposite bank. I can't believe what I'm seeing. A great horned snake is actually sunning itself on the rocks of the rapids thirty yards below the falls. It spots us, raises its massive head and a third of its body and continues to stare, swaying slowly. Sunlight dances off its head as if a jewel were set between the horn-like projections. Then it slowly lowers itself into the water and is gone. I have never seen a snake so large in my life, and I've seen the giant anacondas of the San Diego zoo, on T.V.

I turn to Abis. "Is there another way to get back to the road besides wading back through the river?"

He shakes his head.

"Another way to Love's Island besides following the bank? I mean, without getting us lost."

"Yes. But it takes one day longer."

"Can we somehow go round the river and get me back to the road?"

"No way, Manny-man. Here the river is a snake. He coils up in many, many places. We must cross over the coils. The only way out is back across the coils. Or through the woods to the house of Love."

"I'm not ready to cross the river."

"Then we must go through the woods. To the delicious plum tree pond. No snakes there. We can hunt with our little bow and arrows. Live off the land like two spiders in a web. And be brothers again. What do you think, little sister, do we go on?"

Chufee jumps up and does a flip. We both laugh. Abis rushes at me like a bear, apparently to give me a hug, but knocks me down instead. I get up. We hike. Abis stops periodically to sniff the air and fondle the foliage. "We can tell by the kinds of trees how far we are from the water, Manny-man. So what do you think of the Uktena?"

"If I hadn't seen it with my own eyes, I would not have believed it."

"I will bet with you every bit of euro dollars in my left pocket that you cannot find his picture in your *Paleface Encyclopedia of Animals*."

"Probably not."

"Did you see the wings?"

"Wings?"

"You bet. They have great bird's wings folded on their sides, Manny-man. Perhaps you did not see them because he kept them hidden deep, deep in the water."

"I must have missed that."

"Too bad, Manny-man. *Set damage*. That is French. I am the master of many languages aside English. I tell you what; a man could easily make his life if he could capture the jewel on the top of the great snake's head."

"I think that was just the sunlight bouncing off its wet skin."

"Manny-man, you are such a fool! Some day Abis will catch such a snake and have his crystal. Then for sure Abis will know what is to be."

"Be careful he doesn't catch you."

"This is the very reason I have put off catching this great snake for a while. Asides, I do not have the blood yet to feed this thing."

"Were you scared when you saw it?"

"Last night Abis did not dream of snakes. So he knew today he would not be bitten. Only I dreamt of floating fish."

"Well, I suppose that's pleasant enough. Sara and I kept tropicals. Very restful."

He drops his pack to the ground and lays out his war bundle, the bow and quiver. "Soon it will be dark. We will pitch our wet tent here. But we will not have to hunt for food. Look at all the plums on the ground!"

"Abis, wait!" I shout. But it's too late. He dives for the fruit like a football lineman after a fumble, belly-flopping into the pond. The splash of water is thunderous. Chufee dives in after him. I run forty yards toward them, then walk to the edge, cautiously, looking about for swimming snakes. Abis comes staggering and blubbering out.

"What happened?" he asks as he throws himself on the bank and stretches out in front of me, on his back.

"I think you mistook the reflection in the water for the fruit in the trees."

Chufee climbs up on his stomach and shakes herself vigorously. Abis looks her in the eyes and shouts, "I am a fool, Chufee! It is true! Manny-man, you did not know this before. She knew all along. Is this not so, darling?"

Chufee whines.

Abis points up at the tall, straight tree with the small, greenish fruit hanging from it in gatherings of four or five.

"They don't look ripe to me," I say.

"Plenty ripe."

"Look kinda green, you know?"

"Ripe. Trust Abis. Watch."

He lumbers up the tree like a bear, pops a few fruit into his mouth, squints, then stuffs his cheeks so full he looks like a chipmunk. As he tries to chew his enormous wad, a steady ooze of juice slips out between his lips, runs down his jaw and dollops to the leaf mat beneath the tree.

"See?" he says. "Here, Chufee." He tosses a plum down to her. She backs away and growls. "Okay, you ungrateful slut. I will give it instead to Manny-man."

"Why won't the dog eat any?"

"Hmm, maybe she is not a veterinarian. You eat it, Manny-man. Very tasty."

I pick the fruit up and take a bite. "Abis, this is awful."

He shrugs.

"So hard."

He shrugs again.

"Well, I guess if you're hungry enough, you'll eat anything. And I'm hungry enough. What do you call these?"

"Georgia wild plums."

He tosses a few dozen to the ground, then clambers down himself. For an hour we do nothing but gorge ourselves on that fruit. Then Abis says, "We must make camp over there. Across the bog. Here is the low water line. It will flood when the tide swoops down like sea gulls at a garbage dump. Excuse me, I forgot. Now they are called landfills. Much better. More refined."

"I didn't know rivers had tides."

"This is because you are a city boy." He spits.

"Let's just climb one of these trees and stay in it until the waters subside. I'm not crossing any more snake water. Especially at dusk, when you really risk getting pulled under."

"Hmm, no Manny-man, we cannot do this. When the high water comes the snakes will slither up to the tops of the trees. Then they will swallow Chufee whole. Us in four parts."

"I thought you said the snakes didn't climb that high."

"I lied."

"Well, I'm not doing it. I am not putting my feet into a slime bog. Could be leeches in there. Didn't you ever see *The African Queen*?"

Abis picks up his gear, straps it to his side, and strides to the edge of the bog. "Come, Manny-man."

"I told you, I'm not going."

"Abis will carry you."

"Are you serious?"

"You cannot stay on this side, Manny-man. Hungry packs of swamp wolves may come prowling."

"Swamp wolves?"

"Did Abis also mention alligators? Come. It is no problem to carry my brother."

"Okaaay." I climb on his back. "Hand me that mosquito repellant bark."

He does. I rub it all over myself. Abis does the same. Even though Abis is knee deep in the snake bog, the mosquitoes do not light, though they are swarming about us thick as blood pudding. Stiff-armed, I hold the smelly dog straight out above Abis's head.

Halfway across, this terrible bloated gaseousness overtakes me. I can't help myself. I have to expel a bit of air, almost directly into poor Abis's nose. "Excuse me," I say, quite embarrassed. "I didn't mean to do that to you."

"No, no, Manny-man, it is okay. It is not your fault."

"Whose fault is it, then?"

"It is the fault of the anus. A man does not have to apologize for what that one does."

I'm irritated that he won't just accept my apology. "Why the hell not? It's my anus, isn't it?"

"No, no, Manny-man! Do you know nothing of science? The anus is a separate being. With a mind of its own. It does whatever it wants. Like cock."

"That's ridiculous."

"No, no, it is true. When Abis studied medicine in the swamps of Tibet many years ago, he was taught that the anus and the dick are attached to the body just before birth. Both are swimming around in the mother's womb with you and attach themselves in the two places. This is called the pair-of-sites. That is how the doctors know your mother is about to go into labor camp."

He lets fly an enormous fart.

"You just did that on purpose, didn't you?"

"Ohhh, ohhh," he moans. "Is Abis supposed to say 'escuse me', now?"

"Of course."

He lets go another, bigger, smellier one. "Escuse me, Manny-man. Manny-man?"

"Yes?"

"I am going to say 'escuse me' now for many, many times because I think I am about to fart many, many times."

He lets loose a thunderous stinking whirlwind of gas worthy of the sewers of Paris. This is followed by a long, long burp.

"Escuse me for other end, too!"

He lets fly another, bigger, bag of wind even more foul.

"Whoa!" he shouts. "Sorrrrryyy."

I can't help myself: I expel some air. We both fart in unison. Large whiffs. Huge doses of swamp gas. Chufee leaps from my arms. She splashes hard into the nut brown water, paddles ten feet downstream and dunks her head repeatedly.

"Whoooo!" Abis shouts and farts another time.

I'm not far behind.

"Ohh," I moan and fart again.

Abis's hands shoot straight into the air. I tumble into the water.

"WHOOO!" Abis screams as he farts and falls backwards. Mounds of bubbles break water and pollute the air. A spark would set the world on fire. Stinky mud wells up from the bottom. A small dead fish floats to the surface.

"Ohhh!" I moan even more loudly. My buttocks is lifted upward in the currents with the force of my latest explosion. The water boils around us like in those B movies where the piranha are supposed to be feasting on a carcass. Only no fish, no snake, no beast in the world could, or want to, cut through this bubble wall to suck down a meal.

The thick cloud of mosquitoes scatters and disperses with the breaking, whirling wind. Our intestines twist and distend and expel more and more gas with ever increasing force. It's as if air hoses have been fitted to our bowels.

"Oooohhhh, Manny-man, guess what? It was not plums we ate after all. It was wild laxative fruit!"

"What?"

"I have made a great mistake. Do I do these things on purpose? Is that why I am called Foolish One? Trickster? Did I not tell you I had dreams of floating fish? Does that not always mean intestinal disorder? Take off your pants very quickly, Manny-man. Underwear, too. Hold them up, up, high above your head."

"Ooohhh. All right. Abis, yes. Oh. God."

My head goes under four times as I try to comply. Then we wade as best we can toward and fling our wet things onto the muddy bank. I'm nearly blind now with cramps.

I stagger out of the water and hurl myself onto a log that forms a natural toilet seat. Just in time. Abis climbs a tree, squats and lets plop. The visceral growls and rectal burps would scare off any carnivore. The malodor has got to be killing insects, flies and microbes.

I moan faintly. My eyes shut then flutter open again on their own. Abis rises on his bough, moans faintly, then falls butt first into his own excrement. He sputters, rises, slips, gets up and staggers about like a drunk. He grabs the trunk of a small tree, squats, holds on as if being blown about by a hurricane and lets loose with his bowels again.

Over and over we do this until it is dark and we are both too exhausted to moan anymore or move.

# THIRTEEN

The sky is completely black and so overcast not even one star shines through. The internal storm had raged for hours. I'm not sure what time it is, or where I am, or anything. All I know for certain is that even in the dark I know exactly where Abis is. I'm so drowsy.

When I wake, again, it is still night. But the clouds are gone. The moon has risen. So has Abis. In the light given us we find our gear and wade back across the bog, holding everything above us with one hand and cleaning ourselves in the water with the other. Exhausted now, but unsleepy, we fling our wasted, dehydrated bodies on the far bank and hardly move. At least the diarrhea has nearly stopped.

"This should teach you, Manny-man; a man should never climb on Wakjunkaga's back!"

"What does that mean?"

"Oh, Manny-man, do you not know? I am Wakjunkaga!"

Sleep begins to overtake me again.

\*\*\*

It is morning now. I am lying on a sandy bank beside the fetid waters. Twenty feet away, a snake sleeps on top of my pants. Mosquitoes big enough to carry sparrows in their talons hover about my head in vast quantities. Harpies of the bog. Apparently, they rose early on the off chance they could suck any juices in my body that might possibly have been left after our ordeal. They are successful. I am now a lumpy, desiccated carapace rotting in the sun.

"Oh, hi, Manny-man. You are up. Come join Chufee and me in the warm mineral waters. It is pleasant, like the French Riviera. Saaay, you don't look so good."

He rubs his clean-shaven chin "Know what? Next time we must put up our tent before bedding down. And string up our mosquito net. But now we must see to all those holes the mosquitoes have drilled in you. Without immediate medical treatment, they could get defected. Trust Dr. Abis."

"Shit."

"Ummm, say, Manny-man, I hate to mention it, but you do not smell so fresh this morning. Also I think for the very same reason we must move camp. Maybe you will hop into the stream? Wash your clothes? Have a little splash-about? Did you bring with you some of that nice, soft, fragrant city-boy toilet paper? No? Abis did not think so. Come, I will show you what to do. Come."

I follow him to the edge of the woods.

"Use some of these to wipe up your heiny before going into the water. Less pollution downstream. Mother Nature's very own toilet paper."

"You mean those leaves?"

"You bet. Sure."

"What kind of leaves are they?"

"In your language they are called Virginia creeper."

"Looks like poison ivy to me."

"No, no, Manny-man. Virginia creeper. See how those three leaves are bunched together? That is how you tell it is the soft toilet paper vine of Mrs. Nature."

"You sure? I thought three leaves meant poison ivy."

"Am I sure? Of course I am sure. It is what Indians do best, identifying leafy stuff in forests. As my grandmother has taught me: three leaves Virginia creeper, five poison ivy. 'Three? Wipe thee! Five? Be eaten alive!' That is her little poem."

"I thought it was the other way around."

"Oh, ye of little faith. My grandmother would not lie to you!"

He strides over to the vine, rips off some leaves and rubs them on his face. See? It is okay."

I take some leaves from the vine and clean myself as best I can.

As I do so, Abis says, "Now you see what I have told you is true?"

"About the plant? I guess so."

"About everything, Manny-man. About leaves, about anus, about great pissing snake. Do you not now know they are separate entities from us and can do what they want? Look what anus has done to us last night!"

"But that's just the point. We do have control. None of this would have happened if you hadn't fed us from that tree. Both anus and penis can be controlled to a great extent. Knowing that is what makes for civilization."

Abis laughs.

"Let's try to find something less vaporous for breakfast."

"All taken care of, Manny-man. Abis knows how concerned you are with food, so he has fulfilled your very need. Last night Abis stashed a great and fulsome meal."

"Wonderful."

"Fish! I have buried him to preserve his freshness."

"What?"

"You bet. It is an old Indian trick. Come. I will show you."

He leads me to a mound of dirt and leaves. Chufee is lying on top of it, asleep. Abis gently lifts her off and begins to dig out the mound like a mad canine.

"Peeeeeeeewwwww!" I say, "What is that stench?"

"Uh, oh. I think it may be breakfast. Ooooh. It does not look so good, either."

The fish is covered with maggots.

"Abis, you have just got to learn. Certain causes have certain effects."

"Hmmm. Maybe so." He rubs his chin. "Abis must learn to use both hands. No, no, wait, perhaps it was just a bad recipe!"

"I don't think so."

"Let us take our little bow and arrow and hunt tiny marsh deer for breakfast."

"Abis?"

"Yes?"

"Your face."

"What about it?"

"Why is it breaking out like that?"

His eyes widen. He begins putting his hand up toward his cheek, but stops halfway. "Hmm, maybe it is five leaves, Virginia creeper, three leaves poison ivy."

"What are we gonna do?"

He runs for the water, screeching like a mud hen. I overtake him and dive in myself. He splashes in behind me and begins dunking over and over like a porpoise. Between baptisms he screams, "Rub your anus!! Rub and splash! Get the poison oil off before it causes your skin to bubble like an over-fried egg!"

With both hands I rub vigorously my bottom and my crotch. But it's too late. Already I feel the welts. "Abis," I say, "It itches!"

"That is a bad sign, Manny-man. A very bad sign. It means you are a man doomed to suffer."

"I think I knew that already. How's your face?"

"No problem. I forgot: Abis is not allergic to poison ivy. This is why he has forgotten the count of the leaves."

"But the welts on your face?"

"Ha, ha, I was scratched by a branch just before you got up."

"So staying in this muddy, algae-infested water and rubbing my ass and genitals isn't doing me any good?"

He shrugs.

"So we can get out now?"

"I would do this very thing, Manny-man."

He points. I see the triangular head of the snake as it swims toward us.

"Oh, shiit!" I comment as I hasten toward the far shore.

"Well, this is good in a way, Manny-man."

"What way?"

"She is no longer asleep on your pants."

"Is it poisonous?"

"Semi."

"What does that mean?"

"This little sister is poisonous only if you are allergic to her bite."

"Like poison ivy?"

"Only, in this case, if you are allergic to Mr. Snake's bite, you go toes-up pretty quick, Manny-man. Cash in your chips. Buy the farm. Shuffle off to Buffalo. Shuffle off this moral coil. But you can relax. Most people who are not allergic to poison ivy are not allergic to this snake. Your pal, Abis, is in no personal danger."

"What kind of snake is it?"

"Tie snake."

"The kind that wraps itself around your legs and pulls you under? The kind you were talking about the other day?"

"You bet."

"See, I am learning a little bit about nature."

Abis grins. As my heart rate lowers to just twice normal, I'm reminded about my original problem. I say, "This itching is horrible."

"Try to ignore it, Manny-man. This is what Abis is doing, trying to ignore your pain. Now it does not bother me hardly at all. Do not worry. The itch will vanish, never to return, just like the national debt. It will be gone in a few hours."

"Are you sure?"

"Trust Abis."

"Even so, do you think you could find some sort of Indian remedy."

"Not even a worry, Manny-man. Abis is doing this even now. Meanwhile, you must pick up the bow. First say. 'Little People, I need this.'"

I do.

"Now I will teach you to hunt like a man instead of a city boy."

"It'd be easier to teach you to grocery shop like a city boy. With earned money." I say as I hand him the bow.

"Shuuuush! Shuuuush!," Abis shouts. "Come up the tree. Here comes big game. Chufee, go! Bring in game!"

She runs in the opposite direction.

He turns to me and says, "Hush!! Here. Come. Here. Here."

Twigs break. Branches swish. Heavy footfalls. Louder. Louder. We see movement! Abis shoots an arrow. Someone below yells, "Arrrughh! Help! Icki!" Then we hear the thud of his carcass hitting the forest floor.

I'm paralyzed with fear.

Abis mumbles, "Hmmm, this is not good."

He scrambles down the tree and toward his fallen victim.

"Oh, my God, you've killed him!" I cry as I scramble after him.

When I get to him I see he isn't moving. I can't believe my fate. We've just killed a man. It's devastating. Abis is hunched over, near the body, frantically digging, dog-like, next to a tree. The dead body is laid out with its back against the tree. I cannot believe the amount of blood soaking his shirt.

"Y-you can't just bury him, for God's sake!"

Abis doesn't even look up. He keeps scooping handfuls of dirt between his legs, digging, digging. And humming. Out of tune.

What should I do? Should I help? Maybe this was what it was all about. To make me an accessory. Or frame me for the whole thing. I can't do hard time. I walk off for a distance and sit down near the water. Woozy. My body itches from the poison ivy. I'm more dehydrated and thirsty than I have ever been in my life. My head hurts. My muscles are so sore I feel as though I've been weight lifting. My stomach is a waterlogged coconut in a whirlpool. If I had it I'd gladly give a million bucks to get back on dry land again, metaphorically speaking, the level, steady land of my own library.

I try to take a good look at the corpse but I can't do it anymore than I could look at Sara after she died. Her brother had to make all the final arrangements. I insisted on a closed coffin.

Abis is still digging like a dog. Suddenly he leaps to his feet and shouts, "It's bingo time now!" then whoops and screams and holds aloft what looks like a black fur ball. "This is great, just great!" he shouts.

He breaks the ball in two, tosses one half into the bushes, and with the other half in his hands, rushes at the corpse. Winding up like a rookie league pitcher, he slaps the ball smack into the corpse's bloody shoulder.

Immediately the body bolts upright and screams, "Yyyyoowwww," like a maimed dog. Its unwounded hand makes a fist and begins pummeling Abis on the top of the head, repeatedly. I'm wide-eyed. Abis is whooping. The ex-corpse continues howling. Chufee, out of nowhere, joins the chorus, baying like a wolf at the full moon.

"Good God!" I yell, "It's the melon man! What the hell's he doing here? What the hell is going on?

The melon man continues raining blows on Abis's head. It's as if they're filming a Three Stooges comedy, except real blood keeps pouring from the melon man's shoulder, despite the fungus ball Abis plastered there.

I yell, "Red!"

Startled, both men stop what they are doing and stare at me. Abis wears a face of shock and wide-mouthed surprise. The melon man's face is a mask of such ferocity that instantly I'm reminded of that scene in *The Inferno* where Dante accosts Count Ugolino gnawing the frozen head of Archbishop Ruggieri. The melon man's face blanches. He faints dead away.

"Manny-man, we must get Kanati to the creek and four times dip him up to the eyeballs. Abis had a dream last night of fire. This means his brother will suffer fever."

"What the hell is going on?"

"It is okay-donkey. Only a flesh wound. Ha, ha, I sound like John Wayne now. See?" He holds up his own arm. "It does not hurt me a bit! The arrow only hit the melon man in the rind. He is not dead. He is only slapped down to the forest floor and not even for loss of blood. He is down there for cowardice. He sees his own blood, he goes barf-bag on us. I have seen him do it before."

"I don't feel so good myself."

"Ha, you are a city-boy." Abis spits. He slides the melon man's head-band back around the old man's scalp, slips the two big feathers under the band, then puts his hand to the side of his own mouth as if he were Hamlet doing an aside. "I must tell you what, Manny-man, you must not call him R-E-D to his face again."

"Oh, right. I forgot. Why was that again?"

"I have told you, what, one thousand three hundred sixteen times, it will cause a great storm."

"Storms are caused by shifts in barometric pressure and the presence of fronts."

"Oh, Manny-man, you are soooooooo naive."

"Well what are we going to do with him?"

"Bathe him four times in the stream, then take him with us as long as he wants to go."

Chufee begins to lick the former dead man's blood.

"But what in the hell is he doing here? I mean, we left him in Greece, for God's sake."

"No, no, Manny-man. He lives *here*. Works for William Love. Willy brought him back to the land. He has more right to be hunting in this place than you do. Ha, ha, you have shot him with his own bow and arrow!"

"Me?"

"It is okay. I have already explained to him in his language how you do not know what you are doing with a bow and arrow. I have told him very carefully how you are a fool, anyway. So he cannot blame you for your foolishness. No, no, do not thank me. Abis is only glad to do this to his pal."

"You need to tell me what in hell is going on."

"Nothing in hell, Manny-man."

"First we meet this guy in Greece. Then here. Why in hell would William Love bother to bring a peasant or Indian or whatever he is back and forth like that? It makes no sense."

"Okay donkey. So what to you makes sense?"

"I don't know."

"Okay. So this makes as much sense, then, as anything else, *n'est-ce 'splain*?"

"Is he spying on us?"

"Ha, ha, so you think because his name is Red he is Santa Claus? He is seeing if you are naughty or nice? That is not how reality works, Manny-man. Many people, even when they are old, they do not get over Santa Clause Syndrome. Always wanting someone, parents in the sky, maybe, to be checking up on their behavior. Please, when he wakes up, do not call him what I called him, okay?"

The melon man starts to come around. Abis bends over him, ministering. They speak in that same Indian-sounding language they used in Greece. Red nods a few times. Once he looks in my direction and smiles. I raise my palm and smile back.

Abis turns to me. "It is okay, Manny-man. He can walk. With our help, a little. We will get him to the big river. I have a boat."

"A *boat*?"

"*Si, mongsieur. El boato.*"

"Why didn't you tell me you had a boat?"

"I have a boat, Manny-man. I have sailed it up from, um, um, ah, from William Love's dock."

"Then why don't we just sail it back to William Love's dock instead of traipsing around in this bog with all these fucking mosquitoes and flies and bears and snakes and, and, uh, fart trees, or whatever you call those damn things?"

"Yes, yes. Fart trees. Flatulent forest."

"Well?"

"You have a good idea. No, no, wait. It is a *great* idea! Oh, Manny-man, why did not Abis think on this? It is because I am a fool! No, no, really, Manny-man, it is true! Look, I am hitting myself in the face because of this. Why do I punish poor Abis? If it is true I am a fool, then I cannot help it."

"Yes, you can."

"We will go by boat. In great style. We will have food and insect repugnant, and for your mosquito wounds and poison ivy boils, calamine lotion to soothe your poisoned ass and generals."

"Thank you, God."

"First we must dip this poor boy into the Long Man four times."

"Boy? He must be seventy if he's a day."

"Oh, this hurts your pal, Abis, Manny-man. For now I must tell you the truth. You will feel so bad when I say it unto you, for this man is my younger brother."

"Wonderful," I say as I help Abis lift the old man to his feet.

With one of the old man's arms over my shoulder, and his other arm over one of Abis's shoulders we carry the melon man through what seems like five hundred or so miles of woods, back to the river, or to a river. I don't recognize it when we get there, or anything else on the path we've taken.

The river is wide and deep, its waters clear and almost still. Pine trees, huge cypresses and, I think, sycamores line its bank, which is composed of clean white sand. We immerse the melon man four times and set him down on the bank. The old man moans, but his voice does not sound weak. He leans against a massive live oak tree with great, swooping limbs and Spanish moss draping almost into the water.

"Now, where's your boat?"

"Hummm." He rubs his chin and walks back to the water's edge, looking upstream and down. "Boat, boat. Where does Abis get..." He looks back at me slyly. "I mean, 'leave,' where did Abis leave...."

He and Chufee walk downstream. The melon man and I are alone. I have so many questions to ask him. When Abis is well out of earshot, I turn to the old guy. He is snoring.

I sit down next to him and lean against the same tree, waiting for him to wake.

# FOURTEEN

"Hey. Everybody up, up, out of your deep slumber! Abis is back! Chufee, sweetness, give them a little woofy. Let them know."

She does. The melon man awakens. We both sit up. Abis is walking along the bank, leading by a rope the same way he led the donkeys in Greece, a small boat. In fact, the little boat reminds me of the donkeys in Greece. It's about the same size and color. And like them, it appears to be shedding. No oars. It has a small, rusty outboard motor.

"Why is the engine blackened and peeling like that?"

Abis shrugs. "Maybe she has caught fire once or twice in her lifetime."

"The boat, too?"

"No, no, she is peeling like that because she is very, very old. It is the same reason she is incontinent, a little, too."

"Abis?"

"Manny-man?"

"Are you sure this is your boat?"

He grins and nods vigorously. The melon man points, shakes his head. In the first word I have heard him say in English, he groans, "No."

"Yes!" Abis says. "It is the boat of Abis, the Great Ferry Man of the Pueblo Nation."

"Liar and thief!"

Abis strikes his own breast.

"Stealer of boats!"

"It is my boat. Now."

"No."

"Yes! Yes! Yes!" Abis screams. "It is my boat! I shall prove it!"

He puts the end of the rope in Chufee's mouth then runs off into the woods. In five minutes he returns with a section of log about three feet long and four inches in diameter. As the dog continues to hold the boat's reins, Abis sits cross-legged between us. He takes out his knife and removes the bark from the wood and whittles it smooth until he remains with an oversized marlin spike. This he hones and burnishes until it shines all over.

"Now, Abis is ready," he says. He takes the rope from the dog's mouth and boards. The boat drifts out. At midstream, Abis raises his club again and again, smashing the tiny boat into little bits of flotsam as it sinks downward. Soon Abis himself is dog-paddling in the water. But he continues thrashing about and smashing the few remaining larger chunks of hull. Even when he is nearly exhausted and in grave danger of drowning he keeps raising his club and smashing at the broken vessel.

When there is nothing left but chunks of wood he swims ashore, club in hand and climbs onto the bank, nearly spent. With his last bit of energy he flings his war club into the river. It hits the largest chunk of wood, bounces off and drifts slowly downstream. He turns to us and says, "Now do you see? Does this not prove the boat was mine? Would Abis do such a thing to someone else's precious vessel? Could Abis afford to do such a thing?"

He flings himself onto the damp bank and falls asleep. I turn to the melon man to see what he wants to do. Perhaps we can escape together. But he and the dog are snoring. Me, I'm not all that sleepy.

What to do? I lie awake scratching and wondering. Should I escape? Do I want to escape? Could I even find my way back to that trading post? Besides, after all this, I'd kind of like to actually meet this Willy Love and see if he's really as fabulous as Abis says he is. He isn't exactly the most reliable guide to the universe. But sometimes he does make sense. And sometimes that's more than I can say about myself.

I guess I shouldn't have run away in Greece. I'm glad to be getting a second chance. Does Opportunity knock just once? No. The bugger's always at the door.

I lie between Abis and the melon man and sleep.

***

Abis is roasting small chunks of meat on a spit. The sun is up. The melon man is much improved. Though his arm is in a sling, he is dexterously shredding greens into a bowl. On the old man's head is the beaded leather sweat band, with the two red-tipped feathers stuck into it.

Seeing that I'm awake, Abis grins and jerks his thumb toward the melon man. "He is making poke salad."

"And what are you cooking?"

"Meat. Greens and meat for breakfast. Do not worry; it has already been purified. Ready to eat. Here."

"Umm. Not bad."

"Oh, Manny-man, Abis is very glad. Do you like rat?"

I spit the wad of half-chewed wad into my hand and look for a place to throw it."

"Ha, ha, no, no, Mann-man. This is not rat. Abis was just asking, for future menu magic."

"This isn't rat?"

"No. Of course not. Is a rat so skinny?"

I put the meat back into my mouth again.

"It is snake. With wild mushrooms. Abis is pretty sure it is mushrooms. Manny-man, you are a professor; what is the difference between a mushroom and a toadstool?"

"Excuse me. I'll be right back."

"At last she will not nest anymore in your underwear!" he shouts after me as I run toward the river and consider plunging in and floating to the coast.

Something large and probably poisonous rustles in the bushes. I freeze and listen intently. It plops into the water. Just a reminder of all there is or might be between me and true civilization. When I return to camp, Abis and the melon man are arguing so bitterly they have almost come to blows. I separate them.

"He has remade my tobacco!"

"Which means?"

"Which means he is the evil grandchild of a dildo."

"We ready to travel?"

Abis turns to me and grins."Hey, you bet. We are all packed."

"Then Abis, you go ahead. Red and I will walk behind. I'll support him if he gets tired. In the meanwhile, try to get a hold of yourself."

Abis leads us toward the woods.

"Aren't we gonna follow the river?"

"Oh, Manny-man, this is very unthoughtful of you. No time to dawdle now. We must take the shortest cut to William Love's house. Get our sick man to Will, who will search his wounds and heal him, wickedly-split."

"So you were deliberately taking the long way before?"

"It was your idea, Manny-man, remember?"

Hour after hour we hike up hills and down hills, through pine woods and hard wood forest. Then more woods and woods and woods. Not once do we see a sign of civilization. Not a house, not a gum wrapper.

"Doesn't anybody *live* in Georgia? Uhh, if this is Georgia."

"Oh, Manny-man, the people that live around here, they don't live around here."

"Are you deliberately avoiding farms and villages?"

"How can Abis do such a thing when he is completely lost?"

"What do you mean, 'lost?'"

"This is a new word in your English language vocabulary?"

"I thought you said finding their way through the woods is what Indians do best?"

"This is a stereo-set, Manny-man. Abis is lost pretty damn good."

"I don't suppose you have a compass or a map or something."

The melon man takes out of his pocket a red rock and suspends it from a string held between his thumb and forefinger. At first it remains perfectly steady. Then it begins to swing faster and faster. He points in the direction of the arc, puts the rock and string away and begins walking. We follow him and arrive at the river. Abis runs to the water and motions for us to catch up. We find him struggling to free a nearly new fiberglass rowboat from a tangle of overhanging branches and vines.

"Ha,' he says, "This is Abis's true and only genuine boat!"

"What about the one you smashed yesterday?"

"That was my true and only genuine boat, too. My second-best boat. This one is Abis's A number one craft. No, no, wait, it was number three in the Abis fleet that he smashed. The other is a great and beautiful sail boat with a long grey mast of virgin aluminum on Love's Island. This one is number two. See, it says on the side, 'Number Two.'"

"And a whole lot more numbers. I think that's the boat's registration."

"It is Abis's social security number."

"I doubt you even have one. So, do you plan to smash this boat, too?"

"Wait here," he shouts and runs off into the woods.

He returns with a big stick. Dropping his gear to the ground, he lifts the stick above his head.

"Abis, no!"

His stick rises and comes down like thunder. He smashes his war bundle this time. Then he kicks it savagely into the woods.

The melon man's eyes widen. His face blanches. The old man's hands go to his hair.

"Red, what is it? What's the matter?"

He turns and runs into the woods. His head-dress falls to the ground before us.

"See, look what you have done, Manny-man. You have angered him greatly by calling him right to his face, 'Red'."

"*Me*? *You* scared the hell out of him acting like a looney tune!"

"Why would that scare him? He already knows his elder brother is a looney tune. No, Manny-man, it was you. But it is okay. Once again I forgive you your trespasses."

Abis picks up the melon man's head dress and puts it over his own. But now there is only one feather.

"Okay. So now we go by boat today. This is great! We can relax and enjoy the float down to Love's house. This trip will take only one day, taps. We will meet many, many women there. Meet the big D. You will love her. Also Willy Love. This promise Abis makes to you."

He retrieves his smashed war bundle and tosses it into the little boat with the rest of his gear.

***

As soon as I'm in the boat, Abis pushes off with his foot. We float downstream, leisurely, twice drifting past towns. I'm not anxious to depart anymore. I'm enjoying the ride. And this time, surely, we're on our way by the easiest route to William Love.

Abis finds in his pouch some salve to ease my itch. I have the feeling the initiation, the hazing, I guess you'd call it, is finally over. No more tricks. He's finally taking me in. Acceptance. At last.

At lunch he proves my theory. We pull onto a bank of enormous cypress trees and clean sand to forage. I figure for sure it's going to be the usual; he's going to make me scrounge around for poisonous butterflies or try to feed me a rancid armadillo or something. But no. He takes out a pouch of nuts, collects wild blackberries, eats some, and hands the rest to me. At first I'm skeptical, of course. But soon my appetite overcomes my hesitation. And this time, no evil befalls me, or Abis, for that matter. I guess the strangest thing is that he doesn't just play his tricks on me, but on himself as well. That's why he's always been able to trick me. One never expects a fool to be a fool in his own mouth. His foolishness is a mask he wears, like a dancer in a ritual. It keeps him from getting stuck with the fool before the mask.

In the late afternoon we begin to drift past a good-sized town. I suggest we pull in and have a meal in a restaurant. Abis claims he does not understand English until we have drifted past the pale. At dusk he accepts my idea to go ashore and make camp.

"How much further do you expect we'll have to go before we reach Love's dominion?"

"What makes you think we are not there now?"

"Are you serious? He lives here?"

He grins. "Soon we shall be at his mansion. On the morning of the following day when we arrive at the edge of the sea. This is where he lives when he lives here."

"And you say he's here now?"

"Wilhelm Love has many mansions, many rooms. But verily he has said unto Abis, 'Abis,' he said unto me, "I shall wait nigh unto you. I shall wait nigh unto Manny-man as well, you bet. Together we shall go unto the Happy Isle. There we shall eat pomegranate and grape, peeled by big breasted maidens. We shall sit under the fig tree and the vine, and none shall be afraid."

"What are you doing?"

"Digging a snake trench, Manny-man. This is very, very snaky country."

I begin helping him dig. "I assume this will help keep snakes away from us tonight?"

"You bet. The slithery ones cannot cross a snake pit if it is dug correctly and rope is put along the bottom, like this. The snake, like you, Manny-man, is fooled by the form. In the dark the snakes will think this rope is their dead brother. They will not slither over a dead snake."

"That's very clever, Abis, but is it true?"

"So it is written, I think, in your great magazine called *Scientific American*, Manny-man, in an article by a highly respectable veinologist."

"So it's scientific?"

"Almost foolproof."

"Almost?"

"Is not your friend and pal Abis smarter than any snake, Manny-man? I answer this, 'yes.'"

He drives in the last tent stake. "Except..."

"Except what?"

"The ferocious, blood-sucking snake could avoid the snake trench entirely by jumping down from yonder tree to the tent pole."

"So let's just move the tent away from the tree."

"Too much work to dig the snake trench again, Manny-man. Your pal Abis is very tired now. Besides, sometimes you cannot elimitate all the dangers from life. Sometimes you must take chances in order to enjoy the full, rich melody of living and not just hear the same stale notes over and over. Do not worry so much. Maybe we will get lucky this time and no huge and heavy, fierce, savage, poisonous snake will drop down onto the tent, slither down the pole and cut our throats with its sharp, virulent, noxious fangs like new-honed yet germ-laden stainless-steel daggers."

"Well, if the trench keeps them from crawling into the tent, couldn't we just trench around the tree as well?"

"Could."

"So let's do it."

"But Manny-man, the vast horde of snakes in this forest could just cross from other trees like squirrels. They could already be up in this very tree already, ready to pounce. Do you not see how my little snake dog sniffs around the trunk?"

"I thought she just needed to pee."

"She is a highly trained snake hound, Manny-man. She knows what she is doing."

"All right, all right, if a trench and rope can hold them off, why not just coil rope on top of the tent?

"Oh, this is a great plan, Manny-man, great! Now you are participating in your own fate plenty well. We will do it! Oh, oh, and also we can notch the tent pole all around. This will work like a trench; snakes will not be able to slither down to us!"

"Okay. Let's get to work."

I cut a notch all the way around the tent pole, about halfway through. By the time we bed down I feel perfectly secure for the first time in I don't know how long. It feels so good to be able to trust Abis now.

"What is that you're wearing?" I ask.

"Poncho."

"Why?"

"Looks like rain."

\*\*\*

Sometime in the middle of the night the rain begins to fall in torrents. I wake immediately with the thunder, but soon fall back asleep again, fitfully, dreaming that an octopus, then a giant amoeba, is suffocating me. Suddenly, I'm awake again. Something has grabbed my face! It's all over me, covering my body entirely with its own! Heavy, cold, horrible and constricting, it throws the heaviest part of itself over my chest, its face on mine, sucking out the air!

I try to scream. It grips me hard. I can't move! I try to struggle against its grasp. It growls and makes a ripping sound as if thick canvas were being torn asunder. Then the creature goes cold. My hair becomes wet. Is it blood? My face is in the open air! I can breathe!

"What are you doing, Manny-man?"

"I? I? Good God, what time is it?"

"Middle of the night. You are fully awake now?"

"Yes." I look around. The tent has collapsed about me. The broken center pole lies over my chest. My face sticks out of a rent in the canvas. Abis has a knife in one hand, a torch in the other. His dog is yipping herself into a foam-mouthed frenzy.

"What have you done? You have ruined Abis's brand-new stolen tent!"

"Was it a snake?"

"No, Manny-man. It was stupidity. But it is okay-donkey now. You have fooled Abis with your great joke, cutting the tent-pole halfway through so it will collapse on itself in the middle of the night and scare your pal. Also you have scared hell out of dog. No more hell in her. This is good. We will not ever call her Cereba again. You go back to sleep, now, Manny-man. We are three lucky stiffs all around that the rain is stopped."

He flips the wet canvas over. On the dry side, I lie down next to him and the wet dog.

"Let us hope very hard that snakes do not jump on us since now we are out in the open where they like to hunt and kill. Well, good night, Manny-man. Hope to see you in the morning."

"Thank you," I say. But it is many hours before I close even one eye. I keep hearing sounds. But eventually, drowsiness overcomes me again and I sleep soundly.

***

"Wraaahhhgh!" I scream. Wraaah!" Giant spiders crawl about my face! I sit up. No. It's leafy branches and pine needles covering me. They fly everywhere as I struggle to get out from under them, and from the wet canvas. It's dawn. Abis is standing over me.

"Now what?" he says so matter-of-factly I could throttle him.

Instead, I say as calmly as possible, "Someone seems to have buried me in pine needles and branches."

"Ahh," he says as he walks back to the camp fire, where he's boiling God-knows-what in a pot. "Abis has noticed this very thing himself when he arose this morning. Why is it you have covered yourself like that? Have you forgotten about the red bugs and how they itch the skin? Do you not know about the poisonous ticks that carry over six thousand, four hundred thirty-seven loathsome illnesses, including lemon-lime disease and dipfearia?"

"I didn't do it, dammit, you did!"

"NO! It must have been the giant water rats that fed in the trees last night. This explains the tree-rat droppings all over our campus this morning."

"Where?"

"Hmm. Abis has covered them all up for you, pal, with leaves and pine needles. Not very sanitary. Giant water-rats are very, very dangerous animals, Manny-man. You are lucky Abis has provided for us a rat-terrible dog to bark and chase these evil beasts away and bury their poop for you."

He scratches behind Chufee's ears.

"Look, Abis, you can't pull that crap on my anymore. It could not have been rats, because rats do not eat leaves. They eat dead flesh, garbage and slime."

"Tree rats eat leaves."

"NO, dammit."

He looks hurt. "Do."

"No. It had to be a more cunning animal. One capable of playing practical jokes. Know any animal like that, Abis?"

"Beaver."

"I have read many, many articles in *Natural History Magazine* in the dentist's office all my life and seen plenty of beaver shows on PBS and basic cable television. Not once have I ever seen or read of beavers climbing trees. Beavers don't climb."

"Carolina beavers. You have seen the shows about the western beaver, Manny-man. *Beaverus westernatus*. The western beaver has no climbing claw. The Carolina beaver, *Beaverus carolinus*, it has this very climbing claw."

"No such thing."

"This is the very sentence you have pronounced on the great horned snake until you saw it with your very eyes, no?"

"Well, yes, but…"

"The Carolina beaver's habitap is the south part of Carolina through north coastal Georgia. Very rare. Like the great horned snake. This animal fills a very small ecological ditch. It has sharp climbing claws like a cat. It is the exact same size as a cat, only bigger."

"I suppose it's possible. But you're the one who covered me in pine needles. Admit it."

"Beavers, Manny-man. Very dangerous. They are rodents. Like the venomous water rat."

"We better sleep inside the tent from now on. Can you repair it?"

"I think it is dead."

"Check it."

He picks up the tent, sees its condition, and howls so loudly and so horribly his dog runs into the woods. He wads up the canvas and throws it into the fire.

"No!"

He grins. "No need anymore for it, Manny-man, remember? We shall be in Love's house by nightfall."

"For real this time?"

"For real. Now help Abis catch breakfast."

"I thought you were boiling something already."

"Just boiling water in the pot for practice. Now we must catch a thing for real to put in the pot."

"What do you want me to do?"

"Here is the plan. You get into the tree. I will tie this string to your toe. Dog and I will go to scare up game. Then we will hide in the bushes over there. When the little fawn comes by, Abis will pull the string attached to your toe. You jump down quick like a lead balloon. We will eat plenty good then."

"Have you ever actually used this method of animal capture before?"

"You are pulling my arm now, right, Manny-man? This is the method I have used two hundred fifteen times. It is what is called the deer stand. Deer do not have any natural enemies that hunt from above, so they never look up. It is so effective the deer stand is totally illegal in Georgia."

"Then maybe we ought not do it. I mean, we don't want to be in violation of state laws."

"No, no, Manny-man. It is not a volution of state laws if game is needed for three lost, starving, pitiful fools."

"Oh, well, great. That's what we'll plead in court, then. Give me a boost up the tree. There we go. Abis, let go of my foot. Okay, hand me the string."

"Take off your shoe, Manny-man. We must attack this string to your toe."

"Can't I just attach it to my ankle?"

"Toe."

"Okay, okay. There."

I sit in the tree for three hours before it even dawns on me that I've been taken. Abis has abandoned me. I might as well climb down. Then I hear a rustling. Abis tugs my string. I leap. I grab fur!

"Aaaaaaaaarrrrrraaaaw!"

"Yeeeeeeeeooooooowwww!" I scream as the cougar lashes out at me with its paw, misses completely, I think, and is gone.

Abis is laughing uncontrollably. "No fawn, Manny-man. Bobcat."

"God!"

"You should have caught him, anyway. Good to eat, too."

"My sleeve is shredded."

"Here, Mana-Man, have some cornflakes. These will not bite back."

"You had these all along?"

"Oh, no. Abis went down to the store. Stole them fresh this morning."

"And you let me sit in a fricking tree all this time?"

"For the best. Otherwise you would not let me steal."

"Damn right I wouldn't"

"You would rather starve?"

"Right."

"But not for long is what Abis thinks. Besides, Abis would not rather starve when others have food stiffs they are not eating. So it is best that Abis leave his conscience hanging in a tree."

"Okay, I'll eat. But when we return to civilization I have every intention of sending the store owner a check."

"Why? Abis did not get caught red-handled."

"Come on, let's go. Where's all your gear?"

Abis shrugs.

"Where's your war bundle? In fact, now that I think about it, where's that mask you were carving?"

Abis shrugs.

I smile. "Well, you old dog. You *are* learning new tricks. I'm proud of you. That's how you really got that tent and all that stuff, isn't it? You bartered for it. Pretty soon we'll have to start calling you Abis the Civilized, won't we?"

Abis spits. Then he leads me back to the camp. On the fire is a pot of stew.

"Hm?"

"Squirrel meat, Manny-man. No lie. With roasted green corn, hominy soup, acorn meal bread and spiced bush tea. Abis has prepared all this while you wasted your life away in that tree."

We finish the meal. Abis leads me down the side of one hill and up another. At its crest we are staring down at a paved highway, a small village, and the sea. Boats in the harbor bob vigorously on the whitecaps of the rising wind.

"How long have you been leading me astray?"

"What do you mean by this?"

"You understand exactly what I mean. You've been leading in circles for what, two, three, four days? Starving me, getting me eaten by vermin, making me eat vermin, getting me stung, poisoned, frightened, abandoned up a fricking tree, drenched, scratched, revolted, buried, farted on, farting in return, clawed and bitten. You've made me live off the scum of the land. And all that time we've been within walking distance not only of civilization, but of upper-middle-class civilization, for God's sake."

Abis fidgets. "If your pal Abis has not altogether told the truth to his pal in the past, it is for that pal's good, Manny-man. But now I must tell you the total and exact truth. I have led you here as straight as possible, though the path we have taken was the crooked way."

"We could have been here within two hours of landing on that damn airstrip, and you know it."

"For you, Manny-man, this was not possible. You would not have been ready. You had to shed your old skin like a snake."

"How would you know what I'm ready for?"

"Oh, this hurts Abis deep. Right here. In the spleen."

"That's your testicles."

"Okay, testicles. You know many things Abis does not know. But also you need to know what Abis knows, Manny-man. The heart knows what the brain cannot fathom."

"We've missed William Love, haven't we? He's not down there anymore, is he?"

"No, Manny-man."

"Damn it, I knew it, I just knew it! Now we'll never get to meet him!"

"Abis will take you right to Love's mansion."

"What's the difference if it's empty?"

"Then Abis will take you to the next mansion and the next and the next until we catch up to him."

"How many houses, Abis? How many lies before you confess the truth they're all empty?"

"Why are you in such despair, Manny-man, when you are now so close to reaching the whole heart's core? Live as if, Manny-man. Have faith. You have nearly reached the answer, Manny. You have almost met Willy Love. Then he will tell you everything. You will not believe what he can do until you meet him face to face. He will tell you why he has sent me here to you. Why he has chosen you."

"Chosen me for what?"

"Love is in his mansion, Manny-man. There you will find him. There you will find women with breasts like ripe melons, with pinched waists and strong thighs. One waits down there, just for you. Ha, ha, two or three for me. Oh, I have forgotten, I am supposed to go for only one at a time. Ha, ha, the new mortality. This is what you have taught Abis. Ptewie. Come, we must hurry now. Otherwise we will miss again Willy Love and you will get sore. Come. We will take the launch."

He beckons for me the same way he did at Delphi.

"This whole thing is so crazy, Abis. What am I doing it for? Why *has* William Love sent for me? Am I really going to get some answers? Finally?"

"No damn answers, Manny-man. You cannot measure the human heart with answers."

"What exactly are you trying to say here?"

"That you cannot measure the human heart with answers, Manny-man. So do not try. Just do what you know you should do. There is no meaning of life, Manny-man, life is not a thing, it is an experience to enjoy, not to figure out. Enjoy your life now, Manny-man, it is your eternity."

The sky is darkening even more. On the far side of the village, in the bay, nestled near a flock of small boats are two great, black-prowed, single-masted sailing ships. The tips of their masts describe great arcs and spheres as the hulls beneath them pitch and yaw on the darkening, wind-driven sea. On the horizon is the coming storm.

"You know why there is bad weather coming, Manny-man?"

"Of course. Because I called the melon man 'Red' to his face, right?"

"Right as pain, Manny-man. How did you know?"

I glance back toward the docks. One boat I hadn't noticed before now catches my whole attention. How could I have missed it the first time? Maybe it hadn't arrived then, for the engines are still running. The remnant of a wake is dispersing behind it.

It is obviously a pleasure craft, but an enormous one. Two tall smokestacks and a wide, cream-colored hull. Despite the growing wind, she rides the sea steadily. Yet she looks vulnerable to the coming storm: she has a broad, flat-topped canvas awning that roofs the back half of the deck. Surely they will have to fold back the canvas or it will be rent by the growing gale.

Tiny, wind-driven raindrops stab us like ice daggers. I want to move toward shelter, but find none. Besides, Abis won't budge. I turn my back to the wind and shout to him, "Which one is Love's house? Let's make our way there. He may not be home, but at least we can take shelter."

Abis shakes his head. "He does not live here, Manny-man," he shouts back.

"Wait a minute, now, you said he did! I'm getting angry, Abis. You told me distinctly he lived there!"

"Hmm, no, no, Manny-man-man. He lives out there."

"You mean on the yacht?"

He scratches his chin. "Umm, umm, okay. I will say you are right. It's his motor launch."

"Well, why didn't you say so? See, that's what I wanted to hear."

"I know. This is why I am telling you now. Okay, sure, it is Willy Love's yacht. Come, we will go this very instinct. Maybe this time my little boat will ride out the storm without sinking again. Oh boy, this is great! Just great! We will bounce this way and that, up and down and up and down and side to side to side. Hope you don't get seasick, Manny-man. It always makes doggie here bark and barf."

"Uh, well, look, why don't we just, uh, wait 'til morning. We could go down there and check into to a nice motel. Clean sheets, hot showers in our own private, quiet, separate rooms. Then we get up early in the morning and meet for breakfast in the coffee shop. The storm will be over then. We can check out properly and go to Mr. Love's yacht when the water's nice and calm. Then I could meet him in the right way, you know, bathed, scrubbed clean, ready, and on my own terms. I don't think my tummy could take all that pitching and rolling tonight. I told you before, I get seasick very easily."

"But Manny-man, the boat is still tied to the dick."

"Just the same, it's jiggling about too much for my comfort. Hell, Mr. Love can wait half a day more, can't he? I mean he's not going to sail away before the storm is good and over and the sea's calm again. If he lives on the boat, he'll be there."

"I did not say he *lives* on the boat, Manny-man."

"Hold it right there, Abis. Don't move! You sure as hell said that exactly."

He continues walking down the slope to the village. I continue following after him, exhorting. The rain has let up a little but the tiny, wind-driven drops continue to prick my skin. Darker clouds drift in from seaward. Thunder rumbles over our heads and crashes into the hills. The static charge bristles my hair. The air is thick and salty. Lightening seems to crackle into the hill behind our heads. With each snap and sizzle of lightening comes the odor of ozone.

Chufee shivers and whines. Abis picks her up and carries her against his chest. The poor little bitch is so covered by his arms I'd be hard pressed to say if he were protecting or smothering the little beast. She stinks to high heaven but despite that I feel sorry for her.

I'm so angry with Abis, though, that I ignore his beast and continue to browbeat him. "Abis," I scream into the wind, "you answer me. You said he lived on that yacht. Now does he live there or not?"

"Not."

"Then where in hell does he live?"

I follow him into town, through two deserted streets, and to the edge of the dock. The sheets of rain are now so thick you can just barely see the motor launch and the foaming waves tossing and slamming against its hull like mad dogs leaping at a fence. I cannot tell if the hull is tall enough to keep the waves at bay. The motor launch seems much smaller now that we are close to it. It seems to shrink as the wind picks up and the waves get larger. The wooden planking of the docks is slippery. Abis turns to me and shouts, "William Love lives out there on that island, yonder."

He points to a shrouded silhouette of a small land mass maybe a half mile offshore.

As the thunder rolls and the beats down even more heavily and the gloom descends, the island seems to disappear, to become one with the gray sea and sky.

Abis grins. "We get there in this."

"Are you serious? In this storm?"

"Big boat, Manny-man."

"Not that big."

"Full crew, lots of comforts for a short trip."

"Look, we have to wait until the storm lets up, okay? I have a phobia about boats, especially when they're not tied to a dock. I mean, a little river is one thing, but the wide ocean is quite another. I can barely swim. You know that, Abis. I only agreed to this thing because I thought Mr. Love lived right here on the mainland. That we could get to him without too much inconvenience. You knew that right from the beginning. Now you say we have to get there by sea in this? No way!"

"It is not so far as you think, Manny-man. Right there, see? You will not even have to cross the bar. Trust me. The captain and crew are William's own. The sea is shallow. The boat waterproof. Plenty of life vests, too. U.S. America Coast Guard Approved."

"I'll get sick."

"Never been sick before? You will recover. Besides, see? Storm is already almost over now. Rain, rain gone away. Red has gone away. In five, no, six more minutes, the bay will be smooth as a baby's heiny."

"Look up, Abis. It's gonna pour down again any second."

"Boat is waterproof one hundred ten percent."

"What about the dog? Maybe I better stay behind and protect her."

"Dog is waterproof. She will go with us."

"Why can't Mr. Love come here?"

"He does what he wants, Manny-man. What will you do here all alone? Freeze to death is what."

"It's 80 degrees."

"Hmm. Then you will roast away when the sun returns. Come now, Manny-man. Maybe Love is on board. Maybe he is waiting for us below deck right now. Come inside boat. Sail. His island is so close to shore."

"Well, I suppose if I do get seasick, it won't last too long."

"The storm is clearing out for the rest of the evening, Manny-man."

"I guess I've come this far to meet him face to face."

*It would be good to find out who he is and why he's sent a madman to fetch me. Why does he shuttle Abis and the other one about in yachts and jets the way he does from continent to continent when he could simply and much more cheaply hire two sets of madmen, one for each location? Surely madmen are available everywhere. Does he really own the world the way it seems? God, can you imagine the wealth? With that kind of money, think of who, and what, he must know.*

Abis is in the boat, under a canopy, getting dry. A uniformed crew member is handing him a big, fluffy towel. I follow him down the gangplank and onto the rolling deck. I'm already a bit queasy. As soon as both my feet are on board, another uniformed crew member throws off the line. We part company with land. As the engines hum and the boat speeds out I begin to feel better, though I know my stomach is looking for any opportunity to revolt. Abis, the dog and I stand at the back of the boat, under the great canvas awning and look out to Love's Island. Surely we will be there in ten minutes or so. I might be able to hold off barfing until then, if the weather just cooperates.

But it doesn't. More rain pours down as if it were being shot from a high pressure fire hose. Lightning bolts illuminate the air around us. Thunder cracks and rolls. I try to keep my eyes on the horizon so I won't get too nauseous but the motor launch is slinging about like a bumper car at the county fair. My stomach turns inside out and slithers up my esophagus, looking for an exit sign. I heard once on a *National Geographic* special that of all the ships that have ever gone to sea, fifty percent have sunk. I grip the railing so hard my fingers become white marble.

Abis and his dog are drenched as well. He beckons for me to follow but I can't seem to move. My fingers are welded to the gunwale. He inches his way toward me and tries to pry my hands from the railing. But as soon as he is close, the wet dog stench of Rabbit-Chufee-Ceriba-God-Knows-What-To-Call-Her gags me like a finger down my throat and I projectile puke a *Guinness Book* world record for distance, quantity and smell. Bits of vomit dribble down my shirt. The stench and the rocking waves make me heave again and again and again and again.

"Oh. God," I say, "Oh, God, I just knew that this would happen."

"That is a bald-headed fib, Manny-man. If we knew this would happen we really would have waited. What I tell you now is true: people really do not know what is in store for them, but they really do what they want, despite what they say. 'Oh,' they say, 'I will do this or that when I have the time, I will write a book, I will take a cruise, I will spend more time with my family.' But this is not true. When people really, really want to do something they make the time."

"I'm sure you have a valid point, there, Abis, but you'll have to excuse me, I'm dying now."

"Manny-man?

"What?"

"Why do you want to stay up here in the wind and rain when Abis, dog and you could be dry and fluffy down below?"

"That's not just the engine room and bilge pumps? We can actually go down there?"

"It is where the crew is keeping dry and fluffy, Manny-man."

"I can't move; my hand is stuck to this bronze rail."

Abis reaches out to me. I let go with my fingers and clasp the rail with the crooks of both elbows. He gets me moving toward the doors, shuffling slowly, like someone walking his pet slug.

And then, finally, we're in the cabin, far below. Waves smash and undulate against the hull. I'm lying on a cot. Abis hovers over me, eating a sandwich. Liverwurst and onions. Small bits of it drop from his mouth onto my chest. Chufee pounces on my chest and gobbles them. A considerable amount of water comes in through the porthole seals, streams down the interior walls and collects in huge rolling puddles on the floor. The rivets in the hull plates rattle. They are about to pop. The ship begins to spin. We are being sucked into a whirlpool! I squeeze my eyes together. My face is soaking wet. I know then I am drowning as the boat begins to go under.

An angel touches my forehead lightly. I slide my hand up and feel a warm, damp, fragrant washcloth. My eyes open. She is standing over me. Tall and slender and elegant as the cedars of Greece. Her long, wavy hair flows about my face like the sea. It surrounds her lovely, tanned face like a dark halo.

My eyes close again and I fall back asleep.

# FIFTEEN

When I wake again the sea is calm. I don't know how long I've been asleep. But it seems like a very long time. Sunlight streams in through the portholes. The walls and floor of the cabin are dry. The warm washcloth is gone, if it was ever there. Of course the woman is gone, too. Abis is snoring in a chair, with his feet resting on my cot. Chufee is curled up on the floor. I sit up and look out the porthole. Chufee wakes and barks. Abis wakes and rises.

"Why are we still out at sea?"

"This is because we are not there, yet."

"But we could see the island from the dock."

"We got pushed aside by the sea and the storm, Manny-man. Now it has taken us many hours to get there. Maybe even a day."

"You said yesterday we would see Love by nightfall. You said that!"

"If he was on board this motor launch. He is not on board."

I sit up and swing my legs over the side of the cot. "You said his *house*!"

"This was because Abis was thinking at the time he told you this that Willy was in his little cottage in the village on the mainland. For when he gets off the boat."

"So why didn't we go there?"

"Because he was not there."

"How do you know? We never even checked!"

The cabin door opens. Hume walks in, bringing breakfast. She is with them. The angel. He sets down the food and the coffee.

Hume says, "Good to have you aboard, sir."

"Thank you, I...."

"Must dash, sir. We'll talk later," Hume says, and leaves.

She remains.

"I thought you were a vision," I say to her. "A wonderful dream I was having."

"I'm Diana," she says smiling, "would you like me to pour you some coffee?"

"Yes. Please. I'm Manny Markovitz."

"Yes, I know." She pours three cups. Abis takes one, and three croissants from the basket. He smears them with butter and eats them all. I take one from the basket. Diana takes the other. As we chew, Abis removes the metal cover from one of the dishes and tosses the bacon to Chufee. He eats the scrambled eggs himself.

"Diana, why are we still out at sea? Abis told me yesterday we would get there in a few minutes."

Okay.

"Did not," he says.

I turn to him. "Yes, you did. You pointed to that island just off the coast and..."

"No, no, Manny-man, I pointed out to sea. To sea! You just resumed it was the first island. Ha, ha, you have fooled yourself this time. I never said it was that place. If you are disappointed, it is your fault. If you jump to conclusions and they do not turn out to fit reality, whom's fault is that?"

"Okay, okay, but..." My voice rises in pitch.

"No sense getting upset," Diana says. "We'll arrive quite soon. In the meantime, enjoy breakfast and our company, and the ride. I know you'll like the big house and the archeological digs when we get there."

"What archeological digs?"

"Massive," Abis says. "All over the island. Diana is in charge of them. You will see."

"Come, let's go out on deck. We'll be docking soon."

Dolphins rise from the sea. I'm not sure how long I stand at the railing watching them. I've never seen wild dolphins before. Only on television. Small fishing boats dot the offshore waters. The fishermen wave. I wave back and turn to Diana. But she seems to have vanished again. The fishermen seem disappointed when they recognize it's only Abis and me waving back. Or maybe I'm jumping to conclusions again.

In an hour or so, we approach an island. Green hills rise up nearly from the shoreline, which is dotted with small houses and fishing nets drying in the sun. We enter a protected cove and as we round the bend, an enormous, red-tiled manse and compound of outbuildings comes into view. The outbuildings sprawl down to the sea. The main house is three stories high. From this distance it seems constructed of white marble.

As we sail closer I see terraces on each level, and pillars, streamlined, adaptations of the designs of ancient Aegean columns. A tall, massive figure in white slacks and shirt leans out from the highest balcony. His hands are raised to his face, holding, I think, binoculars.

William Love. At last.

***

A few minutes later the yacht glides through the water of the cove behind the house to a sheltered dock cut from the coral rock. Abis and I stand under the canopy to watch the boat securely moored. As soon as the hawsers are fastened I turn to him and say, "I want to go right up to the big house and meet our host."

"No, no, Manny-man. We must do all things in the proper order here. Order and ceremoney is what he stands for. First you must look over the house and tour the gardens. It is a great and beatific learning experience that you must do, trust me."

"No, Abis. I want to meet him now!"

"This is very, very tough toenails, Manny-man. It is ordeemed that you must tour the gardens. Diana herself will be your guide. I will see to it that your things are taken to your room. Also I must put doggie to bed. See you later. When you are done. Then we will have a grand talk with Willy. It is only through Abis that thou doth know him. This I promise from me to you. What a friend we have in Abis!"

"I'm going to take a few steps over, Abis, so I don't get hit with the lightening when God zaps you down."

"No, no, Manny-man. You are confusing your God with Zeus."

"Maybe so."

"Very common misdeception."

Someone taps my shoulder. I turn around. Diana stands before me, wearing a white Greek peasant's skirt and low cut pull-over blouse molded over braless breasts. She takes my arm and, moving sensually, leads me down the gangplank. It's all I can do to take my eyes from her and look about the house as we enter.

Eventually I do. I am awestruck. Outside of the great country homes and temples of Europe I have never seen so much marble. His whole world must be made of the stuff. The floor is tiled black and white, the ceiling clouded blue.

I move to inspect more closely. Everything is really *faux-marbre*. The trim, counters, walls, and even the built-in furniture are all *faux-marbre*. The couches and chairs are all of the same stuff, all topped with white cushions, dyed or painted to seem marble, too.

Large picture windows look out on the sea. The solid walls are painted with amazingly life-like *trompe l'oeil* windows depicting, no doubt, the actual scenes one would see if the walls were replaced by real windows and the rest of the building become transparent.

The window sills are *faux-marbre*, too, of course, with painted window seats and chairs and painted maidens sitting in them, some in antique Minoan or Aegean costume, some in American Indian garb, with overtones of ancient Mediterranean. Painted maidens lean over painted rails on painted terraces. Some gaze out on an unreal, painted sea. Others stare forever back at us into the real room where we stand for the moment, staring back at them.

The figures seem so life-like you can almost hear them breathe. It is as if once long ago they actually had souls and somehow were enchanted into that painted world of two dimensions.

Pigments of the imagination. Any moment now I expect the painted waves to undulate and one of those painted birds above the window seat to flit down to a painted finger and sing.

Suddenly, one of the birds does move! I'm so started I gasp. Diana pushes me forward. The goldfinch and its gilded cage are real, set into a niche painted to seem as if the wall were flat and the cage and sky behind it painted in. But they're not. They're real. The window behind the cage is real. I misquote aloud, "Nature, half-created, half revealed."

"Come," Diana says, and glides up the stairs.

As I watch her body move beneath the liquefaction of that peasant costume, I say to myself, "Well, at least she's real." But I even have a strange sensation about that, too. I mean, of course she's an actual living human being, all right. I mean, damn, there she is breathing right in front of me and doing one hell of a job of it, too. She's not like one of those ladies painted on the walls or anything like that. She's flesh and blood, and quite a magnificent pile. But everything she and Hume and Abis, too, everything they've told or even done seems, so, so, unreal. As if they are trying to draw me into their fiction, to enchant me into the painted stone like those two dimensional figures on the walls.

Or draw me *out* of the stone into the world of three dimensions.

Hume stops all this speculation with a bit of physical reality so substantial only the most highly trained metaphysician could even try refute it: hot tea and warm, fresh scones. He meets us at the rooftop terrace with tray in hand and leads us to a table. After seating Diana, he places the pots and plates before us, uncovers the tea cakes and slavers them with butter. Diana gestures for me to sample. "Delicious," I say. Hume nods, smiles, and withdraws. Diana pours us both some tea.

"Eat," she orders.

I take another nibble. But I can hardly swallow for staring across the terrace at the thing that has just caught my eye. It's the statue I saw from the boat and took for William Love. Its massive marble form leans over a marble balcony and seems to be staring out to sea. One arm is raised, as if it were staring without judgment at everything that passes by its cold, indifferent eye.

Then I realize this isn't the William Love I had seen from the boat. My William Love had both hands to his face. He had used a pair of binoculars. I shift to glance back at Diana. When I turn again to find the statue on the terrace it seems to be gone. At last I can't find it again among the false and real pillars of the terrace.

I turn again to Diana. "I'll tell you the truth," I confide. "I don't know what the hell's going on."

She shrugs her lovely shoulders and smiles. I smile back. Nothing else matters anymore. We sit and talk away the morning. Hume returns with wine and cheese. He doesn't say a word or make a sound. In fact, I'm almost unaware of his presence until he turns to leave. When he does, I continue telling Diana about my journey with Abis.

Hume is back again. "Lunch, madam and sir," he says.

"But you just served us scones and tea and wine and…"

"That was hours ago, sir."

I look at Hume's watch. "Good God. It's two o'clock in the afternoon!"

"Indeed, sir," Hume says as he places covered dishes before us. He bows slightly from the waist and withdraws.

Neither of us bothers to uncover the dishes and eat. Instead, we continue chattering away, oblivious to the world, and even to what we are saying. But I do remember asking her, "What do you know about Hume, I mean that, that, I guess it's a latex mask he seems to be wearing?"

"He's been undergoing a series of plastic surgeries. Burn scars, I think from a childhood accident. Or maybe the disease. Really, that's all I know, all I can tell you."

I nod. While I have been telling her all about myself, Diane has been telling me in minute detail about the archeological excavations she has been overseeing on the island. It is not what I want to hear right now. I want to learn about him, about William Love. Finally I tell her so.

"First I need to tell you about me," she says. "I think there are some things you really need to know. Personal things. About my lack of future. About my past."

"Is it bad?"

"Some of it. Very bad."

"Will it make me jealous?"

She shrugs.

"Then, no, I don't want to hear it, yet. I don't want to go beyond now."

"But why?"

"Maybe I just want to make up my own mind about things before what you, or others, tell me, prejudices my point of view. I just want you to be what you are right now. If it's an illusion, maybe I just want to keep the illusion going for the time being."

"And what illusion is that?"

"Whatever. I want you to be a mystery. Don't you like to live with mysteries?"

"Not particularly," she says. "But I guess that's just part of my nature, to dispel mysteries. My professional stance."

"I guess I've always wanted a mystery in my life. The great mystery, I suppose. Something to believe in. Maybe there isn't any great mystery in life, after all. Just illusion. I'm not a poet. I'm a social scientist. I believe there are no there are no unsolvables in the universe, only things we haven't figured out, yet. When the physicists unravel it, we'll know everything. What they call the mind of God. The universe is a logical place. I just know it. All the locks have keys."

"Really?"

"That's what I've been trying to tell Abis. He doesn't buy it, either. But it's true. Even if we don't hold all the keys in our hands yet, we know they exist. And we already hold so many."

She laughs. "And yet you don't even know who I really am, and am rapidly becoming. You don't even want to know."

"Not yet."

"All right. Tell me when you do. But I warn you, we're rapidly approaching the point when it will be too late."

So many of the keys already, I think. In fact, I myself already have quite a collection. It's up to me which closets I want opened. Love, for instance. I suppose I could have searched the house already and found him out. But I've made the clear and logical decision to sit here on the terrace with Diana and let Love reveal himself in his own time, and in his own way. I don't care; I can wait. .

"Hello?"

"Oh, sorry, Diana, I was daydreaming. So, where is the master of the house?"

"When the excavations are in progress there may be as many as a hundred men and women working on the dig. We're just about to begin another season. I think he always leaves then, or flits back and forth between the island and his other holdings."

"Why?"

"Who knows? Maybe he doesn't like the crowds. I'm just guessing, same as you are. Maybe it's the noise we make. I think he prefers it out there, in the garden. Alone."

"Well, what do you know about him?"

"He's my boss. Other than that, precious little."

"How'd you meet him? You have met him, haven't you?"

"What a funny question."

"What does he look like?"

"I really can't say."

"Why won't you tell me? It's so infuriating. When I don't want answers everyone's willing to talk. When I want some answers, I can't get them."

"I'm sure if and when he wants to meet you face to face he will. You may have seen him already, who knows."

"What's that supposed to mean?"

"Please don't. I'm sure he'll explain. When you get there."

"Get there?"

"Go to him, I guess I mean."

"Where?"

"Wherever he is."

"I thought he was here."

"He may be. We'll see."

"Why won't you give me a straight answer?"

"I'm sorry. I don't know where he is. I was hoping he would arrive and we'd both see him when you came. Obviously, for some reason that probably has nothing to do with us, he's not here, or not here, yet. All we can do is what Abis suggested when he first brought me here."

"Which is?"

"Just relax and enjoy the wait. He'll show when he shows. Have faith."

I take her by the hand and stroll to the edge of the terrace and peer out beyond the gardens toward the digs. Then with both of my hands on the rail I lean out as far as I can. Suddenly it's as I'm hovering high above the ground on my own wings and the terrace, even the house itself, doesn't exist beneath me. Like a powerful sea bird, I'm riding the currents of air, not though strength or power, which I don't have, but through finesse of the air currents, the achieve of, the mastery of the thing.

But my "achieve of" is really someone else's. My feet are still on the ground, never mind how high someone else has raised that ground above the surface.

Diana leans out, too. I can feel the heat of her body, quite separate from the summer's warmth. Her shoulder touches my shoulder. Her hip touches mine and I'm afraid and thankful for the brisk sea breeze that carries the heat away.

The wind shifts direction. It blows her long, dark hair across her face, hiding it like a mantle. Periodically she reaches up and brushes it away, but to no use. The wind continues to perform its secret ministry, veiling sometimes her dark eyes, sometimes not, bringing the scent of her body to me.

She wears no make-up, and no perfume, as far as I can tell. But she has a pleasant, natural woman's scent and a beautiful profile. Added to her natural allurements, her face has such serenity. As if she has seen into the heart of light, into the mystery that has always eluded me, and found within it the peace that passes understanding.

As I gaze at her profile, now revealed, now hidden by her hair, I have this overwhelming desire to know what she knows. To have her reveal everything to me. But again I'm afraid of the secret, the personal secret she has hinted at.

She is privy to the other mystery, too. She knows. Why do some have that gift and some of us wear the veil forever? Perhaps I do know as much as she, and am now only beginning to know what I know. Or maybe the secret is that there is no secret. Things really are what they seem to be. Maybe the only world is the world of flesh, no matter how much we wish otherwise. Maybe accepting that knowledge is what brings such peace. Or learning to live with the mystery.

On the other hand, she does know more than I in at least one respect. She has met Love face to face. She was hired by him. She's in his employ as she has reminded me, repeatedly. Most likely, she is his lover.

I back away from the railing a bit so that our bodies are not still touching. She turns to face me, her back now to the rail. I look down across the lawns and the garden. "That's it, isn't it?" I ask, gesturing toward the canvas awnings in the distance.

She turns to face them, too. "Yes. What we've done so far. The exploratory pits are over there. The larger scale excavations are to the right."

"How long have you been doing it?"

"Not long, as we measure things. Five years. The actual excavations are only two years old."

"And you've been directing them since their inception? You must have started working here right out of puberty."

"Right out of grad school, anyway."

"Same thing."

"Actually, I took over as chief from my former doctoral director, when he died. Since my dissertation was on this very dig, I was the obvious choice to take over. The surviving expert."

"So how's it gone, so far?"

"Since Dr. Aquinas's death, we've continued to wipe away most of the first surface layer and some of the preliminary conceptions and misconceptions that he had and inserted some of my own. We've been able to dig out two sides of what we assume at this point was the main temple. In addition, we've sunk a good number of deep exploration pits and brought up some extraordinary pottery."

"And how long do you figure it will take you to finish the project?"

She looks as if she is about to cry. "I will never live to see it finished."

"What? I don't understand."

"That's because you a said a while ago you weren't ready to understand. So let's just leave it at that. I'll never live to see the project completed. A project this vast will take sixty years, maybe more, just to excavate properly, let alone evaluate. I have a lot of pressure to finish it right away, of course. You know, make a circus of it. See what it's all about before you go, that sort of thing. Two bulldozers and a crane, and six months later, presto, the new Disney World of Archaeology, complete with rides for the kiddies. But no, done properly, and scientifically, this is more than a whole life's work, even for someone granted an abnormally long life span."

"So it's quite possible you'll never know what you have down there, will you?"

"*I* certainly won't. Not completely. If I'm allowed, I'll just continue for as long as I have to dig and uncover and find bits and pieces and evaluate them in light of what we know already. But I'll never live to see the whole, or even a major part of the whole. It's beyond my lifetime. Beyond my grasp."

"And you couldn't, or won't, proceed quicker? There's no way without compromising the science?"

She laughs. "You sound like someone else I know."

"Well?"

"Proceed quicker?" She shakes her head. "That's the paradox. If I did, I'd end up destroying what I'd hope eventually to find, though at this rate I'll never even come close to finding it. Besides, just to move all that dirt would take an army of workers so vast this island wouldn't even support them. They'd just get in each other's way and slow the project down even further. Diana's Paradox. A working lifetime is not long enough, not even when you get a head start as early as I did and were granted a long life span."

"That's why I like my field best. At least you get to teach what's already known. I just can't imagine your frustration seeking what you know you'll never find. I guess you just have to go on faith that someday it will be found and just go on making your small excavations for others to enlarge and interpret, or reinterpret in light of new findings about what had already happened in the past, perhaps without any consequence to the future, save for the curious."

"Then again, you never know, do you? I mean at any given moment, one of my people could uncover the missing link, so to speak. The Big Revelation. The next shovelful could hit upon a new Laocoön to change the course of art, or raise a whole new, so to speak, civilization back to life."

Someone clears his throat behind us. Startled, we both turn around quickly to face him.

# SIXTEEN

Hume stands before us, with dinner spread out on the table. He places himself behind one chair, waiting to seat Diana. His features seem sharper now. And darker. Perhaps he's wearing a different mask. Maybe it's the diminishing light.

I can't believe he has set the table so elaborately without us even noticing he was on the terrace. But there it is, table for two, table cloth, glass-shaded candle, covered dishes, and two bottles of cooled, white wine from Crete.

We're alone again. Just us and the snapper almondine. It smells and tastes wonderful, but neither of us has much appetite. Mostly, we drink the wine. She looks down at the tablecloth. I touch her wrist. She looks up at me. I say, "How did you wind up here? I mean, really?"

"What do you mean?"

"I'm not sure. Well, okay, look, start from the beginning. Where are you from?

"Minnesota."

"So how come you have dark hair? I thought everyone there was a corn-fed blonde?"

"You're thinking of my mom. But my father was a full-blooded Chippewa. They met when my mother went to the reservation to do missionary work. She's the one who converted."

"So being half-Indian gave you a leg up on this occupation?"

"What do you mean?"

"Well, didn't you learn the secret lore of the Indian on your papa's knee?"

"Actually, my father didn't know any of it. He learned it from my mother. Just as I did. And she learned it in missionary school. You can imagine what version of reality they taught her. I unlearned most of it in grad school."

"So this stuff about occult, unrevealable Indian rites passed on from generation to generation is just bunk?

"Nobody revealed them to me, that's for sure. I got from my father and my family on his side a reverence for our past. A respect for my ancestors. Puts me in a funny position. The Indian side of me says, 'don't dig up the bones of your ancestors. Let them return to the elements so the spirits of the dead may be free, while the archeologist side of me, the European, says 'ignore someone else's superstitions in favor of your own. Dig and learn whatever trivia you can to add to the wealth of trivia that may one day become your own, or more probably, someone else's insight.' So, drawn and repelled by both sides of my ancestry, my past has become what I am making it. And I've tried to make it as good as the real thing. To me it is the real thing. With as much consequence, or more, to my life. As an undergraduate, I worked on the Neolithic findings in Greece, at Magassa, around Sitia, and on Crete. That's where I first heard about William Love. He had an estate there and much interest, financial and intellectual, in the excavations. I was just beginning to recover from a very painful love affair. My third in four years. He put me through grad school. There I met Dr. Aquinas, who put me onto this site and switched me from Aegean to American Indian archeology and groomed me to take his place."

"How does Love make his money?"

"As far as I know, he made most of it in the Mediterranean and Middle East long before he came here. Changing grape juice into wine and olives into oil, other things, imports, petroleum, arms, international art, only he knows what else."

We are standing next to the terrace railing once again. Our wine glasses rest on the top of it as we stare out over the gardens, festively strung with tiny white lights in the trees. It reminds me of the pictures of Rockefeller Center.

"Come," she says, and picks up both glasses.

I follow, stopping briefly at the table to snatch the second bottle of wine, already partially empty.

We descend the spiral stairs at dizzying speed, run across the lawn, through the garden, and don't stop until we reach the edge, where grass and flowers cascade into the shallow salt inlet. We stand and watch the lights of the ships rise and fall with the waves in the open sea. Small boats play in front of them in the bay waters. Bright white lights on their bows shine into the bay waters.

"They're fishing now," she says. For shrimp and crab. Spreading their nets, too, I think, for fish."

"It's all so romantic, and marvelous," I reply, gazing out at the reflections. When I turn to face her again, she's gone! A wave of fear comes over me that I have been abandoned again. I can't move. Then I recover enough to search for her along the edge of the garden.

I see her silhouette in the moon and run to catch up. When I get close, I begin to walk. She faces me. "You may kiss me now," she says.

I kiss her passionately. She backs away. "I wasn't expecting that," she says.

"But you said...."

She lets out a sigh."A friendly kiss."

"I didn't want to give you a friendly kiss."

We walk slowly along the pebbled garden path. Watching fireflies light and mate. We kiss again, even more passionately. We are off the garden path and on the ground, shielded from the garden lights. I begin to remove her blouse. "No," she says, "no."

We kiss again.

"I promise," I say, "I will never hurt you." My hands are on the bottom of her blouse.

She sighs. I drop my hands. Her eyes close. My hands return to her waist, and the bottom of her blouse. "What the hell," she says, and raises her arms for me to remove it.

\*\*\*

We make love off the garden path so many times we both lose count. "What passion," she says as she lies with her head on my chest. I am thinking the same thing. Neither one of us knows the time. Obviously, it is pretty close to dawn, for the sky is beginning to brighten. She sits up and looks at me. "What is that rash?"

"The remnants of poison ivy."

"But how?"

"Abis. Don't ask."

"If Abis is involved, I don't want or need to."

We rise, dress and leave the garden. As she turns to put on her blouse, I notice for the first time a tattoo on the side of her left breast. It is exactly like the one Abis has, only in miniature. I mean to ask her what it signifies, but right now I'm afraid to know.

She leads me back to her room. We make love again. Finally she says, "We can sleep now. Just a little while."

"I'd better go back to my room."

"Why?"

"I don't know."

"Stay here."

\*\*\*

I wake with a start and glance at her clock. It's been two hours. I feel guilty as Adam on his first night out of Eden. Here I am in William Love's house, his guest. Drinking his wine. Eating his food. Sleeping with his mistress.

Diana snoozes peacefully. I'm so discomposed I actually say aloud, "What am I doing?" before I catch myself. But Diana doesn't wake. Still, the original sentiment stays with me. I mean, here's this woman that, really, I hardly know, and somehow I'm committed to her in a way I hardly understand. I have felt her incredible vulnerability beneath her veneer of confidence and professional demeanor. Along with it, I feel my own vulnerability.

So what's bothering me now? It isn't that I'm not ready for Diana. But it is so impossible. My real world is thousands of miles away. Or. Everything is so ephemeral. Like I'm a new-changed moth. And you know how long they live. Maybe I'm thinking too much. Too far ahead. The whole relationship with her is too new, too much like being in a dream world. But there she is, breathing. Lying next to me. In William Love's bed. I'm ashamed.

"Hey! You should be ashamed!"

"What?" I shout, startled.

Abis is standing over us.

"Not you, Manny-man. Her. Shameless hussy, taking advantage of a poor virgin like you. Terrible. Terrible. See, I have put my hands over my eyes."

"You're peeking," Diana says.

"You have caught me. Now I am as shameless as you!"

"How'd you get in here?" she asks.

"Do you not have an open door policy?"

"No."

"Next time, use Mr. Key."

"Can you at least turn around so we can cover up?" I ask.

"Sure, sure."

Abis turns and sets the tray he's carrying on the edge of the bed. He pours coffee from the porcelain pot into three cups. "Here, you two drink this." Then he turns to me. "Manny-man, Abis came to your room to take you out in his real and genuine boat. Does he find you in your room? No. So I begin to count. "One," I say, "Two." This was how far I got. Only to number two. One and one. Then I say to myself, I say, "Self, *Circe la femme*. That is Latin."

He laughs so hard he spills most of the coffee in his cup, which he wipes up with his sleeve.

"Come, Manny-man. We go yachting."

"Diana?" I say, turning to her.

"Not me. I've had his Baptismal before. You go. I'm sleeping in."

"Come, Manny-man, the water awaits."

He stands at the foot of the bed, grinning.

"Well, uh, why don't you wait for me on the terrace, or wherever you're having breakfast."

"What? You are ashamed before me you are naked as a jay bird? Not so modest before. Okay, okay, I'll go. Oh, here, take this pot. Drink plenty. Humey will bring us a nice hot breakfast with American cheese spread just as you like it. Maybe American candy bars for later. Then we sail!"

When he leaves I turn to Diane. "You sure you don't want to go?"

"Oh, yeah. I need to sleep in."

"Me, too."

"He won't keep you out long. Do you good. Learn a few things." She snuggles up and I hold her. "I'll be here when you get back. Sleeping."

We make love again. Then I find all our clothes on the floor, mingled in a heap, pick out what belongs to me, put most of it on and return to my own room down the hall, carrying the rest. There I shower, find new clothes someone has laid out for me, and go up to the terrace.

Abis is seated in a chair, munching croissants, his feet resting on the railing. A porcelain coffee cup even more elegant than the ones he brought to Diana's room rests on a small round marble table next to him. Another cup waits for me on the other side of the table. But when I reach out to take it, I realize it has already been used. Who has Abis been talking to? Could it be William Love? Hume appears with a tray. He lays out silver for me, a basket of rolls and butter, and a fresh cup. He smiles, rather furtively, I think, and in silence takes the other cup away. I'm pretty sure I see from the corner of my eye that just before he leaves the terrace, he takes a sip from it. Or is that what he meant me to see?

After I down a few rolls with wolf-like delicacy, Abis says, "ready?"

"Why not?

I follow him down to the dock, past large motor launches and sleek sailboats, each big enough to sleep ten.

"Which one?"

He points to a diminutive sailing craft on the end of the dock, hardly more than a toy.

Seeing my dismay, he says, "It is a fast pleasure boat. This is the very dictionary definition of 'yacht.' Great, no?"

"No. I'm not getting in that thimble."

"Manny-man, it is safe. Trust me. Even upside down it floats. I know this personally from many demonstrations. And we will not go far. Only in the bay. Very shallow there. Do you know how to handle the sail and tiller?"

"No."

"Easy as cake. Today you will learn in this. Like riding a tricycle. Before you take on this great sailboat for me to cross the bar. Eh?"

He steps into the microboat. It sinks down in the water fearfully and sways exaggeratedly with every movement of his body.

"No," I say, taking a step back. "And I mean it this time, too. You can't persuade me."

He gestures with a low, over-elaborate, bow for me to enter, and holds up a Greek captain's hat with golden braids for me to wear. He waves it slightly and the gold braids glint in the sun. I back away one more step, right into a cleat. Immediately I jump forward in pain and nearly fall into the water.

"Boat is safer than the dock, Manny-man. Come on, you will be the captain. I will be the crew."

"No."

"What will you do? Go back and tell Diana you have returned to her protection because you have lost your balls? What will you do with no balls, Manny-man? Sing her serenades in a high voice?"

He sings a few notes in falsetto. "Hey, she will not be amused with that too long. Belieeeeeve me."

His 'believe me' has such lewd conviction it makes me angry. I don't want to go back to her. I'm gonna to show him I am a man who can make up his own mind. I board the little boatlette.

Before I can even settle in, or think about what a stupid choice I have just made, he unties her, pushes off with one foot, and raises the striped sail.

"Listen, Abis, I don't know that much about sailing, but isn't that canvas too big for this little boat? It looks like it's twice as tall as this boat is long."

"You bet, man-man. And three times wider. Makes this yacht go plenty, plenty fast."

"And you're sure that's all right?"

"Sure, sure. Nice cool, brisk wind. See that feather on top of the mast?"

There's a kind of wind flag featuring what looks like a long rooster's tail.

"Bald eagle feather, Manny-man. No boat can ever go wrong with an eagle feather on it. When it points that way, you point the sail like this. Then it fills with oxygen. Away you go to sail the seventeen seas. When you want to go back, you cross like this–oops, watch the boom–and it fills with oxygen on the other side like that. Pregnant with air. Back and forth, you zigzag home. Here, man-man, you take the reins."

I grab the rope from him and put my hand to the tiller. He opens up the little cooler and takes out an icy beer for each of us.

"Remember, we go out with the sun on this shoulder and in with the sun on that shoulder. That way we never get lost. Even over the horizon."

"We're not planning on going over the horizon, are we?"

"No, no. Not planning. But sometimes Abis gets carried away."

"We're going pretty fast!"

"It is the wind, man-man. We just go with it. Watch with one eye on the road. One eye on the feather. Shift the sail as the feather shifts. One eye on the horizon."

"That's three eyes."

"Need three eyes. Use one of mine. I will watch the horizon."

We sail on and on. I'm actually having fun. Beginning to relax. Hand on the tiller. Captain of my fate. Then I panic. "Abis, where's the island?"

"Over the horizon. Umm, over yonder, I think."

He points behind us with his thumb.

"Oh, shit! Let's go back! How did you say we turn this thing around?"

Abis shrugs.

"Excuse me, are you saying you don't know?"

"Used to know. I forget."

"Well, think, Abis!"

"Umm, give me a minute. Ah, yes, you do it with that."

He points to the tiller. "Turn, but do not ignore feather. Sails must always be a little bit pregnant. Always need oxygen."

"Oh, shit, a freighter!"

"Relax, man-man. He has not hit us, yet. Enjoy the wait. No worry, anyway. See? Abis has this."

He holds up a little chrome-plated whistle. "When he gets too close, I will blow and he will put on his brakes plenty fast. Then he will come to a complete and total stop. Abis thinks this is a rule."

"Whose rule? Yours? Do they know the rule?"

"Manny-man, do not worry so much. Of course they know the rule. Relax!"

The ship looms closer, still heading right for us, or more correctly, we toward it, since we're the ones out of control.

"Blow the damn whistle!" I scream.

"Not to worry, Manny-man. I trust in you," he says and casually tosses the whistle overboard. It makes a little plopping sound and is gone, an artifact to drive future archeologists wild with speculation. Item: hollow lump of metal with a ball inside. Found underneath crushed miniature sailboat containing two crushed and badly mangled human skeletons....

"Oh, shit, Abis, help!"

I try to turn the sailboat, but can't keep the wind! We're going to be rammed and run over! We're much too small to be seen in time.

Now I can make out men on the deck of the freighter. They all have dark beards and stubbles. None of them is paying attention to us, or even looking at the water. I scream. One of the crew members turns around.

143

But not toward us. We can't be heard over the noise of the big ship's engines. They're going to ram us. They're fifty feet away!

"Oh, God, Abis, take the tiller!"

"Hmm. Things look pretty serious, now, Manny-man. Maybe Abis should not have thrown his whistle away."

"Shiiiiiiiiiiit!"

"No, do not dive overboard, Manny-man," he advises, grabbing my collar. "Then they never see you. Also maybe you will drown."

"Where're the fucking life vests, dammit!"

"Life vests, Manny-man?"

"The fucking life vests, Abis, it's the fucking law!"

"American U.S. Georgia law?"

"Oh, shit, Abis, shit! He's twenty feet away!"

"It's pray or scream time, now, Manny-man!"

I do both, screaming, "Oh, God, oh shit, oh God, oh shit!"

Suddenly one of the crew men points toward us! The others turn around to look! Too late. They can't turn aside. By the time they even get the message to their pilot he'll have already run us down! I can feel the vibration of their huge human-sucking propellers in the water and the mass of the iron hull drawing us in. I can't even read the name of the ship that is going to kill us because it's in a foreign language. The water foams and flecks and bubbles as they come hard upon us and just miss! They pass our side within five feet. Crew members shout to us. A few make crude and unusually obscene gestures. One uses the same hand signs the bus driver used at Delphi. Abis waves his handkerchief and smiles. I'm sitting rigidly now, my legs stiffly splayed out in front of me, my arms stretched out stiff as well, and my knuckles white from gripping the gunwale. The little sailboat rocks so violently it takes on water over the bow. I close my eyes and chant a prayer I hadn't chanted since childhood. I think it's called the prayer for the dead.

"Wheee!" Abis yells. "Like wild west days, Manny-man. Ride 'em cowboys! Wow, that was fun!"

I open my eyes. The freighter is steaming past us now. It's over. We are still alive. Unsunk. But badly foundering. Abis hands me a small translucent plastic bailing bucket. "Manny, do you drive your car like that?"

"I resign as captain," I mumble and drop the braided hat on the deck.

"Too late, Manny-man. Your crew has mutated."

He takes the flopping tiller and turns the sail into the wind.

"Didn't you tell me to keep the sun over the other shoulder to get back in?"

"Damn thing moves, man-man."

"Oh."

"Ha, ha, I fooled you. It is the earth that rotates."

"Hardly makes sense at this point. You turning around?"

"You bet."

"Where are we going?

"Hmm. I am hoping it is toward Love's island."

***

So we are sailing back and I'm beginning to relax again. I take off my shoes, lie back, and watch the still, white cumulus clouds and the flapping eagle feather. It makes a kind of pinging sound each time it hits the aluminum mast. The air is warm. Nothing can go wrong. I snooze.

"Oh, shi—" Abis cries. But he gets out only half the word before we are both pitched into the water.

The little boat is upside down! We have been tossed ten feet from it. I try to swim back but we're caught in strong rip current. "Abis!" I yell as I start to go under. I'm drowning.

His hand comes across my shoulder. I go limp and float as he drags me toward the overturned hull of the boat, kicking powerfully, but losing ground. Losing ground. "Kick, Manny-man, kick!" he screams, and I do.

We gain some on the capsized boat. Not much. But some. After a time, though, we're gripping the overturned hull. He clambers onto it, then pulls me up. We stand on the keel, leaning against the big fin, I forget what they're called, the one that sticks out of the hull and keeps the sailboat from sliding sideways in the water when the sails are up. Anyway, the fin now juts at a thirty-five degree angle from the horizontal. Abis begins to jump up and down on it. I can hear the fiberglass cracking. He hears the cracking, too, because he says, "uh, oh," and stops.

He leans back on the fin as if he were in a chaise lounge and folds his hands behind his head. "No use, man-man. The mast is stuck in the sand. On bottom. Only one thing to do."

"What's that?"

He looks intently at me. "One of us must swim down into the shark-infested waters and free it."

"Fifteen feet? In this current?"

"You go, Manny-man. I am tired."

"I can barely tread water. You know that. Hell, you just had to save me from drowning."

"Then there is only one other thing to do,"

"What?"

"Enjoy the sun."

"We're going to fry to death out here within an hour, Abis."

145

Fifty feet from us, the beer cooler bobs away with the rip current.

"I thought that eagle feather of yours was supposed to protect us from this sort of thing."

"They were fresh out of eagle feathers at the store, Manny-man. Abis had to substitute one large seagull feather. From its butt."

One of my shoes floats halfway between us and the beer cooler. The other is not in sight. They were the same shoes I had lost in Delphi.

Abis sees it, too, because he says, "Man-man, you must learn to hold onto your things or you will lose them. Did not your mother teach you this? Ah, well, no worry. They were ugly shoes. Abis did you a great favor to drown them, again. Did I not try to do this for you once before? No, no, Manny, do not thank me. You were not even grateful the last time I tried."

"If we live through this, I'm going to kill you."

"Okay, okay, I will fix everything."

He puts one hand to the side of his face and yells, "Taxi! Taxi! TAXI!"

"Stop that. You're embarrassing me. Let's just die with dignity."

"TAXI!," he shouts and waves his arms.

A motorboat with two fishermen comes by. They laugh and point, then chug on by. When they are out of sight, Abis says, "I know those two. Both their mothers were whores. That is why they are such bastards."

Another boat comes by. Abis waves and smiles. The fishermen wave and smile back. It occurs to me that they don't realize we are really in trouble. Abis is being too casual. I scream, "Please, help! Help!"

They turn around and circle us. I wave both arms frantically. They come close and toss us a line. We tie it to our keel. Abis says, "When the mast comes free of the bottom, we must jump on the keel board. The boat will flip upright. Hold on right here, man-man. Lift both arms. As the boat rights itself, we will rise up with it and end up inside again. And not even get wet again."

This is exactly what happens.

As I sit in the bottom of the boat again, with my legs straight out, I say, "Obviously you're been through this before."

Abis grins. "Good thing Chufee did not come, huh, Manny-man? She is a dog who does not like this salt water swimming. Also and too she is just the right size for a medium-small shark snack. Ha, ha, no wonder she ran off to hide under the bed when Abis suggested this sailing trip." He grabs the tiller and sail line, and says, "Okay-donkey, here we go, pal."

"Can we head back, now?"

"Sure, sure."

"Aren't we going the wrong way?"

"Manny-man, we must make the big chase, first. Here, you take the bucket. Help Abis bail. Good thing I have tied this bucket to the floor."

"If I take the bucket, what will you use?"

"Abis must drive the boat, Manny-man. Make the big chase before it gets away."

"Before what gets away?"

"The beer cooler, Manny-man. Do you not see it is nearly on the horizon bobbing to the Happy Isles already?"

"What about my shoes?"

"Gone, Manny-man. Ugly shoes. Soon Abis will give you a pair of almost brand-new high-class tire-sole sandals just like his. You are one lucky stuff, Manny-man"

"Wonderful."

The salt begins to itch as my clothes dry and stiffen.

"Okay, Manny-man, here it comes. Got it! Want beer?"

"Might as well. Are we headed back home, now?"

"Back to Love's Island, Manny-man. Not home."

"Whatever."

With the sail fully up we slam into the dock, nearly crushing the thin hull of the boat. I scramble out as quickly as possible and run back up to the big house. Diana is under the canopy of the terrace. Hume arrives with ice water and *ouzo*. As he mixes then he says, rather wryly, "Did we have a nice sail?"

"Interesting," I answer without looking up.

"Did we overturn, sir?"

Now I look at him and squint. "Yes."

He nods, gravely. Chufee trots up, sits on Diana's left foot, smiles stupidly, pants, and salivates on the marble tile floor.

Diana scratches her behind the ear. "Did he get the mast stuck in the bottom?"

"Yes."

Hume nods.

"He does that regularly?" I inquire.

"Every time, sir"

"Ahh."

"I believe he forgets to observe the feather, sir. For changes in the winds."

"Ahh."

Diana smiles. "Abis, in case you have not noticed, it yet, darling, has a short attention span."

"Like the Gods," I say.

# SEVENTEEN

Diana and I sleep most of the afternoon, waking now and then to make love. Around six she leads me down to the kitchen, where she finds a wicker basket, packs a cold picnic dinner and hands it to me. We are headed toward the digs. As we walk along the path around the garden, a flash of insight keeps trying to enter my consciousness. Like a dream nearly remembered.

But it will not form.

Like the shadow of a dream, an impression of something important. I try desperately to recall it, but it won't surface. "You know when Abis and I were out there clinging to his little boat," I say, "and in genuine danger of drowning, I had this vague, almost dream-like notion, almost like a hope, that William Love himself would save us rather than those two fishermen. I mean directly. Love himself."

"Why?"

"Because then I could finally meet him face to face and know he was real, so to speak. Not that I don't know that now. If only because you told me so. But if Love actually came to me and did that, can you imagine how grateful I would have been? How much linked to him? How much I would feel for him, and be obliged to him?"

"More so than to the fishermen who did save you?"

"Yes. They just happened to come along and throw us a line. But I feel like I'm already so obliged to him now."

"In what way?"

"Well, his hospitality, for one thing. And for you."

"Oh? Was I a gift?"

"Please don't be annoyed. I didn't mean it that way. I'm just trying to work things out in my head."

She says nothing. I try to think it out myself. I know I can't. But if he *had* been there, if he were here and I did finally meet him face to face, what would that have done to me and Diana? How could we go on? If I knew I owed my whole life to him? It'd be more like sinning than not. We'd have to break it off. And I'm not sure I could stand that now.

I turn to her and say, "Yet, in another way in my dreams. I was glad he didn't show."

"Why?"

"Maybe living with that slight doubt gives me wiggle room, so to speak. Of course there's always the very real possibility that he was watching over us all the time. From the terrace up there. Through binoculars. He could very well have dispatched that second fishing boat to us when the first fishermen didn't help."

"A bit far-fetched, don't you think?"

"It's just that I want so much to meet him face to face."

Diana is about to say something when Abis appears, leading a donkey. "Hey, Manny-man, who do you think you missed not being in your room last night?"

"Don't tell me!"

Abis points back toward the dock. The big yacht is gone. "In his little house on the mainland now, I bet. And guess what else? I think he was there the other day when we were on the mainland. We fooled ourselves again."

"Then he was here all this time we've been here?"

"Who knows? His yacht was here. But him? Who knows his ways, mysterious to be?"

"*You* know, God damn it! Why has he been hiding from me? Why can't I meet him face to face?"

I'm practically shouting. Diana seems genuinely shocked. Obviously she thinks it is an overreaction. But I know Abis is mocking me. He puts this knitted-brow-look-of-confusion on his face.

"Abis, why didn't you tell me he was here for sure? Why can't you be honest with me?"

"I am honest with you, man-man. In all big things. But sometimes I must lie in order to tell the truth. *Canpiss*?

"No, I don't *capite*. That's my whole problem."

"Manny-man, Abis did not know William Love was here on the island until Diana led you down this garden path. Did you know, Diana?"

She says, "Don't you get it? Neither one of us has seen him."

"But look what he has sent us by way of my taking, Manny-man."

He reaches into his saddle bags. "Champagne. The good stuff. Dumb Paragon. Two and one half bottles!"

He lifts out the bottles. Two are unopened, a third is half consumed. All drip with condensation. He smiles at us like the cat who has just eaten one sixth of the canary, wags the bottles to interest us, then sets them down on a flat rock and steps back three paces like a hunter setting a trap. As we step forward he ambles back quickly and fishes out from the saddle bag three tall, thin, stemmed champagne flutes. With a great flourish, he reaches in again and pulls out a tin of English crackers, Fortnum and Mason, then a jar of black caviar. The label is in Russian. I spread the caviar with a plastic knife. Diana pours wine. Abis spreads a checked table cloth that looks as if it had been stolen from an Italian restaurant, complete with spaghetti sauce stains. We toast William Love in his absence. Always in his absence.

The wine is cold, fragrant, dry and seductive. The bubbles nip at my lips and tongue. I think of Sara in Freeport on our honeymoon. I close my eyes and feel the tropical heat of the island. The fragrance of her perfume and her body. When I open my eyes again Diana is in front of me. And Abis.

He unstraps three canvas folding chairs from the donkey's back, sets them on the ground overlooking the digs, then sits on one, stretching out his feet, stiffly. A champagne glass rests on the table cloth in front of him. On his lap, a mound of crackers, caviar-laden. He opens Diana's picnic basket and passes around sandwiches and fruit. There is enough for everyone. How did she know to pack enough for three?

The donkey clomps up to Abis. She stands by his side, just off the tablecloth and shifts her feet about uneasily. Her skin shudders along her back and sides as flies buzz about, land, and fly away again. Could she be the same donkey he had in Greece? Diana and I move our chairs to the other side of the table cloth, upwind of the animal.

"Tomorrow, Manny-man, Abis has a great, great treat in storage for you. The game. You will get to play. This is a great and mighty privilege."

Though I know he wants me to, I refuse to ask.

He drinks two more glasses of champagne.

"You will play, Manny-man."

"Will I?"

"And be a star. Have your own dressing room. Women will flock to your side as if you were made of chocolate. Rub up against you. Kiss your knees and toes. Get your shoes wet with slobber. Tomorrow I will give you a little stick to beat them away. You will let them take it away from you. Eh? Eh?"

Diana glares at him. Either she knows he is up to his old tricks again or she is jealous. Mentally, I gird my loins. This time I will not be suckered in.

"Come," I say, then finish off my cheese sandwich and pick up my wine glass. "Let's descend into the pits."

Diana leads the way. Abis brings up the rear, carrying the Dom Perignon. Leaving the donkey to roam. Already the evening is beginning to settle in, casting deep shadows. We shuffle gingerly across bridges that consist of little more than two by fours, and sometimes narrow strips of thin plywood, over pits, deep test shafts and the gaps and dips between the grids. We are descending into the terraced slopes. Beneath the trees I feel a cold breath, as if the pits were filled with ice and we are being pulled down to the chilliest place in the universe. Over the deepest pits I am afraid to look down into the dark, squirming shadows until I have crossed.

Each hole is stranger than the next. Some are only inches deep and seem as if they were clawed out of the earth by the paws of beasts. Some are wide and sink many feet, with sides perpendicular and floors hidden by the gathering gloom. Several are so deep they seem to descend to perdition.

Diana's official tour guide voice drones on as the last of the sun is swallowed by the rim of the high terrace. We are so far down that the surface of the earth is hidden, though the rapidly darkening sky is visible between the canvas awnings. She switches on a string of dim lights. They sway and vibrate in the wind. The bottoms of even the shallowest pits are soon engulfed by their own writhing shadows.

At each shaft she stops and comments on some aspect of the excavations. I peer dutifully into the gloom to see what she sees, but all I can discover is layer after layer of discolored dirt and evil smelling muck like the odor of rotting garbage. Surely these can't be human remains. But Diana insists each layer is a whole generation of human lives, that in the deepest pits we are peering down and down into so many lost generations of the past, that we have become voyeurs into prehistory and engulfing, clouded myth. Where she sees light I smell only the dank earth and the hydrogen sulfide reek of decay. And yet, I am so mesmerized by the depths and by her voice that twice I almost fall from the beam and tumble into the abyss. Twice she grabs my arms and steadies me.

The more I pass into her realm, the more she transforms from a warm, tenderhearted woman into a dispassionate, scientific lecturer spouting Insights which are lost on me. The meanings and significance of terms like Early Cycladic and Canaanite whirl about my head and disperse thorough indifference, incomprehension and Dom Perignon. My mind rejects the meanings of her words and whirls on another axis.

I'm too distracted by my own wandering thoughts, by Abis, alcohol, William Love, and her eyes. I try to understand her discourse. Duty bound, I peer at every pit and patch of soil she points out to me and try to imagine the homes and palaces and pillars she says were here. Why can't I see anything but bits of rubble and discolorations in the soil? Because that is all there is. My imagination is not good enough to see what she sees in these holes. I'll have to see the artist's renditions or the animated special effects movie version to make this place real. All I can manage now is to follow her about like Abis's dog, smiling and sniffing and nodding, understanding little but the intonation of her voice.

"...and we know for certain there were at least eight levels of civilization at this level and below. But there may have been as many as thirty-one. We know the temple, at least, was rebuilt that many times. Usually after destruction by fire."

"'First comes the wind, Manny-man, then the title wave, then the fire. After the fire, the still, soft voice.' This is an almost exact quotation from your Bible, Manny-man, except I have put your name in it."

"The temple was rebuilt thirty-one times?"

"At least. Over the span of a few millennium."

"And each time dedicated to a different god?"

"We don't think so. We think they prayed to the same Godhead."

"Just different manifestations?" My voice is dry.

"Various shapes and forms, sure. Just as we do now. Because we don't know God's true one. I don't think too many of us get to see God face to face."

"Not around here, anyway."

"Manny-man, that is the very thing that drives people crazy, huh?"

"What is?"

"Impatience. Everybody wants to know now. They don't know it, but they are dying to find out."

"Some God, Abis. A sadist."

"Hey, you can't blame someone else for crashing if you're driving the car, Manny-man."

"We haven't drunk enough wine yet to solve the problem."

"Whom's fault is that?" He holds up a bottle.

Diana continues to tell us what we do know, or think we know. She points out a large, level field in the distance. "It is our most important single discovery so far," she says, "We call it our Stonehenge."

I see an enormous, magnificent circle of apparently equally spaced stones, each ten feet high, forming what she says is a sophisticated astronomical observatory similar in function and form to the Celtic ones in Europe. Then we turn again to the more subtle finds, the discolorations in the soil and bits of stone. I drift away again, hovering between my own world and this one and the world to come.

When we finish the tour, I turn back to Abis. He's reeling from the champagne. I'm hoping I'm as rational as I think I am. "Hey, Abis, this is very good wine, huh?"

"The beast, Manny-man."

"Willy Love's a generous soul."

"Don't ask, man-man."

"To give me so much."

"What you mean?"

"Well, wine and lodging, great food, clothes, wonderful company and all, though he doesn't even know me. Except what you've told him."

"Me told him?"

"But you know what I think, pal?" I put my arm around his shoulder.

"Do not say it, man-man."

"I think he had Diana more in mind when he sent that champagne down."

"Oh. Oh, yeah, sure, Man-man." Abis laughs. Then, "No," he insists. "He said he has sent everything especially for you, Manny-man. Because you are his latest and most especial guest."

"He actually mentioned me? By name? I mean, when he gave you the wine to take to us?"

"Oh, you bet, sure, Manny-man."

"So he does know I exist."

"Of course he does. He is one of your best friends and admirers."

"Oh, I wouldn't go quite that far, would you?"

"What? You are kidding me now? He knows all about you. From me! He loves you like a brother, Manny-man, for Abis's sake. Because you are my pal."

"Really? Well, what did he actually say?"

"Oh, umm, umm, he said he thinks you are a good man who has been through hell. He says he admires your courage, Manny-man."

"Did he, now? But what did he *actually* say. I mean his exact words."

"Um, um, okay, he said, 'this Manny Markovitz, he is a good man, Abis. I admire his courage.' These are the exact replicas of his words."

"And where did he say he was going?"

"To the mainland, Manny-man. To live in the little house for a little while. Like a monk. This is because he has so much mainland business to reindeer. Then he will come back here, pronto. Meet you. Talk all night. Drink good ouzo and Metaxa all the way from Greece. Live in high style, again. Eat shrimps and crabs. These are the actual things he will do in a few days from this very minute. Maybe two weeks, tops. You relax. Hold on. He will return for you."

"So he's back on the mainland?"

"The motor yacht is gone. This is how I know."

"What about your little yacht, Abis? Couldn't it make it all the way to the mainland?

"Wouldn't want to try."

"Why not?"

"Umm, too small."

"But some people have made it all the way across the Atlantic in six foot canoes."

"Some people are as crazy as loons on fermented figs, Manny-man."

"I guess it's all in what you want to do. And if you want to do it badly enough."

"Abis wants badly enough to stay here, Manny-man. Relax. Eat well. Wait. Play the game tomorrow. Make you a star in the heavens."

"How far is it to the mainland?"

"Forget this very thing, Manny-man."

Diana quickly adds, "He's right, this time, Manny. Forget it. Too far. I wouldn't travel with that maniac as my pilot to open water if I were you. Have to change his name to Charon. Remember, he has the attention span of a movie star magazine. Can you imagine him trying to monitor the winds all the way to shore?"

"I can't imagine anything," I say. But in reality I can imagine quite a bit; another plan is forming in my mind.

# EIGHTEEN

"Ha, ha, get up for shame, the morning is half over and you two still in bed? You know what, Manny?"

"What?"

"Abis did not even look for you in your own bedroom this morning. Humey did not even put sheeps on your bed. You two when you are doing this nookie-nookie could be more like me, discreet. But no! You are the talk of the island. This makes your good pal Abis blush. See?"

"You're holding your breath."

"Is that not the right way to blush?"

"For you, probably."

"I take this for a great compliment."

"You take everything for a great compliment."

I think, "So everybody knows. Everybody that counts, anyway. Abis, Hume, William Love. And he doesn't seem to care. At least he doesn't say anything. Not to me."

"Time for the game now, Manny-man."

"Screw the game."

"Amen," says Diana.

"Whatever it is," I add.

"You cannot screw the game, Manny-man. It is a *macho* game. Tell you what, man-man, it is a well-known fact that it is bad to make the two backed beast before a sporting event. Saps your energy. You will be energy sapped, Manny-man. Hope you did not do it more than once or twice last night."

"I want to go to the mainland."

"No good, Manny-man. Weather sucks. Could drown."

"I can wear a life vest."

"Only one life vest."

"You can swim."

"All right. I will take you."

"You will?"

"After the game."

"How can we play this game of ours if the weather is so bad?"

"Bad weather is good weather for the game."

"No. I want to go to the mainland now. After breakfast."

"After the game I will take you. This is a great compromise."

He snaps his fingers. Two maids and Hume enter with breakfast for three. Only Hume stays to serve it, though.

"So you have decided to play then, sir?" Hume asks as we finish.

"Yes. Though I have no idea what it is I'm playing."

"Reality being what it is, Sir will need this."

He holds out a small, silver, covered dish. As I reach out, Hume quickly uncovers it to reveal a clear, nearly transparent gel-like mouth guard. "Most efficacious for the prevention of brain concussion, sir."

I stare down at the thing. "Thank you, Hume. I won't be needing that."

"To use or not to use, sir, is not a question of moral choice but of reason and experience."

"Beg your pardon?"

"Reason and experience, sir. They tell us what is. Our moral feelings tell us what ought to be."

He continues to hold out the tray and its ominous contents in front of me.

"Let me put it this way, Hume," I say, adopting his tone. "It is not a question of physical imperative or moral insight. It's a question of rational choice. I don't need that damn thing because I ain't playing. I do not participate in any sports that involve even the remotest possibility of brain concussion. Therefore, whatever game Abis intends this time, he shall play alone. Or at least without me."

"*Not* playing. Very good, sir." The hand and tray withdraw. "Then perhaps Sir would allow me to use it, as I have been rather in need of a new one myself."

"Wait a minute, *you're* playing?"

"Indeed I am, sir. Every real man on the island physically capable of doing so is playing. Except you, sir."

My face is as red as a congressman's nose. But I will not be suckered in.

Abis grins. Can he sense my resolve has softened the way a bear can sense fear? To mask my true emotions I grimace. Abis eyes me coyly and says, "You will be hooker."

"No," Diana says. "He'll get hurt."

If she had addressed that comment to me, I would have been all right. But no, she has to talk directly to Abis and Hume, as if I'm an irresponsible child. And if that is not bad enough, she turns to me and adds, "Manny, you're just not built for it. You're too thin. Your legs are too skinny."

Is she for real, or have they planned this diatribe together just to suck me in? Either way the effect's the same. I snap my fingers and motion for the mouthpiece.

Hume smiles and holds it out.

"No, Manny!"

"Stay here in your warm bed, woman, I have man's work to do."

Abis and Hume withdraw. I swagger into the bathroom.

\*\*\*

Now we're on the field, "the pitch," everyone is calling it. "So what are we playing, by the way?" I ask as I crack my knuckles and spit. Nothing about the goal posts or the shape of the field reminds me of any game I have ever seen or played.

"Rugby, Manny-man."

"That's sort of like American football, right?

"It is English football. Always played without pads or helmets."

"Sort of like our touch football, then? Couldn't be too dangerous. You familiar with flag football? Sort of like that?"

"Yes, Manny-man. I played this flag football once on an Indian reservation in New Jersey, U.S.A. Hurt my knee and had to wear a cast from toe to crotch. Itched like hell when my scrotum sweated all summer."

"And you've never been hurt playing this game?"

He smiles slyly. "Want one of these?"

He holds out a small gelatin capsule.

"What is it?"

"They call it class II drug."

"I don't think so. But thank you for offering."

"Umm, no, really, here, Manny-man. The whole team takes 'em."

"The whole team plays under the influence of restricted narcotics?"

"Oh, sure. You bet."

"Does the other team know about this?"

"They gave them to us. Makes the whole game more fun. You see pretty colors, too."

"I'll pass."

"Hey, Manny-man, where are your spiky shoes?"

"Oh, gosh, must be in the luggage you lost for me, Abis. I've never owned a pair of spiked shoes in my life."

As I re-tighten the laces on my sensible walking shoes, players are gathering about me like hyenas about a small dog. Massive, mean-looking hyenas. They're all wearing these strange lace-up cotton shorts. Most have muscled legs that for girth a bull elephant would envy. Abis tapes some of my fingers together with surgical tape. I don't want to know why. But I'm beginning to think I should have stayed in bed with Diana.

Hume appears, without his mask. I don't want to stare but I seem to do so every time he looks the other way. He has no face. It appears to have been completely burned away. No ears at all. No nose, just browless, lashless eyes, two nostril holes and a lipless mouth. The thickened flesh is pulled so tight it shines. The greatest irony is that it seems as if this pink, shiny, faceless face were really the mask, and the mask he usually wore, his real face. I suppose it is. It's the one that lets him meet other faces and live, as best he can, a normal life.

I nod and smile.

"Ready, sir?"

I think of the opening lines of the Christian Testament. With Hume, the word made flesh is turned inside-out. The flesh has been made the word. I would not have known him save for the mild, sophisticated, kind and mellow voice that drifts on the air to me from the throat and his slit of a mouth.

"I am," he says, "one of your props, sir."

I blink, the way deer do.

"Since you will be our hooker, Mr. Markovitz, I shall stand on this side of you, Benedict on the other. We will arch our backs, lean over, and lift you gently off the ground, ever so slightly."

Abis tosses me a jersey with horizontal stripes in red, black and yellow, the same colors as the canvas canopy on William Love's yacht and tent. He, Benedict, Hume and the rest of our team are wearing the same colored jerseys, of course.

"Like this, Manny-man," Abis says. "First you put your arm around Humey's back, grab hold of his shirt on the other side. Along here, where the ribs are."

Hume's body is so wide and muscular, my arm can barely stretch around his back to reach the rib cage on the other side. When I do so, I can feel the scar tissue under his jersey.

"Okay, now you do the same with Benedict on the other side."

Benedict sidles next to me like a Clysdale positioning for the harness. He's an enormous, dark-haired guy who could be Jewish or Syrian. How can you tell without the scorecard? Actually, he's more like two or three Jews or Syrians zipped into one body. His black Fu Manchu mustache twitches as he smiles. When he grins, I see he has lost a front tooth. From the last Rugby game? I sling my other arm around him. Together they arch and flex their backs and lift me two inches off the ground.

"No worry, Manny-man. Rugby is a gentle and friendly, peaceful, pastoral game. We play all the time. Most players are the local guys and some who come to work the digs in the summer and such."

"If it's so friendly and peaceful, why the mouth guards, Abis?"

"Also, you should war rugby shorts like these, with rubber buttons."

I'm about to ask why as Benedict and Hume put me down but stay in position beside me. I let go of their jerseys when my feet touch ground. As I look over at about Benedict, though, something about him disturbs me; I've seen him before in an unpleasant situation. Of course, the ship! He was one of the foreign sailors on the freighter that almost ran us down! I'm *sure* of it. Almost sure, anyway. But how could he be? No, that's impossible. No, wait, I've got it; during the storm, on the passage here to Love's island, he was a member of the crew on the yacht. But that's impossible, too.

Unless William Love's returned.

If he has, he's probably watching from his tower on the top floor terrace right now. Drink in one hand. Diana in the other. I look up but can't tell anything. There's something up there, but it's probably that statue again. Of course, there is always the possibility that any one of these players is William Love in the flesh. Even, I suppose, though admittedly not very likely, Abis. I look around. Which one? I hope it's not Hume.

Actually, now that I am looking around, I realize nearly every one of the players has some scars or physical deformity of some sort. Is it all from playing the game? I tighten my clench on the rubbery mouthpiece and ask Abis, "Now what?"

"They will lift you up, Manly-man. Like that. Good. Now see how your mighty frame is supported on their puny backs? When your feet are off the ground, you can fight with them to hook the ball and send it back toward your team."

"That's it? That's all I have to do?"

"These men here will get behind your props and push. I am one of them who is pushing you."

Another of them of them is Odysseus, the melon man.

I walk over to Abis and whisper. "Wait a minute, you telling me this old guy is gonna play this game."

"Oh sure, you bet, Manny-man."

"Well, if he can do it, I shouldn't have any trouble, right?"

"You bet, sure."

*Or, maybe, he's not as old as he looks.*

"Manly-man, you duck your head like so. The top of it will fit into the top front of bad guy from other team's arm pit. His head will fit into your arm pit. It will be very snug and cozy. If you do not duck your head soon enough, his head will fit into your chest. Sometimes this is not comfortable. If you duck too much, your head will hit his head. This could make one or both of you maybe dizzy."

I look up at the other team, mulling about, disorganized. Their uniforms, shirts, socks, shorts, and shoes are grayish-purple and they are gathering like a great storm cloud, tightening their formation into a slowly turning funnel, and slowly, slowly drifting toward us. I swallow hard. The closer they get, the less civilized they look. Like the bad seed of humanity gathered from every miserable corner of the earth. I try to convince myself they are probably just graduate students working on the dig. How fierce could graduate students be?

Some of them toss a fat, white football to and fro. Some limber massive, muscled legs. Then they gather into formation, "scrum," Abis calls it, as he moves in behind me.

"Manny, watch your ears."

"What does that mean?"

"Hmm, see that big Indian Hindi guy opposite you?"

"Yeah?"

"Ha, ha, this is so funny, he bit the whole ear off our hooker last year. That is your position."

"He bit a man's ear off?"

"Ha, ha, bled like a stuck pig, Manny-man."

"He bit a man's ear off?"

"He is playing opposite you. When you are up close together, say nice things about his mama."

"Abis, I don't...."

But I get no other word out before I'm swept up in the maelstrom, caught by Hume and Benedict and heaved off my feet as my props assemble to assault. It's as if the statue of the Laocoön is being combined with the one of the Marines raising the flag on Iwo Jima. The other side forms a mirror image of our formation and looms in closer.

The Hindustani guy with pushed-in cheekbones grins obscenely, then begins to growl at me like a mastiff. At least one of this guy's parents has got to be an ox. His neck is squished down as if both it and his head had been gouged out of wet clay and thrown with great velocity into his shoulders. His roundish face is slightly askew, as if it had been pushed in at the top and side while the clay was wet. One thick, black, scabby eyebrow runs the length of his forehead. He has not shaved in a week.

The teams pile up into a great circle, tighter and tighter, drawn, it seems, by their own rotating, gravitational mass. The umpire comes with the ball. He begins to drop it at my feet. But some of the men jostle out of scrum too early. So instead of dropping the ball, he blows his whistle. The jostling immediately becomes shoving. Fists begin to fly. He blows his whistle again. With that, the crowd on the sidelines screams and jeers in every rude language of the universe. They make all sorts of obscene gestures garnered from across the globe.

One girl, a sweet looking, petite young innocent in a spotless, bright yellow Rugby shirt and very, very short shorts strolls onto the playing field. The official waves her off with one hand, violently. She screams, "Just drop the fucking ball, you dickless cretin and let them play!"

He blows the whistle even more loudly and waves with both his hands and arms for her to clear the field. Both teams have dropped their name calling and mayhem and face her reverently as if saluting the flag. Slowly she hitches up her Rugby shirt and ties it off at the midriff. Then she turns around slowly and walks off toward the foul line. Both teams are watching her intently, as she has an excellent walk. Five feet from the line she stops, bows toward the crowd at the waist, and in slow motion reaches behind herself with both hands. Slowly, she pulls down her shorts, and moons the judge.

The crowd, the judge, and both teams cheer and whistle her magnificent performance and, I must admit, her magnificent, well-tanned ass.

"Abis sings loudly, "We see her heiny, ain't white and shiny. No Rugger wishes she'd put on britches."

Slowly the moon is eclipsed again. She walks off the field as the audience continues their enthusiasm. As soon as she steps across the line, the umpire drops the ball and we lunge forward. As he does, I look up one last time to check for life on the terrace. My head jolts back as if kicked by a kangaroo. The world goes grey, sated with exquisite pain and shooting stars. The Hindustani's head has smashed into my ribs. Now we are stuck together as if I were the tar baby. I had forgotten to duck my head. My ribs are crushed and stabbing into my lungs. I can't breathe.

The ball squirts out. The players separate. Someone on the purple team picks up the ball and runs. The Hindustani man leaps to his feet and chases after him. My props drop me like a bad stock option and run after the ball. I collapse to the ground. Somewhere in the distance I hear footsteps and the thud of my own broken body hitting the turf as I lie unable to move for the pain, trying to suck in air. The earth becomes even blacker again, nuller and more void than when Ricky Baumgarder kicked me in the testicles in the seventh grade.

I feel the vibrations of the hooves of the other players, the real ones, as they run across the field and back again. I taste the damp, chalk soil in my mouth. It has an earthy, fragrant aftertaste. My head floats like a bubble over the earth. There's sand between my toes. Gritty as the garnet paper in my grandfather's workshop. I can feel his strong, hard fingers on my shoulders, gently urging me down again to earth again. I'm on my back. Faces overhead in the mist stare down at me. "He's coming around," one of them says.

Abis is one of them. "Hey, Manny-man, how come you don't play hooker anymore?"

"My ... ribs ... they're ... crushed ... I ... think ... they're ... broken," I gasp out through gritting teeth.

"Yeah, so?"

"So?"

"So this means you will not play anymore?'

"My lungs are pierced. I'm drowning in my own blood."

"This is no good, Manny-man. Now we must find a new hooker. Where can we do this now? We had to take an officious time out, too. You have interrupted the whole game. Shame on you. You make your pal Abis look real bad in front of whole team."

"I'm, I'm sorry."

"Should we substitute for you? Usually in this game no substitutions. Like combination dinners at the Chinese take-out place."

"Yes."

"Let me think on this, pal. You really, really won't come back and play anymore?"

"Yes."

"Okay-donkey. You trot off field. I will be hooker."

"Can't breathe…can't…move."

"Hmm. Okay, I will get the Rugger-huggers. They will help you off the field. Maybe goose you in the crotch as well."

Some players off to the left stomp about, neighing and whinnying to themselves. Steam rises from their backs, heads and wet jerseys. Two handsome Amazon women appear from behind them, the kind you always see wearing hiking boots in granola ads, with shaved, muscular legs and large, ripe, melon-shaped breasts. As they lift me to my feet, I groan out, "I…hurt."

They gently swing my arms all the way up and over their broad, soft shoulders and bear me off the field.

\*\*\*

I wake in my room in Love's house. My eyes water from the acrid smell of the antiseptic. A dim night light glows like a distant moon on the far side of the room. Diana is there. And Willy Love. I hear his voice distinctly. He's an American! God, I knew he would be! I'm not fooled by that phony British accent.

Abis is sitting on my bed. The sun is up. Leaning forward, close to my swollen face, he says, "You should have played on class II drugs, Manny-man."

I nod, painfully. Even my throat is sore, as if I had been given anesthetic. "Could use some now."

"You got plenty already."

"Last night?"

"And now."

"Am I under the influence?"

"Who knows."

"My ribs broken?"

"Maybe bent a bit. Like a car fender."

"Not broken?"

"This is what the doctor said. Or maybe she is, what you say, a nurse."

"A nurse? She made the diagnosis? A licensed, registered nurse?"

"She is registered."

I try to sit up a little. "A real, registered nurse?"

"Hmm, how do you say, registered alien. No worry, Manny-man. She is a doctor, big time, once. Delivered babies."

"A medical doctor?"

"Has a degree."

"Abis, answer me straight. Is she a doctor of medicine? An M.D. with a license to practice?"

"I will go find out."

"Wait!"

He continues toward the door, reaches it, turns and says, "What?"

"Was he here?"

"Everyone was here."

"I mean William Love. Abis, wait!"

But he's gone. Hume comes in. "A mimosa, sir. Drink up. Now there's a good gent."

"Where's Diana?"

"On the mainland, sir. She flew."

"With William Love?"

"All I can say is that she had to go for her usual reason and should return this evening, if she is up to it. Or tomorrow."

"Was William Love here?"

"Really, sir, I could not say. Eggs Benedict. Now that is what you really need. Coffee. More juice and the remains of this half-bottle of champagne."

"I *am* famished."

He smiles and leaves. I try to lift a forkful to my mouth. It is too heavy. I fall asleep.

\*\*\*

When I wake, the food is gone. Benedict, the huge prop with the mustache, is sitting on the chair next to me, with his feet up on my bed.

"Come ta say how sorry ah am fer yer injury. No offense."

"It wasn't your fault, was it?"

He shrugs. "Here ya go. Yer supposed ta take one these here pills now."

I take the bottle. One of those standard green plastic ones you get at any pharmacy. Except the label doesn't list the name of the pharmacy, or the pharmacist, or even the doctor. Just my name and the name of the drug, which is not one I'm familiar with. Which is odd, considering all the pain medicine they prescribed for Sara.

Benedict is holding out a glass of water.

"I guess it'll be all right," I mumble, and take a few.

"Ah reckon ah shoulda helped you some when you went down. Fact is, ah didn't know you was hurt so bad as you was. You ought not be playin' Rugby with them skinny legs a yourn."

I nod, and ask, "Do I detect a hint of a southern accent?"

"Little county crossroads near Cascadia, Alabama. Actually, Cascadia was th' big city fer me when ah was growin' up. Teach now in Golburn, by God Texas."

"So you're here for the digs?"

"Well, shoot ah reckon. Whole damn bunch a us're pouncin' down now like army worms on azalea. Season's nigh on here."

"Sounds like you've been here before."

"Ever year fer five years now. Almost since th' project done begun."

"I didn't realize it had been going on that long."

He scratches under his left armpit, really digging in hard. "Pro'bly 'bout, oh, seven year, if ya consider the p'eliminary site work they done."

"Maybe I misunderstood, but I could have sworn Diana told me the hole was less than three years old."

He smiles. "Maybe she's tryin' ta subtract a few years off her own calendar."

"No, there's something far stranger going on here. You know Abis, the guy who took over as the hooker for me in the game yesterday?"

"You mean Abdul? His name's Abdul ben Wabbi."

"Abdul ben Wabbi?"

"Eccentric multi-trillionaire, ya know. A-rab, ah think. Some them guys is double dipped in petroleum oil. Money sticks to 'em like cornmeal on a egg-battered bream. Owns this whole island, ya know."

"Whaaaat?"

"Got to, showin' out like he does."

"What do you mean?"

"Oh, you know. Walkin' 'round, doin' this 'n that, and not actually doin' nothin'."

"Sound more like an unsupervised employee to me."

"Weell, mebbe so," he concedes. "Mus' be payin' him by th' hour, then."

"What about William Love?"

"Who?"

"William Love. You've never heard the name before?"

"Oh, oh, right. William Love. Now ya mention it, ah have heard that name hung out on the wash two, three times."

He looks around as if he's about to confide a great secret to me. In a low whisper, he says, "Now some folk say *he's* the real lord of hosts aroun' here. But ah ain't never seen hide nor hair of him. Say, you mine if ah chew?"

"Chew what?"

"You're a funny guy," he says and pulls out a foil pouch of tobacco together with an old, battered coffee can that has most of the paint scraped off the outside. Seeing me eye the pitiful can, he holds it up and says, "It's m'Holy Grail. Been with me a good-God-a-mighty long time. Sure it's okay ef ah chew?"

"Go right ahead. Long as you don't light up or miss the bucket."

He nods, proceeds to unroll a silver-foil pouch, grab up a wad with his fingers, and stuff it into his mouth with the same ferocity Polyphemos ate the shipmates of Odysseus. "M'wife," he says, "she tol' me once ta choose. Either this here pouch or her." He shakes his head and shifts the big wad from one cheek to the other. "Yes, sir. Good woman. Livin' in Mobile now. Remarried to th' lawyer what handled th' divorce. Bless his heart, that ole boy was *good*. Done took me fer ever damn thing ah owned except this here coffee can. But damned if he didn' get the coffee that was in it. Guess they was grounds fer divorce. Know where *I'd* go to if'n ah ever needed me a lawyer. Uhh, what was you askin'?"

"About William Love."

"Right. William Love, William Love. Nope. Never seen him, nor spoke to him, none, neither. So far as ah can r'member."

"Never?"

"Well, see now, ah'm the wrong guy ta ask. Ain't never been too swift with names ner faces, neither. Artifacts, you bet. Show me a shard n' ah kin tell you whether ah seen it ten years ago or no. Can name you ever arrowhead ah ever found, an' where ah found it since th' time ah was a puppy. An' ah found me plenty."

He spits a disgusting slop of fecal-colored spittle into the coffee can. The brown slaver hits bottom with a dull thunk. I can't imagine what it must taste like or why anyone would want to chew on it.

"But," he continues, "ah couldn' tell you the name a one farmer whose land ah found it on. Ah couldn' name you four kids ah went ta high school with. No sir. Who was we talkin' about?"

"William Love."

"Oh, right. William Love. See, he 'parently don't come here too offen. Way ah hears it he's like a old codger what don't like people too much. 'Course this is just rumor an' ya ought ta take it as such, but they say he hates this dig an' what it's doin' ta his island retreat here, 'cept, of course it's gonna turn this place into one little gold mine of a tourist attraction. That's why this big ole house, you know. It's all a big facade."

"What do you mean?"

"Look at it real close some time, man. Damn thing's built to be converted into a hotel jus' as soon as us diggers cleans him a big enough hole and clears out our own selves. Way ah hears it pretty soon we're gonna have ta vacate th' premises n' go on back to livin' in tents during paleface season."

"Paleface?"

"Oh, hell, you know. Th' great untanned horde from Spokane. Little ole men with them little cameras an' skinny white legs a-stickin' outta them polyester plaid Bermuda shorts. Cellulite dowagers armed with four-color maps ta take back home to th'mahjongg club in Yakamoto."

I nod very enthusiastically, knowing my actions are too animated. But I can't help it. It's the pills they've given me.

"Hey, ah hears you teach, too. An' workin' on a book. Hope it's a murder-mystery. Man, ah love 'em."

"NO!"

"Whoa, not so loud, there, buddy. You'll break my eardrum."

"It's okay! I feel great!"

"Sounds like you're about two grams past Mars, there, feller."

"You bet!"

"Whisper me this, then. What's yer spy novel about?

"No! No! Not a novel. Careful scholarly research!"

"Oh. You must teach college, then. Suppose ya gotta do that stuff to get you some tenure. Couldn't stand it m'self, scrounging all about diggin' up minor points 'bout minor people, knowin' all th' time all the good stuff 'bout the big guys already done been done and said."

"Well I don't know about that. Knowledge is power."

"Shiiiiit, man, that's somethin' smart people without power say. Hell, knowledge ain't power, son. Power is power. Comes from money."

"I mean, research is, is, life. It's the meaning of my existence. That's why I love the library so much more'n the classroom. I mean, the sense of power that pure research conveys. And the bliss you feel among the closed stacks!"

"Uh *huh*."

"I remember in graduate school once we were all sitting around one night in the *Rathskeller* drinking beer and talking into the dawn about our hopes and desires for the future and I remember telling them my fondest wish would be that God would grant me a huge endowment from the NSF so I could spend forever doing research and publishing my findings for the world to read and marvel at. Was that the beer talking then? Hell, I don't know. Am I making sense here, or what?"

"Uh, yeah, sure. But calm down a bit, okay?"

"I'm calm as a cuke."

"Yeah, but yer hands is shakin' like a two dollar tripod."

"No, no, really, I gotta explain this to you, see it's so important! Okay, okay, now, look, see, take my field of sociology, it has become very, very, very clear that the new redirectionalist sociological-emotionalist theorists have a valid point, maybe even a major one. I mean a whole new lingual-historical, fully text-obligated way of looking at things. And not a-political, either. I mean perhaps a whole new way to propel both our ontology *and* epistemology into exciting new modes of steleological thought. It almost makes you want to shout amen!"

He squints his eyes respectfully and expectorated into his coffee can. "Ah reckon you kin get you a grant an' reinvent the wheel, you know, make 'em square, an' see ef that works better, an' if it don't work better, get you another grant and make 'em squarer. Me, ah like to come here in th' summer, drink me some beer, play me some ball, and dig in the dirt. Makes me feel like ah'm uncovering th' past 'stead of reinventin' it."

"So you teach high school? Must be a pretty big place if it has an archeology department."

"Don't rightly teach archeology. History. Prehistory's a sorta hobby. Mostly ah'm th' head football coach. Got me two line coaches, two backfield men, a quarterback coach and a kicking guy what almost made it to the NFL. Sonabitch *still* got him one hell of a foot. Played him two years in the Canadian Football League. 'Course ah make mos' of ma money endorsing stuff 'round town and doin' the Couch Benedict Show on Sunday mornins. Come on right after Bible Hour and right before NFL football."

"This is a high school?"

"Southeast Central Commerce District of the Permian Basin."

"Ahh, that's right, Texas."

"Serious football folks, Texans. Serious. You never did play no ball before, did you?"

"No. Didn't play any sports beyond one year of Little League."

He shakes his head, sadly, with sympathetic concern, as if I had just told him my testicles had never descended.

"Soo, what can you tell me about William Love?"

"Kinda obsessed with th' ole boy, ain't ya?"

"Not really, but I do think he's the one behind what's going on here. Hey, you think it's hot in here? I'd kind of like to get up and move around a bit. Think that would be possible? You know, maybe dance around a little?"

He picks up the pill bottle. "Ah b'lieve yer only suppose ta take one a these at a time."

"What I take, four? I don't think Abis is bright enough to be running this operation. You like boxing?"

"Ah wouldn't be sellin' that Abis, or Abdul feller, whatever his name is, short, if ah was you. But what's th' diff'rence, anyway. Ah mean, why worry 'bout who's in charge? Don't change nothin'."

"Can't help myself. There's something strange going on here. They've got me involved in it somehow and I've got to know if it's ethical or not."

"How you gonna do thet? Some things ain't so simple ta get answers to like why Couch run th' quarter-back sneak on fourth down 'stead of kickin.'"

"So what should I do?"

"Son, you skinny, but yer full grown. You been 'round long enough ta know we ain't in control of nothin.' Ef we really had us some sayso 'bout how th' universe's run, we'd all be good-lookin' an' get laid a whole lot more. An' if you stay on this island fer a piece, you're gonna figger out real soon we sure as hell ain't immortal."

"No, you're right. We're not immortal. And some of us are a whole lot too mortal a whole lot too early."

"Thet's right, son. An' when you go, ain't nobody takin' nothin' to the grave in no U-haul. Everthin's a loaner. Even our bods. This island and the elements that make it up ain't William Love's or Abdul's, or anyone else's, no more'n it belonged to that king and his people buried out there somewhere fer us ta rediscover. We walk the earth a space an' share it with th'other living souls while we're walkin'. Th' body decays, the elements thet made it pass on to the next generations. So no use lettin' all the dirt in the world to worry you. We're here now and the dead ain't; they don't live unless we revive 'em. An' we got some control over that situation, too."

"Not so much as you think," I say. "Sometimes the past just pushes in and takes over."

"Well, sure, theys plenty of stuff on the bottom of th'barrel what's sure to get stirred up once in a while, but ef ya stay calm, it'll settle down again."

I nod.

"Soo, what're you doin' on this island if ya don't dig an' ya don't play ball?"

"I have no idea, to tell you the truth. Abis brought me. The guy you call Abdul. Hey, you hear someone laughing down the hall?"

"Thet's you, son."

"Oh. Woops." I stop.

"Now, if ah was you, which ah ain't, by the way, ah b'lieve ah *would* try ta find out." As he gets up to leave, he says, "'Cause, ah gotta tell ya, they's some mighty strange things has happened here in the past."

He opens the door. "And that Abdul feller you call Abis, why he may not be the strangest one around, but tell you what, he's gotta be in the top three. An' ah'll tell ya somethin' else, too, you ain't the first one he drug up here."

"Wait!" I shout, "Wait!" But he's out the door.

# NINETEEN

Yellow sunlight streams in through the window, lighting up the swirling dust motes in the air. Birds sing their sweet, intensive songs. Sea gulls glide in the air above the bay, occasionally swooping down to pluck a fish from the water. I'm sober again. And in pain. I consider calling for help, but my ribs are so sore, I can't abide the thought of expanding my lungs enough to shout. Benedict walks in.

"Here," he says, "hold this a minute."

He hands me the sacred coffee can. As best I can I try to keep it at arm's length. It hurts to do so, but the smell is worse than the pain. He slips a fat wad of tobacco into his cheek, stuffs the pack into his back pocket, and takes back the can. "So, how ya feelin' bud? Ya look like road kill, if ya don' mine my sayin' so."

"Hurts."

"Want some them?" He points to the pain pills.

"No. I think I prefer the pain to the high."

"You ain't a Baptist, are ya?"

"Pain gives you a sharpened sense of reality that over-happiness blurs. That's why tragedy has always been more important than comedy."

He spits, scratches under both arms and sits. "Maybe in readin' but not in real life. Don't nobody see better through pain. Makes you too short-sighted. Like when you was five years old and everything referred back to you. Observed a lot of pain all my life, and most of it self-inflicted."

He clasps his hands behind his head and puts his boot-clad feet up on my bed. Clods of dirt fall out from the treads of his rubber soles and bounce onto the sheet. He spits into the coffee can again. "Yep, we're slaves, ever damn one of us. Slaves to th' passions, self-pity, misfortunes, an' bad habits, an' that's pure fact."

As he talks he gets up from his chair and begins to look around the room like he's spying invisible beings. He bends down and looks under the bed, stands again and peers behind the curtains, and feels along the baseboards. I sit up a bit and say "Wha…"

But he puts his index finger to his lips and shakes his head vigorously, then silently mouths, "hidden microphones." In a normal voice, he says, "Yessir, slaves. An' fools. An' if you forgets it for even a dog's minute, why somebody'll come by an' oblige you with a good swift kick in th' sitdown an' a friendly word or two as a reminder."

As he talks, he goes to the doorway, pokes his head out, looks both ways, up at the ceiling, then finally returns, closing the door behind him.

In a slow, low voice, almost a whisper, he says, "kin you go outside? You feel well enough?"

"I suppose so. Why?"

"B'cause some things is best said in th' wind. Know what ah mean?"

"No."

But he motions for me follow him and helps me to my feet. We go out to the terrace where he helps me into a white wicker chair and pulls its twin up next to me. "You gotta get off this here island. Kin you do that?"

"I don't know. Why?"

He looks around furtively. "B'cause ah cain't. Ah'm contracted ta stay. An' it'd arouse too much suspicion."

"About what?"

"'Bout what they's really doin' here! Last few weeks, ah've been doin' me some investigatin' on mah own. Ah been listenin' to you terday an' yesterday an' ah reckon ah kin talk ta you. Ah b'lieve you kin be trusted. Think you kin get off th' island and go to th' authorities?"

"What authorities? For what?"

"Don't know rightly what authorities, damn it. Mebbe th' Georgia Bureau of Investigation. No, no, they may be in on it. Mebbe th' U.N. Yeah, that's it, UNESCO. No, no wait, maybe jus' go to the press. We needs publicity here, and th' more th' better. To stop what they's doin.'"

"Stop what?"

"Altering prehistory, son. Altering th' facts! Systematically tryin' ta destroy the real finds here and salt th' pits with items not originally found on location. Turn this place inta somethin' it ain't."

"But why?"

"Look, ah didn' want ta scare you none with any of this yesterday, 'cause ah figured you wasn't in no shape ta hear it. You sure you're ready now?"

"Why not? Why you think they want to alter the finds here?"

"Fer one thing, ta make money an' lots of it. Fer a major other, to cover up the murders!"

"Whaaat?"

"Look, ah'm still not sure ner nothin' but ah overheard Diana an' thet, thet other guy talkin'."

"Surely you don't mean William Love, do you?"

"Well, hell, after talkin' ta you, now ah ain't sure of nobody's names no more."

"All right, okay, what about these murders?"

"Ritual killings. And castrations of the priests. Way ah figgure, this place might actually of been a actual site of a temple of Cybele. Maybe even Agdistis. Mebbe th' onlyest true one in all a North America. Hell, mebbe th' onlyest one left in th' whole world!"

174

"Oh, you mean murders that took place here when this was still a village upteen thousand years ago, or whatever. God, you scared me. I thought you meant now."

"Sorry 'bout that. But hold that thought. What ah meant is the murders what took place when this was a Cybelian temple site."

"Slow down, you're confusing me. What in hell is a Cybelian temple site?"

"Cybele was th' Phrygian mother-goddess. Even th' Greeks was afraid a her. They practically purged her name from their own literature. She's a sorta product of a wet dream a Zeus's."

"Huh?"

He spits into his coffee can. "One night, according to the legend, ole Zeus had him this wet dream, see? Oh hell, you know what ah'm sayin' here. Don't look so puzzled. Anyway, ole Zeus was apparently sleepin' outside at th' time. Naked as a jaybird, ah reckon. Them gods was always naked. So where his seed done soaked inta th' ground, see, this disguistin' lookin' hermaphrodite creature rose up like a weed th' nex' day. Even th' other gods was horrified. Not b'cause this thing was so plug ugly, bless its heart, but 'cause of its power. Of what it could grow up ta be. So they gone an' cut off its dick an' balls. Then like morons, they plants them genitals an' wouldn't ya know it, they become a almond tree overnight, with almonds what got them other goddesses pregnant. One a th' offspring was Attis, who later on was killed in a jealous rage by Cebele. She cut off his balls an' he bled ta death, poor mythical bastard. Then he turned into one them big, tall pines that grows around them islands in Greece, an' 'round these parts, come ta think of it. Like that one right over there."

He points toward the digs.

"But that's just nonsense, myth."

"It ain't nonsense if you truly believe it and act on it as if it was true. No myth is nonsense if you b'lieve it. Then it's your religion and you'll kill to protect it. An' these folks b'lieved in Cybele so much her priests castrated theirselves, just ta keep the ole tradition goin', ah reckon. They was eventually banished from all a Greece. Put in boats with plenty a food an' set adrift. Theory is, see, they ended up here, on this barrier island, where the whole sect transplanted theirselves along with their strange rites and them pine tree seedlings. Once here they just kept on practicin' their strange rites and all, which included killin' babies an' drinkin' their blood. God knows where they got them babies from. Probably slaughtered the native Indians here. 'Course it's a well-known fact they'd use adult captives if they couldn't get no kids. Virgin boys, if they could get 'em, though I reckon they was always in short supply in ancient Greek cultures. Anyway, they'd take their captives out to the temple and cut off their balls and eat 'em."

"So you really don't mean murder, you mean ancient blood sacrifice, right?"

"What's the difference why or when? Murder's murder, right? Ain't no statutory time limit on murder."

"Okay, murder is definitely murder, coach, but all this happened centuries ago. Victims and victimizers are all the same dust now. Not like they did it yesterday and are still running around loose and need to be caught and punished. Not like they're still doing it."

He looks me straight in the eye. "Ah ain't so sure."

"Whaaat?"

"You know how much money is involved in this here project? Any idea?"

"Millions I'm sure."

"Hunnerds a millions. And they means to make ever cent of it back some day. Ta do that they means to protect ever damn cent of their investment from anybody, you an' me included, who threatens it. By any means necessary."

"From us? Why would anybody worry about you *or* me? That's ridiculous."

"Why? Th' future tourist trade is why. You thinks them little ole blue-hair ladies from th' Doodle Town Library History Club is gonna come all the ways out here ta see where heathens drunk babies' blood and ate genitals fer dessert? Hell, no. What them little ole ladies wants is somethin' like Bullfinch's Mythology in th' original, bowdlerized version. So them folks 'round here knows they's gotta alter the truth an' make this place some kinda transplanted temple to Artemis, goddess of chastity, an' leave out what really happened here so ole Aunt Molly from Toonerville Trolly, Arkansas don't flinch an inch to come on down on the church tour ta visit. An' if they gets away with doin' that, they'll have gotten away with destroying th' real past, mebbe even obscuring a whole lost civilization. Th' Vandals will of won again and we'll never learn."

"If you're right, of course I'll help. But we've got to have real proof."

"Civilization as we don't know it, so ta say, needs yer help."

"If I do try to get off this island, will you help me?"

"You bet, an' we can't spend no coon's age doin' it, neither."

He sticks out his hand and we shake.

"Whatever it takes," he says, "so long as its ethical."

"Of course. And legal, too."

"Ta quote ole Billy Blake, 'no man is improved by the hurt of another.'"

"So what's your proof?"

"Nothin' tangible, yet. But ah knows it's true in my heart a hearts."

"Coach, we've got to have physical evidence, okay?"

"The heart knows more'n the mind can fathom."

"That's what Abis says, more or less. But you can't bring your heart to court if someone sues your ass for slander."

"Okay, tell you what. You meet me right here on this very spot tomorrow an' ah'll have you real proof. That's a promise from me ta you."

"All right."

"Well, gotta go and drink me some beer an' dig me up some civilization before somebody ups an' destroys it or dumps another ringer in the pit. Come on down an' dig yer toes in the soil of prehistory when you feels like. 'Bye."

"'Bye."

***

Maybe ten minutes after Benedict leaves, Hume comes up to the terrace, carrying breakfast and my pain pills. I continue sitting in the wicker chair as he hovers above me, waiting, I assume, to make sure I take the damn things. Why do they want me drugged up all the time? Hell, what do they want of me in the first place?

"Hume?"

"Sir?"

"Has Diana returned?"

"Still on the mainland sir. Hunting."

"Hunting?"

"She enjoys the chase. And the killing, sir. I believe it's the blood that stimulates her. A bit of the old Clytemnestra in all of them, sir."

"William Love, too?"

"The killing? One would imagine not, sir."

"Hume, must you wear that mask around me? I mean, it's not as if I don't know what you really look like."

"I prefer it, sir."

"Okay. But could you answer a few questions for me?"

"About what, sir?"

"William Love."

"I'm afraid there isn't much I can say."

I lean forward.

"All these years." He looks down at me as through imaginary bifocals. "And I know next-to-nothing."

"How long have you worked for him?"

"I have worked for no other."

"So you see him often?"

"No, sir."

"He doesn't come here very much?"

"As I understand it, hardly at all."

"Then it's true what I've heard, that he hates these digs?"

"I'm sure other duties keep him absent. I'm sure he would like to be here more often."

"So why did Abis bring me here, then, if not to meet Love face to face?"

"To paraphrase Mr. Cowper, sir, Abis moves in a mysterious way, his wonders to perform. Perhaps he thought you would enjoy being here, or needed to be. Perhaps he simply liked your company. I'm sure that would not be so hard to accept, sir?"

"Well, it just doesn't figure."

"Perhaps sir should simply accept that little miracle. Testimony for it is so strong it would be more miraculous for it to be false."

"Hardly scientific evidence, Hume."

"The sciences rely on feeling just as well as any other human endeavor. Ever read Camus, sir?"

"Years ago, when he was 'in.'"

"He says somewhere that the misery and the greatness of this world offer no truths, only objects for love. Absurdity is king. Yet love saves us from it. Enjoy your day, sir. Look down on the diggers today, if you feel up to it. Perhaps down there you will find what you're looking for. Though I have met him face to face, so to speak, I know him best through his writings."

"You actually knew Albert Camus?"

"Not him, sir. William Love."

"William Love is an author?"

"I daresay more living souls know him that way than any other."

"Has he been published in America?"

"Of course."

"Then how come I've never heard of him before?"

Hume shrugs. "Seek and ye shall find. Ye might want to start seeking in our library."

He withdraws. Wild thoughts run through my brain. Sinister ones. Obviously Abis is not running the show. William Love is. From afar. He's the one who sent Abis to find me, or if not me *per se*, then someone who looked like me. Someone of my general physical type? I'm getting goose bumps. Why did they disable me? Obviously it was done on purpose, to keep me here. And what about Diana? Bait, to keep me here? No, she has got to be what she seems. Well, what if everything else is what it seems, too. Maybe I've just caught a touch of paranoia from Benedict. But what was Abis doing in Delphi? He had to be waiting for me.

And what about Love? Maybe he doesn't even exist. But he has to be real. I saw him on the terrace when I arrived. I'm pretty sure I talked to him the night I broke my ribs. Well, the next step is to find him in the library. And what about my promise to Benedict? I can't get off the island unless they take me. With my ribs crushed, I can't take Abis's boat. I wouldn't be able to put a life vest on for weeks. Besides, when it comes to that, would I have the courage to go out into open water in that little thing? Especially now that I know how easily it can overturn? Or was that on purpose?

Well, I'm stuck here for the present. And what about Diana? I have to get to find out more about her. Discover the truth. Make decisions rationally. If I really do love her, after all, I may spend a lot of my life on this island. If things are less than sinister. I'll need a few things to find out. A flashlight, for one. And some rope.

***

"Wonderful lunch, Hume."

"On behalf of my staff, I thank you, sir."

"Now, where's this library you told me about?"

"Down that hall, sir. It's the same hall, by the way, that leads to Mr. Love's room. Only you won't be going quite that far. This lad will guide you."

He gestures to a serving boy in the doorway. Is it the same child that held the reigns of the donkeys in Greece? I'm not sure. I rise and follow him through the long, wide hall, gawking like a county bumpkin at the flawless workmanship of the wood paneling, then rushing ahead to catch up to my rapidly striding guide. Staring up at the exquisite plaster work on the hallway ceiling slows me down. Is it real? Yes. Probably. I shuffle forward and run right into the kid, who is standing in the middle of the passage, gazing down at the Persian rug hall runner. My poor ribs. They feel as though they've been slammed with a two by four.

When I'm sufficiently recovered not to see blue stars and yellow trumpets, I realize the boy is smiling and pointing to one of the wall panels. It looks like all the others to me. So I ask, what's the matter? Why are we stopping?"

He says nothing but continues to point.

"You're supposed to take me to the library."

He says nothing, just points.

Then it occurs to me, maybe he doesn't speak English. "Are you an exchange student? I ask. "What country are you from? Do you understand what I am saying to you? Library? *Biblio,* uhh, *bibliotheque?* Umm, *biblioteca?*"

"The library," he says in the imperfect, broken English they speak in parts of New Jersey. Then he stretches out his hand like a young Moses and strikes the paneled wall.

It moves! I mean, part of it actually seems to give way before his advancing fingers, swinging back on silent, invisible wheels, turning aside on silent, invisible hinges.

"Well, I'll be," I say and move forward. But the boy stands in the middle of the doorway, blocking my entrance. Then I realize what he wants, reach into my pocket, pull out two fifty cent pieces, and give them to him.

The boy laughs and looks at the shiny new coins. With his thumb, he flips the silvers one by one high into the air. Then, turning slightly and swaying out his hips, he holds his slit pockets wide with his fingers. The coins fall right into the slits and disappear. He turns and saunters off while I enter the library, alone.

It is much, much larger than I had ever thought it would be. I mean, I had expected it to be large, but this is on the scale of a wealthy eighteenth century gentleman's collection, reflecting a time when young men spent vast fortunes on books and their bindings instead of rock concerts and electronic equipment. I'm absolutely dazzled by the hand-painted wallpaper, the gold-leafed plaster work and the high, vaulted ceiling. For who knows how long I stand rubbernecking like a farm boy in the big city.

Benedict's words come to mind. This room could be converted into a hotel lobby easily enough. Just remove the bookcases, or turn them on their sides and make them into check-in counters.

Light floods into the room from skylights. It makes the room seem larger than it really is. That and the sparse furnishing, only the bookcases and one massive, warped, early Renaissance library table. The illusion of greater size is further enhanced by the brightly colored wall murals, exactly like the ones at Knossos: young boys with brick-red skin struggling with heavy strings of grey-and-yellow dolphin, beautiful, chalk-white, bare-breasted women leading bulls with golden horns to slaughter, scenes of everyday life in a vanished world. Everything is as bright and as vivid as if the mural had been painted yesterday, which is probably not too far off the mark. And the room is not so large as it seems on first impression.

Here and there on the bookshelves rest oddments from the past: shards glued clumsily into gaped and useless, but gloriously decorative amphora and damaged bull's head rhytons, broken stones and broken clay torsos, broken busts and fired terra cotta pots with Native American Indian and Aegean designs painted on their sides.

Have these things been spirited away from the digs? Do they provide proof of what Coach Benedict has been saying? Mostly, they seem to me like the usual run-of-the-mill broken ancient European torsos. And they don't seem to be broken in the right places for what he suggested. Because of their great age, though, they must be worth quite a bit. Even those in poor condition. How can Love trust all those workers and servants not to loot? Abis alone could carry off the whole collection in a day. And what about me? To William Love, I'm the most unknown quantity of all.

Maybe he knows all this stuff's too hot, too traceable, for thieves to sell. Perhaps they fear him too much to try anything. He must have considerable power in the world, power too great to be put upon like that. It would be like trying to sell treasure stolen from the Vatican. Of course there is another possibility.

Perhaps none of it is real, and everyone but me is in the know. Maybe he's got the real stuff locked away. Or, if Benedict's correct, perhaps he's destroyed the pieces he doesn't want anyone to know about, or sold them off himself on the black markets of the world. Maybe they were sent to museums, or legitimate collectors, or are hidden in a vault somewhere on the premises. Maybe that's how he makes his money, surreptitiously, by living off the past.

With the right market, one could live quite comfortably, especially in places like rural Greece and rural Georgia. When Diana took us on her tour, I didn't see even the slightest hint of anything actually unearthed, let alone vast treasure-troves of the past such as Benedict claims is coming from this womb. There aren't even tents set up to temporarily house such a collection, nor, as far as I know, any displays anywhere, except here, hidden in this secret library. You'd think he would want to start the publicity and the speculation. Maybe all there is, is what's on these shelves. And these things may not be real. And if they are, maybe Love brought them here from Europe to salt this find and give it the look of an ancient, mysterious place, Atlantis Lite.

But the books on the shelves are real. Row after row, in big, white, *faux-marbre* cases with massive Greek columns supporting a whole second level of bookcases, complete with walkways, railings and moveable stairs. Because of the pain, I climb the stairs gingerly. When I reach the top I start to laugh aloud. All the volumes on the second floor are phony! Every one of them! They're leather-covered facades made to look like uniform sets of the great authors.

If I'm going to find Love here, I'll have to find him in the lower depths. I descend the stairs to begin my search again. Of course I'm distracted, as usual, by this or that ancient volume, which I have to take to the desk and examine, standing before it like a priest at the altar. As I set one of the volumes down, for the first time I really notice the massive desk chair. It's antique, and seems to be covered with the original leather. Once, no doubt black, now its surface is mostly worn away. The worn cushion is one deep, deep impression from someone's seat. I can imagine William Love working here, hour after hour, quill pen in hand, thinking and writing it all down. So here, after all, is physical evidence of his existence.

"Hello, Manny-man. Good to see you up."

"Abis, you scared the hell out of me."

"Ready for a picnic?"

"I don't want to go on a picnic. I want to stay right here. Why are you trying to lure me away?"

"Diana will not be back."

"Whaat?"

"Not for two more days, Manny-man. What will you do, sit around and mope? Two more days, Manny-man. Your penis will fall off if you do not use it until then."

"I'll stay here."

Abis looks into my eyes, staring from one angle to the other like an ophthalmologist. "You cannot. Your eye whites already look like a route map of the London Underground, Manny-man. If you stay here with these musty bookies, your whole body will shut down like a clogged toilet. Then you will curse and blame Abis. You will say, 'Why did my good friend Abis not take me to meet all the easy women of the village?' This I cannot let you do, Manny-man. You must come. I will show you the patch. We will have Royal Danzig. It is party time for mice while the cat is treated on the mainland."

He takes me by the arm. I stand firm.

"Manny-man, why are you here but to enjoy life while you can, huh? Has Abis not told you this before? Some day much sooner than you think, you will no longer be able to. Then you can re-pant and God will say to you, 'no problem, Manny-man, We'll let it go this time.' And you will be on God's good side again. Trust me. It will be okay-donkey. Do all things in moderation. Everything will equal out, the good and the bad. If you do not do some things, such as celibacy and soberness, then you must do their opposites twice as much. Then everything will even out in the end and you will make God happy, no matter which God you choose to please."

"You have a strange sense of logic, Abis."

"No, no, Manny-man. Not strange. Logistics all the way and perfect mathematic proof, *n'est-ce pi?* Listen. I will prove with the pure mathematics of reason."

"By all means."

"Okaaay. Now, follow my difficult formulas closely. Two plus two is four, right."

"So far."

"So four is your representative on Earth of the perfect balance, right? Because two plus two is everything in balance-moderation."

"Okay."

"So, also then three plus one is four, right? "

"Right."

"Okay, so now here is the tricky theological part, Manny-man. Four plus zero is what?"

"Four," I say, reluctantly.

"Okay. So more of one and less of another, is still perfect balance, Manny-man. Somewhere in this world eight someone elses will be celibate and sober for us and the two of us will be drunk and wild for them and all the Earth will be in balance and God will be happy and we will be happy and picnic. Come."

With perfect timing he then reveals the picnic hamper he had hidden behind his back all this time, probably the same one he had at Delphi. Then as now it is filled with meats and cheeses, fruits and bread. I begin to remember the good times we had that day, or do I? Anyway, I begin to relent. He lifts the cloth inside the hamper to reveal an enormous bottle of Royal Danzig vodka as he raises and lowers his eyebrows repeatedly, like Groucho Marx. Then he grins.

"Come, Manny-man, I will show you the patch. Then we will go into town and seek local girls with big bosoms."

"What do you mean by 'patch'?"

He laughs. "Come. I will show you."

I figure I can put my search for Love's book on hold for an afternoon. With a little help I can always find my way back into this library. What intrigues me most is the prospect of going into the village. At worse, I will be able to speak to the locals and maybe get a handle on things. Maybe even look into hiring a boat from one of them. Maybe gather some evidence about what's really going on at the dig, and most of all, find out about Love. After all, if what Hume says is true, I can always find him in any library with good holdings, even on the mainland. That's why God gave us Interlibrary Loan.

"All right," I say, "what're we waiting for?"

"To the patch, Manny-man. Maybe some of the students are in there now. Nubile, big breasted students who can help us each to count to four."

# TWENTY

"Down this way, Manny-man. We must turn left through the trees and cross the field into the grove. The patch is at the far end of the wood. All the boys and girls will be there."

"So what is this patch?"

"Come."

"And you say I'll enjoy this?"

"Does a frog bump his bottom when he bounces?"

He leads me through a stand of huge, dusky, live oak trees, dripping with silvery Spanish moss. Green ferns grow on the top portions of their massive boughs and grey-blue lichens on their undersides. We cross a large, unkempt garden plot. It's hard to tell where the weeds stop and the rows of vegetable plants and bright, fragrant flowers begin. As I stop to admire a large plot of red flowers with drooping heads, Abis doubles back and starts to drag me away by the arm. His dog grabs my pants leg and pulls me, too, with a growling, shaking motion.

"Not for you, Manny-man, in healthy prime of life."

"No, wait a minute; I want to look at these. What kind are they?"

"In this very place we must watch out for the poisonous cotton mouth water moccasins and copper heads who love to eat the giant, greasy, disease-bearing rats who love to eat these vegetables and flowers," Abis mumbles.

I move on, checking quite often the ground beneath and around my feet and just ahead. We pass a grove of unattended fruit trees. Plums and peaches and pears. Beyond it stretches a tall fence of woven reeds and cut twigs which seem to hide a patch of land from Love's house, the digs, us, and the rest of the island. We reach a primitive gate, which is shut. But not locked.

I sigh, place my hand firmly atop the crude latch, turn to Abis and mutter, "Here we go again, don't we."

He grins and nods enthusiastically. Then without hesitation he pries my hand off the latch, opens it himself, and enters the patch. I follow, close the gate behind us, turn and look about.

"Oh, Jeeze," I say, "Jeeze!"

Abis quickly raises both eyebrows twice.

"Oh, Jeeze!"

Growing everywhere are tall, lush, sweet-scented bushes that are not okra. College-age kids, boys and girls, fill the garden, walking about, nearly naked. Quite a few, in fact, have dropped the "nearly." Some are playing musical instruments, flutes and drums and guitars, some tending the plants. Some are picking and shredding the leaves and putting them out to dry on wire mesh racks. Most are just lolling about, smoking joints, or eating some strange fruit I saw growing just outside the garden walls. Off in the distance, by the fence, on the far side of the patch, three people are making love, omelette style. Everyone but me seems oblivious to them.

"Who put this place together, Hieronymus Bosch? Oh, Jeeze, Abis, Jeeze!"

"Great, huh? Like southern California, where Abis grew up."

"Those plants, is that their real color? They're so, so *green*. They look artificial. Oh, God, why am I asking dumb questions?"

Abis is shedding his clothes. First his shirt then his sandals. With just his loose, white trousers on he dances over to the naked boys and girls, shaking his shoulders rapidly, and joining in their circle. I have seen every one of these kids before. They are, or were, the staid student-workers of the dig. But now? Now they have become their bodies, slim, muscular, beautiful torsos, arms and legs in poses like those of the sea-ruined statues in the basement of the Athens Museum. And I think, "here they are again, before the fall and the ruination by the elements, and withering time and chance and..."

So many of them here look so, so dissipated, pale and jejune, despite their youth. So unhealthy.

Abis turns to me, flashing a lascivious grin, still shimmying his shoulders and shaking his hips. The students turn to me as well, waving their hands slowly and languidly, as if in a synchronized, agonizing, underwater dance. As if struggling in slow motion for life, like animals caught in a tar pit. We all seem caught up in the middle of a dream, a lush, decadent, nineteenth century French imagist poem of a dream, a living, slow-moving tableau or a naughty turn-of-the-last-century French postcard.

Other half-or-less-dressed students mill about, or loll in the grass, in those poses, mild-eyed and solemn. Two rise languidly, like smoke, and come to me, their hands and long, thin arms outstretched, offering home-made cigarettes.

"No, thanks," I say, "I don't smoke."

Abis laughs. "Manny-man, you must take what is offered you. Participate."

I stare at him, then at the mild-eyed boys and girls, then at the burning joint.

These cigarettes don't have names printed on the sides, do they?"

"Hand-rolled, Manny-man. Custom-made. Great shit, Manny-man."

He grins even harder. The languid children each hold out home-rolled cigarettes to me like offerings to the gods, and I think, "not so long ago when they were true children, we adults were gods to them." And now they are holding out to me the tips of long, thin fingers and pale, Giacometti arms.

"I'm sorry, Abis, all of you, I've never done anything like that before, except almost once when I was a student, and I was ashamed of myself afterward."

The mild-eyed boys and girls continue to hold the honeyed offerings out to me.

"It will make your ribs feel great, Manny-man," Abis says and takes a long, long drag on one of the cigarettes. He holds his breath for, it seems like two minutes, then, finally, lets it out slowly, slowly.

"You see, Manny-man, just one puff does not defect you at all. Just takes the edge from the sharp corners of life."

He doesn't seem stoned, or craving harder drugs. In fact, his long drag doesn't seem to faze him much at all, except that his eyes are redder now. Maybe the stuff does serve to soften life a bit.

I falter at this self-deluding proof. The girls hover about me still, offering their gifts. One caresses my cheeks and makes what can only be describes as sweet moan. Another musses my thinning hair. A third unbuttons the top two buttons of my shirt. My cheeks are flushed and hot. The first girl takes her cigarette from her mouth and places it between my half-willing lips.

"Take it in," she says, "Slowly, slow." Her voice is deep, and nearly breathless.

This is how Eve's voice must have sounded to Adam.

"Now," she says, "now, or the fire will go out."

"No," I say, "no...."

With a lilt in his voice, the way you speak to children, Abis urges, "Come on Manny-man, you can do this thing. You know you want to."

And I do. With my whole heart. I long to be a part of it all. To participate. But I'm so afraid. I look about at all the longing faces, all the pretty, youthful, hollow, leaden eyes staring back at me, and Abis grinning like a woodland deity, like Bacchus, Pan, a Priapus.

The blonde young nymph smiles up at me. I shrug, "Oh, what the hell. I grow old, I grow old, I shall wear the bottoms of my trousers rolled." Flashing into my mind is the image of Gustav Aschenbach in his flannel trousers, dying alone in a chair by the sea. The polluted sea. His "innocent" Tadzio aware and not aware. All those years ago, seeing *Death in Venice*, reading it, I never thought to live it, though. And here I am, Tadzio and Aschenbach, but it's my soul, not my art that is fastened to a dying animal and I think, "oh my God, I don't want to die alone."

I turn to her. "I'm not sure how."

"Like this," says my Lorelai. She sounds German but looks Scandinavian. She removes the cigarette gently from my mouth, takes the smoke deep within her, holds it there, half closing her eyes, then closes them all the way, softly, like a sea anemone shutting over a fish. Not one wrinkle on her pale brow.

She holds this pose forever, then exhales, takes the cigarette from her lips and places it between my lips again. "Puff now. Puff now. Take it in, deeply."

I tilt my head and suck the smoke awkwardly into my lungs, expecting at once a garden of earthly delights. Instead I'm drowning in liquid tar, coughing violently, giving up the acrid smoke that is hot like dragon's breath.

They encourage me to take another puff. I do so now, more readily than the first and hold it in as if my breath were my soul, though, still, my throat is burning. Then I cough again, but this time holding in most of the smoke. And later, much later, I let the narcotic escape at my will, expertly, willfully. With a rounded puff. A perfect ring of smoke.

Everyone in the world is laughing. Even, I think, I ...

They urge me on again. I inhale a second time. A third. It becomes much easier. With familiarity. A fourth. I find it's true about my ribs. They don't hurt at all. I feel them in their place, but they've become liquefied. And now I don't really mind them at all. It's so much fun to have floppy ribs. Loppy, loppy ribs. My nibs are so much fun. I'm fun. And my gums are soooooo shiny. I giggle.

At the edge of the garden path Abis spreads the large, checkered tablecloth. And the munchies. He opens the bag of chips and they crawl about a bit before they're caught and eaten by the children. Then he brings forth from his basket of plenty such edibles as when the world began. All-American delights: corn chips and dip and cinnamon flavored popcorn, cheese flavored Nachos and chicken flavored crackers. He spreads out everything he had in the basket but the Royal Danzig vodka as the children circle about the feast like buzzing flies, then hone-in like piranha. One nubile young maiden sits down opposite me. She's wearing a thin, gauzy, silken blouse with no brassiere under it. Her nipples are poking through. They're dancing. Their colors are actually dancing and I love to watch them dance. I long to see the rest of her nubile, naked body, to lie with her, to devour her youth before time does. I watch her watching me, probably looking for signs of life. I've been part of such a phenomenon in school. In class, no less. And in my office. But I've never allowed myself the pleasure of appreciating it before. Not while I'm on duty. And they are not women then. They are my students. My kids. My sacred trust.

"Hey, Beatrice," Abis shouts, tossing Rabbit, or Chufee, or Whatever He Calls Her Now, a few scrunchy corn chips, "nice blouse!"

Beatrice smiles. But, I think, not at us, and all-too-soon, moves off to join the other children. We have lost her, Abis and I. We have lost them all. The whole generation of them. Abis was too gross in his account. On the other hand, I'm not too sure how long she had been sitting there with us. It is starting to get dark. Dark clouds form overhead. Everything is drifting, drifting slowly with the slowness of a continent. The universe is drifting slowly on its axis.

"Hey, Manny-man, you ever do it under the influence of drugs?"

"Only alcohol."

"You try this," he says and holds out a small mirror with a line of cocaine stretched out on top of it.

The mirror is in front of me. I lean over it. All I can see is the line of white powder. Nothing else reflects. "No thanks. I've had enough new thrills for me."

"No, no, you take. It will make your ribs disappear forever. Give you a six foot dick."

"That's grotesque."

"Of course it is! Like a Priapus! Like me!"

"From what I'm told, I don't think a Priapus is wanted on this island."

Abis scowls. Does he know about Benedict's theory? To cover up, I quickly say, "So where are we going?"

He rises. "Come. We go. Leave our stuff here. Hume will come to tidy up."

On cue, Hume appears and begins putting away the picnic things.

"Come on, Manny-man, before we go, you snuffy-snuffy."

"I don't know how. No, really. You'll have to show me how."

"Only enough for one."

"Then you do it for me."

"I cannot do it for you."

"Then take most of it."

He shakes his head.

"Half."

He takes out his wallet, extracts a nice, crisp Euro note, rolls it into a tight tube, like a soda straw and snuffs half the coke up his nose, a quarter load into each nostril. "Ta-da," he says and bows.

I begin reaching for my own wallet.

"No, here, Manny-man, already rolled for action."

I take his Euro and snuff up the narcotic as he did, a quarter load into each nostril. Nothing happens. I feel no different. I'm still me. And mortal. Except I'm taller now. I'm peering over heads. Also the background is receding. My head is puffed up like a loon balloon. If the weed has slowed things down, this stuff has speeded it up again to near normal. Maybe a little on the fast-forward side.

Now Hume is at my ear. "Did you see him there?" he inquires.

"Who? Where? What?"

"Mr. Love. Down in the digs this afternoon."

"No! He was there?"

"I told you he would be."

"Youdidnothingof the sot."

"Indeed I did, sir. I told you to look down there to find what you were seeking."

"Ooosaid the library."

"There, too."

"Th'place wasa phony."

"Only parts."

"Well ya gotta wade through a lotta chaff afore you find the grain in that place," I say.

"The grain is there, nevertheless."

"Lissin here. If yer so smart why donyou find the books yerself an' bring 'em up to me?"

"You would like me to minister to you, sir? To tell you what you must do to find the true way? Rather than point you toward the books so you can figure it out for yourself in your own heart and of your own free will, sir?"

"YES!"

"Hardly the Protestant Ethic, sir."

"Hardly a Protestant, Hume. Can ya doit?"

"I'm no priest, Mr. Markovitz. Besides, how would you ever know I was right?"

"Pure faith, Humster."

"Faith is not necessarily truth, you know."

"Bu' look at all th' anxiety ya avoid when ya believe."

He shakes his head.

"But you'll do it?" I ask again.

"Indeed. Hold your breath until I do. Sir."

"Wow, ya'really mean that? Because I can really do that now. See I don't have a nose anymore. Oh, God, I shouldn' a said that to you. Please forgive. But do you really, really man that about th' books? About Love? I mean, literally?"

"I mean, sir, only half of what I say and all of what I do, literally."

"Well that certainly explains it."

Abis takes me by the left elbow.

"Where you taking me to?"

He drops my arm and moves back into the dark. His disembodied voice says, "Nowhere, Manny-man. Only where you want to go."

"Great. Abis, where are you?"

I move forward, away from Hume. "Ahh, there you are."

He's at the picnic basket again, pulling out the bottle of Royal Danzig vodka. "To the village, Manny-man."

"No, man. Let's stay here! Hume is gonna do it all for me."

He shrugs. "Okay. Here."

"So what're we gonna do?"

He comes closer and whispers, "Come. We will be peasants once more. Come into touch with the dust again. From which we rose. Here in this woodland place. I toast to you again. Ashes to Phoenix. May you rise again." He comes even closer and whispers even lower, "unlike these other folks. Look, here is vodka, drink of the peasant. From my mother Russia. Where I was born. On the steps of the Steppes. We will drink this peasants' drinky and be peasants and brothers once again. To brotherhood. Family, the one thing you can count on in this world! 'Ah, Love, let us be true to one another!'"

"Oh, oh, I get it. From a poem. We're on a darkling plain. No wonder we can't see shit!"

But I can see the children from the corner of my eye. They are milling about the edge of the gathering gloom, like shades out of the underworld. The gate is wide open and their faces lit up from behind by the tiny lights strung up in the trees beyond the woven fence. None will come forward out of the dark, though Abis holds the magic bottle high and wags it lasciviously. Then he does lewd things with it, makes pornographic gestures that, I'm ashamed to say, make me laugh with delight.

"More, more," I shout with joy when he stops.

He bows, lights a torch, sticks it in the ground next to him, and opens up the bottle. "What shall we drink to, Manny-man?"

I shrug.

He grins and raises the bottle. "To Lynn Ado's ass!"

"That the girl that mooned us?"

"Woman, Manny-man, woman."

"What a wonderful, spontaneous performance!"

"Oh, Manny-man, I spit two times on spontaneity! And I think about it first before spitting. Man-man, you are naive as my puppy. The only man over twelve who was actually born yesterday."

"You saying she planned that show?"

"Oh, Manny, Manny, Manny, did you not see how tanned that ripe, luscious ass was, eh? Much careful training went into that. Careful, timed exposure to the sun over many weeks, cautiously at first so as not to burn. Tanning each cheek slowly to perfection. Over weeks and weeks.

Over months. Ha, ha, it is not a thing to be taken lightly! Then, careful watching, watching, waiting for her time in the sun, probably bribing that big Syrian who is her boyfriend with exotic sexual favors behind our imagining to get him to begin that shoving match and to throw punches to start the fist fight. Did you not notice it was he who called Melos Kikones a son of a whoring donkey to start it all? It is true as rain, Manny-man!"

He puts his right arm, holding the bottle, to his heart. "Oh, Man-man, you are soooo naïve. Now we must drink this wadka to her and her carefully planned spontaneous performance. Ha, ha, we drink Russky peasant style."

He carefully places the bottle on the ground, next to the torch. Then he fishes into the deep pockets of his baggy pants, pulls out two greasy shot glasses of thick, course, uneven, bubbly, silvery glass that seems to shimmer in the firelight. Next he pulls out a pepper shaker.

"Okay-donkey, watch now closely, Manny-man. We pour in the wadka like this. Then we shake in the pepper. Now, as the granules sink, they attract the fusel oil impurities in the alcohol. They go down to the bottom harmless as a toothless snatch. Then you toss off the shot like this."

He jerks the shot glass to his mouth and throws his head back violently. The liquid tosses into his throat without, it seems, ever touching any part of his mouth. Every grain of pepper remains in the bottom of the glass.

"Ahh!" he says and sighs, smacking his lips a great, loud, satisfied smack. Then he wipes his mouth thoroughly, since he's fully dressed again, with his sleeve, burps loudly, and fills both shot glasses until the vodka curves up over the rim. He pours pepper on and hands me one glass. His dog growls.

"I think that pepper is just an excuse to down the vodka that way," I say.

He smiles and shrugs. "Downing wadka this way is a great skill you must have, Manny-man."

I toss the liquid back and take it straight to the belly.

"Nistrevia!" He shouts, dancing up and down like an enormous, overgrown elf. Then he fills the shot glasses again. And again. And again. We stand, hanging onto the trunks of trees by the side of the road, the woodland lawn, and puke like Indians at a black drink ceremony. I think I stay under the trees for a long while, maybe passed out. I think I might be a little high. When I wake the lights are all turned off except for one dull string of low wattage bulbs off in the distance, hung between some trees. Abis is gone. Hume is gone. The children, too, are gone, though in the distance drifts the sound of tinkling, delightful laughter.

# TWENTY-ONE

Someone is pulling my leg! Hard. A voice whispers, Murray, Murray, listen to me, please! You gotta get up!"

"Benedict?"

"Shhh, not so loud. We mustn't let 'em hear."

"I can barely see you."

He switches on a small flashlight and shines it on his own face. He's on his belly, holding a finger to his lips. I sit up and lean back against a tree. As my eyes focus more clearly I can tell, even by this light, his face is pasty-yellow; the whites of his eyes look more like egg yokes than albumen.

"You all right?"

"Can ah have some uh that?"

He points to the bottle at my feet.

"Sure."

As he gulps down a full glug, I say, "What's the matter?"

"Jesus Christ in arms, Manny, y'ain't gonna b'lieve it!"

"What?"

He looks around in his most furtive manner, and shudders. I look, too. As the moon comes out from the clouds I see, faintly, Abis standing off in the distance, in the shadows, peering, it seems into the dark, at us. Chufee sniffs the air.

"Tryin' hard as hell ta spy," Benedict murmurs as he switches off the flashlight, grabs me by the arm and makes me rise. He leads me further down the garden path back in the direction of the house and away from Abis's ears. "You an' me gonna raise more sand than th' chickens!"

"What now?"

"Man, you ain't gonna b'lieve it!"

"Probably not," I say.

"Ah'm tellin ya. You won' b'lieve it. Ah means it makes that other cover-up look like mah Aunt Mae's Sunday crocheted tablecloth!"

"What, already?"

He looks around again. Abis is coming up the garden path. "Manny-man?" We hear him shout, "Manny?" The dog woofs.

"Look," Coach Benedict says, "Ah gotta go. Don' want that Abdul guy findin' me."

"Why? He's harmless."

"Let go mah arm, Murray! Ah gotta get!"

"But why?" I repeat, holding onto his arm.

Abis is getting closer and closer. We hear him say more quietly, "Manny-man? Come. Time to wakey-wakey, go to town!"

Now he's nearly on top of us, but I will not let go of Benedict's arm.

"Let me free!" Coach cries, "ah gotta get outta here!" He's in a full panic now. "Please!"

Of course Abis can hear him.

"Ah swears, ah'll meet you at the digs. Ya gotta do it, Murray."

"It's Manny."

"Okay, fine, have it your way. Manny. Ah got it all, all th' proof! An' more! Oh, God, wait'll ya see th' new stuff ah got! They cain't hide this one, buddy. Uh, uh, not from me they cain't. This's waaay too big! Oh, God, lemme go!" he stage whispers now. "Ah swears ah'll meet you at th' digs tomorrow!"

"Okay. When?"

"In th' mornin.' Close ta first light as you ken get away. Oh, God, Manny, you're gonna hafta 'scape soon as ya can. Get away from them an' tell tha' whole story to someone an' send help. You'll hafta do it once ah show you this new thing ah uncovered. Oh, God, Manny, ah know they gonna try an' kill me! God, ah jus' know it! Yer gonna come in th' mornin' an' fine mah lifeless carcass by th' side of th' road all stiff an' cold and startin' ta smell real bad already. Ah jus' know it! Shot through the head with a big ole bullet hole and bleedin' like they done to th' other guy!"

"What other guy?"

"Hush up or he'll hear us!"

"Calm down," I whisper. "Nobody's gonna kill you. Unless you do it yourself with a heart attack from worry. Here, drink some more of this."

I hand him the rest of the bottle.

"Yeah, oh yeah, thanks, man. Yeah. This is great. Don' taste like nothin'.

He takes another long, hard swallow, which seems to have the right effect.

"No, no, that's okay," I say as he tries to hand it back. "You just keep the whole bottle. I'll get back to you in the morning."

"Yeah, but listen here, ah been thinkin' mebbe you gotta try ta leave tonight, ya hear? Go right to th' FBI or the GBI. They couldn' be in on it! Get help. Ah'll be waitin' fer you in the mornin' like ah said, don' you worry. But if ya don't show up, ah'll know ya either 'scaped or they got you, one."

"How am I supposed to escape?"

"Hell ah don' know! Try to hire you a boat, mebbe? Yer goin' inta town with Abdul, ain't ya? Break away. Talk ta one them villagers. They'll help you if ya pay. Ah don' think they's in on this! Look ah gotta go. But tomorrow we meets, an' ah'll also tell you the real reason why they brung you here!"

"Wait, I...."

But Abis catches up to us. He strikes a match and with it lights his torch again. Then he looks at Benedict and squints. "You all right?"

"Yeah. Just had me a panic attack. Suffer from 'em on occasion."

Abis nods. "Such a thing happens here in the woods. Pan comes out, shocks you. Ha, ha it is called 'panic.' No, no, wait, I almost forgot which side of the ocean we are on."

"I'm letting him keep the rest of the vodka, if that's okay with you."

"Sure, sure, Manny. Great idea. You are a genius for thinking it. The Aristople of vodka giving, the Einstein of consideration."

He pats me hard on the back. "Okay, come, we will go to the village now. Look for virgins to defile. Not so easy to find on this island."

He nudges me in the ribs. I wince. "Come, Benedictine, you come, too."

"Sorry, cain't this time. Saay, ya'll don't happen to have you a bottle Jack Daniels, do ya?"

We both shake our heads.

"Didn' think so. Sad."

He takes a few steps and is swallowed by the dark like walking off the edge of the earth.

When he is sure Benedict is really gone, Abis blows out his torch."That one, he is crazy as a Canadian."

"Are Canadians crazy?"

"You bet, Mann-man. Must be to live in a county so cold that long body parts can freeze off. South Canada is north of North Dakota. Is that not crazy? Well, let us go to the village."

He pulls my elbow. Chufee tugs my trouser leg. Together they nearly topple me over. I'm not very steady on my feet.

***

"Where are we, Abis?"

"Parking lot."

"What parking lot?"

"It does not matter. Only the good surface it provides matters now because I am going to teach you my native Russian Cossack dance. From the Caucasian chalk mountains. Where Abis was raised on goat meat and Royal Danzig Vodka. Watch."

He squats, folding his arms in front of him, then violently tosses first one leg then another, stiffly, out in front of him, nearly keeping his balance twice.

"You try it, Manny-man!"

I do, but keep slipping onto the pavement. But at least the expenditure of energy seems to be sobering me up. And wearing me out. Finally I just have to sit. I don't have the strength or energy anymore to fall. My ribs begin to ache. But Abis keeps it up, balancing better and better each time he tries, dancing his dance in the parking lot on and on into the night.

\*\*\*

Next thing I know, we're inside a building. I'm sitting at a small table with a full glass of vodka before me. Abis is dancing with three young, pretty, well-stacked woman. Sweat pours off his brow. His arms are raised. Sweat has soaked his armpits and his back. He puts his hands to his hips and continues gyrating, then raises his hands again and snaps his fingers, not quite in time with the music.

As he and the trio gyrate close to me I shout, with the timing of a .125 hitter, "Abis, why were you at Delphi? Why did you find me there and bring me here?"

"Manny, look to the three Fates."

I can barely hear him above the music. I think the next thing he says is, "Even the gods, even the minor deities," but his voice trails off as he dances away from me. A few minutes later he walks out the door with a former virgin.

I'm too busy to care. I've been talking for the last few minutes to three local fishermen at the table next to me. Actually I only speak to the one in the middle. He's the only one I can understand. The other two speak with such thick dialects I can't make sense of any two consecutive words they mumble. I buy them a few rounds but nurse the single vodka in front of me. I'm beginning to feel a whole lot more sober and rational. My head is beginning to throb, in this case, a good sign. With Abis gone the place is quieter, more a rumble than a thunderclap.

"So you guys fish for shrimp? You have a little boat or something?"

"Me, mah brothers here we owns us outright from Daddy th'fines's scrimps traller ever done builded in these here parts an' it ain't no little boat neither," the middleman says, showing me with his arms how big their boat is.

"Would it be adequate for, say, mainland passenger transport? I don't mean necessarily as a regular routing, but perhaps on a contingency basis, for instance?"

"You ain't fum 'round here is you?"

"Why do you say that?"

"Well, 'cause you tawk so funny. Like a tax collector or sumpen. Hey, no offense ner nuthin' but it's kinda hard follerin you."

"I'm not a southerner by birth, if that's what you mean. I suppose you're having as much trouble understanding me as I am understanding you, and especially your two companions, particularly when they mumble."

"They ain't no companums, mister, they's muh partial brothers. Half-brothers, really, an' I got me a hard time cipherin' m'self sometime." He leans forward and says in a lower voice, "See, they comes fum what we calls th' dumb side uh th' fambly, bless their hearts." He leans back again and says loud enough for them to hear, "see, now, mah momma ain' his momma, ner his momma ain' his. You follerin' me? Carl here, he's th' eldes,'we reckon he fell offen his grandaddy's mule wagon a time too many as a small boy. Know what ah'm sayin'? Th' boy picks up stations on his radio what ain' on th' air."

The old guy, Carl, grins exaggeratedly.

"I got a feeling you guys are slightly pulling my leg. Anyway, seriously, can you guys cross to the mainland in your boat?

"Well, shoot ah reckon, son. Done tol' you we got us th' second biggest fishin' boat on the whole damn island."

From the corner of my eye I see Odysseus, the melon man, eyeing us cautiously. He gets up from his bar stool and starts dancing with a disreputable-looking young woman, coming closer to my table step by step, no doubt to eavesdrop. "What a world," I say, "with old men dancing with new women."

"They does it different up north?" the middle fisherman asks.

I think about all those parties back at my school with graduate and undergraduate students and their lecherous old professors getting drunk together, and shrug. "No, guess not."

Odysseus dances even closer to me. I rise to greet him. He bumps into me, hard. My ribs sing out as harsh and painfully horrible as a John Adams opera. "Sorry," he says as he fumbles to put something in his pocket, and dances away. He didn't even seem to recognize me.

I sit down for a while to recover, then say to the fishermen, "Come outside a minute, all of you. All three. I have a business proposition. Come outside where there's less noise."

We find a table in the open air. I look around for spies, then ask, "Can you take me to the mainland in your boat? I'll pay you whatever you ask, within reason."

A waiter comes and we order beer all around. As he begins to walk away, the older fisherman calls him back and whispers something in his ear. The waiter smiles, looks at me, nods, then leaves. We sit in silence for a moment. Rather, I'm silent, the three fishermen talk among themselves excitedly. I can make out about three words, "shoot," "and," and "ahreckon."

As they chatter, I'm thinking I've got to get help for Coach Benedict. If he's right, I have to get people with the right influence to stop the fabrications and destruction, and preserve historical truth. If he's crazy, I have to get him some guys with white coats.

Two of the fishermen are smoking. Number three has begun a conversation with a pretty, plump, girl in a low cut, peasant dress similar to the ones Diana frequently wears. Only this girl's cleavage is more waterfall-like.

Diana! What to do? Aloud, I say, "When I get home, I'll call."

"Wha'?" The oldest fisherman asks.

"Can you do it?

"Th'mainlan'? Reckon we could tote you on over. But, damn, man, why ya wants ta go there? We got us everthin' you needs right here."

The waiter returns with only two glasses of beer. The three fishermen share one glass. I have the other to myself. The first gulp tastes funny. Too bitter. The second gulp is okay. Except it gets me a little nauseated and dizzy.

"In many ways," I tell them, "I don't want to go. Believe me. But duty calls. If everything checks out okay, though, I'll be back in a day or two."

He shrugs, and turns to the other two. After more animated talk, he turns to me again and says, "When ya fixin' ta go?"

"Tonight?"

"You gotta pay us now, fer th' troubles."

"How much?"

He scratches his chin. "Big. Big. Cain't do it cheap, now. Here, looky this." He takes out a small pencil and a crumpled piece of paper that smells like dead shrimp, writes something on it and hands it to me.

"A hundred dollars?" I shout. "My God!"

"Too big?"

"Yes, too big!"

The three men huddle again. He writes another figure immediately. Meanwhile, waves of nausea wash over me. He hands me the paper.

"Twenty-seven? Is that your lowest offer?"

With great dignity he straightens out his collar. "Twenny-seven dollar. That ain't but nine buck a piece. No, no, that ain' right. Gotta figgur gas cost, too. Better make that forty-two dollar ef ya wanna goes right now. We ain't takin' lessn that." He pauses a bit, considering. "Ken you afford thet? Mebbe we could do it a might sight cheaper effen you can wait 'til daylight. See, we don't have no run-in lights, an so, yeah, shoot we could do it fer forty-seven."

One of the other men whispers something to him. He whispers something back. I don't know why they're whispering. I can't understand them when they talk among themselves, whisper or shout. Finally the spokesman says, "No, no, wait a whole minute, stop, time out. Do over. M'brother here says if'n we waits 'til day, we gonna have ta charge you four time that figgur then, on account of that's when we're out makin' big money scrimpin.' So if you wants ta wait 'til dawn, gonna cost you one-oh-eight, fifty. Thet's one hunnerd and eight dollar and fifty cent. Somebody gotta pays fer all them fishes and scrimps we left swimmin' on the far side a th' nets an' not gettin' no money fer."

"All right," I say, "then we better go right now."

Standing somewhat stiffly, I start to reach for my wallet to pay for the beer. But the oldest of the three shakes his head vigorously and pulls from his pockets coin after coin after coin.

"A coinucopia," I say aloud and laugh. That's the kind of humor I use in my classes.

Meanwhile the eldest is still pulling out more pennies. He slams them all on the table.

"Mah half brother, here'll pay fer this little thing n'soon you ken pay for the big'en."

He says this with the ominous portent of a prophecy. I realize at that moment they could kill me for my wallet and toss my lifeless body overboard where nobody would find it and it'd drift out to sea and be eaten by the starfish. There was this case in the papers not too long ago where these guys ripped somebody's belly open while the guy was still alive so the body wouldn't fill with gas and float.

But, damn it, I'm going, anyway. I have to try. I promised Coach I would. But these guys are unsavory looking, to say the least. One hasn't even shaved for a week. The other two are more drunk than I am. But, God, I have to trust them. If I stay on the island, it could come to worse. And I gave Coach my word.

"Okay, let's go to your boat."

***

Their boat is unsavory, too. It doesn't seem to have been painted, scrapped, or cleaned since it was built.

"How old is this thing?"

The spokesman scratches his chin "Weel, lemme see, now. Tell you what, she's a good boat. Damn sight better'n most. But ah reckons she ain't bran new. Lemme ast m'brother here. He's the builder."

I look at the old guy. "He built this boat?"

"Done inherit it fum Daddy."

"Your father built it?"

"No, no, his daddy's daddy. Big Daddy."

"His grandfather built it?"

"Inherit it."

I sigh. "Never mind."

"Damn good boat. Yessir. Straight. Sure. Solid wood. Ain't rot hardly none atoll, 'cep' a little bit where it don' show none. In two, no, no, wait, in four places. Shoot, thet ain't so bad fer a boat this ole."

"What's that awful smell?"

He sniffs all about with his nose in the air like a skunk downwind of his own trail.

"What smell?" He asks quite innocently.

"I clamber aboard, open a door, and look below. "Is that water seeping in down there?"

"Well, shoot, son, don't worry none 'bout thet. We fittin' tuh turn on th'sump pump in a bit, ef we ken get 'er runnin.' Don't really need it hardly none, though. Boat don't leak none atoll, 'cept a little in them four place I tol' about where the wood's all rot outta her."

"Look, maybe this isn't such a good idea after all."

His eyes flash fire. He strikes his chest with such force I jump. "Listen here, you sonofabitch, this here's a damn good boat! It was ma own brother's grandaddy's boat and his daddy's afore him! Three generations, mebbe four what fish fum this here boat ever goddamn day uh their lives! Through ever storm, an' high water God Hisself send this way in ever season. An' when his time come, by God, ma son and his sons is gonna fish it, too! An' you comes here and turns yer snooty-ass nose up at ma brother's boat? Well you ken jus' get yer snooty ass outa here. Go on, off the boat! Yeah, tha's right, get!"

"Hold on a minute, okay? I didn't mean to insult anyone, all right? This is a very nice boat. If you and your brothers fish in it every day and trust your lives to it, who am I to argue? The sky is clear and the wind is warm. It'll be fine, I'm sure."

He huffs and turns his back to begin preparations. I look about. "Please, God," I pray silently, "just one more time. Just one more trip before she sinks. Don't let it go under. Don't let me be sick."

The thinnest brother, the one with the grizzly stubble of beard, points toward the back of the boat. He's a slight, balding man with a thin, flabby neck, thin arms and remarkably good teeth, unless they're false. I doubt if the three men are really brothers, even half-brothers. They look so different.

I smile at him and ask, "Do you know William Love?"

He grunts and points again to the back of the boat. I do what I'm told, walk to the railing, and hold on.

They work on the engine, frantically trying to get it started, banging on various parts with wrenches and a funny little hammer that looks like a toy. One brother stands and begins to howl. The engine sputters once.

Then it cranks up. The brothers pat each other's back. Then they all shake hands, vigorously.

I don't participate in the jollity. I'm too busy hanging onto the railing. My stomach is horribly queasy and we haven't even left the dock. The oldest one revs up the engine. It sounds like a small lawnmower. Maybe they have a sail to put up once we're out in deep water. It does have a mast. I mean, I guess that's a mast.

"Okay, so, where ya want tuh go?"

"The mainland."

"Big target, Mister. Mebbe you could pinpoint er a bit more?"

"Love's house."

He points back to the island and the mansion on the hill. It's bathed in moonlight.

I laugh. "No, no, not that one, the one on the mainland."

He doesn't laugh. "Mister, he don' by God have no house but this'n."

"Yes. The one on the mainland."

"Ahm on take you to th' closet dock n'drop you off just soon's we sees the green uf yer money."

"Fine," I shout over the wind and the unmuffled sputtering of the little engine.

"So what was you, one them fancy-ass guests a Mr. Love?"

I think for a moment, then grin. "Yes, I guess I am. Or, rather was."

"So what you do, piss 'em off?"

"No!"

"Then why you leavin' in th'middle the night? You ain't stealin' ner nothing is you?

"I'm just going because he's gone."

The man scowls.

"To the mainland, that is. He's on the mainland."

"He lives here, Mister. On our island. If he's gone, he ain't long gone. He done promised ever one of us if he lef' any time, tuh always be right back, an' that settles it. He is, by God, gonna be right back. He done said it an' ah believe it. If you wants ta see William Love, you go on an' wait right where you was!"

"There's no evidence of his returning anytime soon, if at all."

"If you wants ta fine him quick, how come you ain't takin' one of his boats? He got him a powerful passel of 'em."

"None available. Or at least none at my disposal."

"Shiiiiiiiiiiiit."

I go into the cabin. I'm feeling as sick as I did on Love's motor launch. So I lie down gingerly on a pile of greasy cushions. Masked behind the odor of the dirt is the same canvas smell that William Love's tent had, the one in Greece. I think I'm allergic to at least sixteen of the fungi species growing in the cabin and on its contents. Mercifully, I fall asleep. But it's a fitful sleep.

# TWENTY-TWO

One of the brothers rouses me. It's nearly dawn. Through the open porthole I can see a rosy sky. A brisk, cool, flower-scented breeze blows through. I try to stand too quickly and my knees buckle. As I regain my legs, he points out the porthole. The mainland stretches out before us like a midnight blue apparition in a haze. Not quite reality yet, but a memory, a dream of it rises from the sea and focuses more clearly as we get closer.

I make my way on deck, still quite nauseous. My head aches. My ribs throb. My mouth is dry. I can feel my heart beating weakly in my chest. I've always thought I have a heart problem, despite what the doctors tell me. But the air is crisp, the sky bright pink and green and blue. At the helm the spokesman steers. He points. I nod and grin in pure joy. I'm going home again. I'm free. When I get in, I'll call Diana. Or I'll write. Or both.

Within the hour we are gliding into the dock.

"How much I owe you?"

"Fifty-two dollar."

"I thought you said, 'thirty-two.'"

"Okay, forty-seven."

I nod and smile and reach for my wallet. "Oh my God, oh, God, oh, no, my God!"

"Now what?"

"My wallet's gone! I've been robbed!"

He give me a stern, sideways look. Then he narrows his eyes like a snake's.

"No, really. Look!" I shout, turning all my pockets inside out. "I have nothing! No money, no credit cards, no wallet, no identity at all!"

He spins the wheel hard around. The boat makes a sudden u-turn. I nearly topple.

"What the hell do you think you're doing?" I shout. But it is quite obvious what he's doing. The only thing I can do is stand forlornly against the railing at the back of the boat and watch the mainland recede against the light of dawn.

As the sun grows in strength, my own strength ebbs away. Yet somehow I am able to grab his shirt and scream, "What have you done with my wallet?"

The other two brothers turn to see what the commotion is about. The translator shouts to them in dialect. Suddenly the old man leaps at my throat! His elbow hits my ribs. I go down in agony. He jumps on top of me and starts hitting me in the face. The other two pull him off and send the tough old bantam rooster to the front of the boat. Me they pick up and escort to the cabin below and confine me there. What have they done with my wallet?

But that doesn't figure. Why would they have wasted their time and diesel fuel on this farce of a trip without tossing me overboard in the middle of the night or just dumping me out on the mainland if they were the ones who stole my wallet? No, it had to be the melon man, Red, who took it when he bumped into me at the pub. Was it at Love's command? Why does Love want me back on the island? What does he have in store for me?

Immediately I go back on deck and apologize, profusely. They accept, reluctantly. Though tepid handshakes are exchanged all around, still, I know they view me with profound distrust. I slink back down into the hold and stay there, searching, stealthily, for my wallet.

On the cabin wall opposite me, a rickety old bench is bolted to the wood of the hull, directly under a rotted porthole. Piled and scattered beneath it, a collection of old, torn, oil smeared canvas and plastic cushions rise and sink on a tide of bilge water, smelling of rotting fish guts, stale beer and diesel fuel. I take the driest cushions I can find and stack them atop the bench. Trying to keep my feet out of the sloshing water. Actually, I must admit, there's less slosh than I thought there'd be. Maybe the sump pump is working.

I press my palms below my eyes for a minute. When I look up again, I see the vicious old man who attacked me has come below. His sinuses look more swollen than mine. So does one eye. Wow, maybe I did that. Maybe not. I shrink back as he shuffles toward me, grunting and glaring. He shuffles to an old cabinet, opens it, and pulls out a long, crisp, clean brown bag. Inside is a fat loaf of Italian bread from a bakery and a child's rectangular, plastic, bright yellow thermos, with pictures on the sides of Daffy Duck.

At this incongruous sight of the scrawny old man and his duck, I can't help myself: despite how much it hurts, I raise my arm, point, and laugh hysterically. Startled, the old man stares at me. I sort of shrug, and smile. He continues staring. I point to the picture of the duck. He looks a bit embarrassed. Then we both burst out laughing wildly. Each of us points to the duck in turn. This sets us off howling again. Pretty soon we're holding our sides, then holding onto each other, laughing and wiping tears away. Every once in a while, I've got to stop and grab my throbbing head or ribs or stomach, as the pain or the waves of nausea get the best of me. But in a minute or two we're with back at it again, laughing our fool heads off.

The engine stops and the other two brothers run down into the hold to find out, no doubt, what's going on. The old one tells them, I guess, and they grin. That's when I become aware of how few teeth they have among them.

We end up sharing what little coffee is in the thermos, and the bread. They're kinder to me then they have cause. Why? As far as they know, I tried to trick them. Maybe what saves me in their eyes is that I was drunk at the time, and fooled myself as well. I try to think of a way to repay in kind.

"Listen, all of you, you have my complete permission to go ahead and do your fishing for the day before putting me ashore. Really, don't mind. I'll be fine."

Now the interpreter bursts out laughing. He says something in dialect to the other two. They laugh as well. Finally, wiping the tears from his eyes, he says, "It don't make no shit load a diff'ence what you wants, chief; we the ones what needs ta be out here fishin'."

"You know, I hadn't even though of that."

He snorts. "Mista, tha's why yer such a asshole. Lucky fer you an' us we needs ta put in fer supplies. When we gets back to th'island we puttin' yer sorry gone-ass ashore an' goodbye to it."

I can't be mad at him. I deserved that. Well, at least they revealed their plans to me and can relax. Besides, if I stayed on board all day I'd only be a burden. I shouldn't have tried to run away from my obligations on Love's island, in the first place. Damned if I haven't done that too many times in my life. Too many times lately.

"Wind's picking up," I say.

"Tha's what it do."

They leave me in the cabin. I sit hunched over my borrowed bread and coffee, still wondering what in hell happened to my wallet. Did the melon man really take it in an attempt to keep me on the island? He is, after all, in William Love's employ. Or did I lose it long before?

I wander back on deck. The morning sun is full upon the back of the pilot's head and makes it shine as if surrounded by a gold halo. He's so skinny his clothes hang as if they were covering no flesh at all, only soul. In this state he reminds me of those saints' icons, interchangeable and beatific, I saw in the Athens Museum. So gaunt. All three of them. Three brothers in the unflesh.

Maybe that serenity he projects is only an illusion. Not serenity at all but stupidity. Maybe it's not a transfiguration of the flesh by the soul but a wasting away of it by alcohol. Maybe it's ignorance that keeps him on the literal plane, not sublimity. Maybe his is a mind incapable of the grandeur that transforms to metaphor. He is what he is, the flesh and no more. Come to think of it, maybe that's the definition of a saint.

A school of dolphins swims by.

"Did you know the ancestors of the dolphin were once sea creatures that evolved into land creatures and re-evolved into sea creatures?"

"Evolution's bullshit," he says without turning to look at me.

Now I'm convinced. He is a saint. Made of that same stubborn stuff that makes martyrs. No sense arguing with him. Instead I stare out to sea and watch the various islands pass. The dolphins jump and roll in the foam of our wake. One leaps clear out of the water to get a good look at us. He seems to be smiling.

The other brothers come out on deck from below. They share the last of the coffee and the bread with us. I had no idea any had been left from the last communion. When it's done, they return to their duties down below.

Why are they so nice to me? On the other hand, why didn't they just put me ashore on the mainland rather than ferry me back across? Why not take a chance? They had nothing to lose, and to their minds, true, maybe I wouldn't send them the money I owed. But maybe I would.

Unless it was all a ploy. Maybe they, too, work for William Love, and he wanted to show me how much control he really has over me. Maybe this whole voyage was part of his Grand Plan. Well, if he really wants me back, he has me now. Might as well go to the digs and see if Benedict is still there.

\*\*\*

He is. But I can't believe my eyes. He's propped against a Priapus tree, looking as if he'd been holding onto it all night, sleeping off a drunk. Of course, I ask the Universal Stupid Question: "Are you all right?"

He looks up at me with baleful, yellow, bloodshot eyes. Still clinging to his tree, he says, "How could ah be, knowin' what ah knows now?"

"Hell, that could apply to all of us, Coach."

But he's in no mood for lame humor. So I begin to uncoil his arm from the trunk.

"Hey, hey, ah ken do it."

He proves it, lifting himself momentarily, then slithering down to a sitting position with his back against the trunk. I squat next to him. He smells like the inside of a full whisky barrel. "So what do you know?" I ask, gently.

"Thet they's converin' up horrible atrocities, fer one."

"So you said."

"No!" he says more quickly than I thought for a man in his state. "Ah mean recent ones."

He sits upright.

"How recent?"

"Real recent. One them pits in th' back th' digs ain't fer archeology a-tall."

"So what's it for?"

"It's a mass grave, Mel. With recent bodies in it, some hardly decomposed a-tall!"

"What?"

"Ah done seen it with mah own two eyes! It's a fuckin' graveyard with ah'll bet a hunnerd people, maybe more, buried in it. Ah mean people ah knew. People who was workin' on these here digs an' somehow's disappeared over the las' few years ah been comin' here. Hell, ah jus' figgured them folks done gone home or sumpin.' But they's *dead*, God damn it, *dead*! Old 'uns and young 'uns, an' students an' supervisors, th' whole frickin' nine yards a twine, son! Some of 'em ah knowed fer a fac' was workin' here late as las' summer, an' a few ah reckon was here *this* summer! Mel, they done *kilt* 'em, don't you unnerstan?"

"I'm sorry, Coach, but you've got to be hallucinating. I mean you've obviously been here drinking all night!"

"You don' b'lieve me?"

"How could I?"

"Then hep me up an' ah'll show you th' hunnerd proof!"

"Come on."

"Ah'm comin'," he says.

He begins to walk toward the open pits on unsteady pinions. I stay very close to his side, to catch him if he falls, and also to hear what he's mumbling. He quickens the pace. "Come on, keep up!" he says.

I catch up and grab him by the arm. "Listen here, Coach, what do you think really happened, huh? I mean, what you're saying makes no logical sense. Why would so many people be killed?"

"Ah thinks they been ritually murdered, tha's what ah thinks. Ah thinks it's a part a their Cybele worship."

I laugh. "Come on, man, wake up, smell the ozone; this isn't three hundred B.C.E. Nobody worships deities like Cybele anymore."

"Shiiiiiiiit. You don't buy thet sop about ever pagan puttin' down they old religion an' takin' up Christianity just 'cause some Emperor a thousand mile away done declared it th' official state religion, do ya? Hell. Ah'll lay you odds th' number a Jove worshipers in 380 A.D. was purdy damn near th' same's it was in A.D. 379. An' ah'll lays you odds they's still some folks up in them hills still payin' homage to th' ole boy right now, this very minute. Son, they's alays been pockets a pagen worship somewheres. Zeus, Odin, Satan, Baal, you name it an' ah'll guarandamntee you thet right this moment they's somebody somewhere on God's Green Earth right now burnin' incense or sacrificin' God knows what to knows who. Hell, man, don' you read *National Geographic*? Ah says they's worshipin' Cybele right here on this island and doin' it th' ole fashion way, drinkin' warm human blood!"

"Human sacrifice? Oh, come on! For God's sake, Coach, this is the twenty-first century. People don't slaughter people like that now. It's absurd!"

"More absurd'n people takin' babies outen they mama's arms and dashin' they heads against a tree? Nazis done that in civilized Europe not so long ago. More absurd'n strappin' dynamite to a teenager girl's body and havin' her walk into a school yard t'blow up little children in the name of God? You *know* thet stuff's goin' on right now! More absurd then…"

"All right, yes, I get the point. There's irrefutable proof for all those things you mentioned. But do you have proof of what you're saying. I mean about what's going on here now?"

"Ah'll show you."

He leads me on for a pace or two then stops again. "What ef ah tells you thet yer good ole buddy, Abdul, or Ibis, or whatever you call him, and yer little girlfriend, Diana, is involve' with this Cybele worship?"

"Whaaaat?"

"Ah ain't kiddin.' They's priest an' priestess."

"That's ridiculous."

"Is it? Well, hell's bells, boy, maybe you better come with me an' find out."

"Don't worry, I will."

He nods.

"Now," I say as we reach the edge of the pits, 'you show me what you got."

"Okay, here." He totters forward, motioning for me to follow around two of the grids. "We gotta go way on beyond them two shallow trenches way over there on th' other side, then over that there grassy knoll. Careful when we crosses over them nex' four boards. They's narrow as a rattlesnake's penis an' them holes they crosses is the deepest ones on the whole damn island."

As we get to the pit I hesitate. "Whoa. This isn't safe, Coach. Those boards are waaaay too narrow to cross without a handrail or something. Doesn't NASHA or NOAH, or whoever it is check these things for safety? Let's go around, okay?"

"R'lax, will ya?" He gives me that same contemptuous look the kids at school used to when I wouldn't take a dare. But when he sees how scared I really am, he says, "come on, man we crosses them bridges all the time. Ever one of us. Ever day. It ain't nothin.' Nobody falls, fer God's sake, trust me."

"Maybe so, but no sense taking chances. How deep you say these pits are?"

"Not more'n fifteen feet, an' them boards is a good six inches wide. More'n enough."

"Hard wood or soft?"

"Pressure treated southern, by God, yeller pine. Hardest damn wood on God's Green Earth."

I stand before the first pit, take in a deep breath, and hold it in like a man in the gas chamber. Then I let it out slowly and say, "Okay, okay, I'll go first."

I slide the toes of one foot forward and test the wood for steadiness. The other foot remains firmly planted on the ground. Then, slowly, cautiously, I shift my weight. The wood is wet. The ground around the wood is wet. Why? It hasn't rained, I don't think.

The board is smooth and springy under my feet. Like a fiberglass diving board. I step back onto solid ground. "Coach, why don't you bring your so-called proof to me later this morning? When we're both more rested."

He pushes me aside with a wave of his arm and strides out to the center of the plank with no more concern than if he were on the sidewalks of Manhattan. Then he turns to me with both palms up and springs up and down a few times to show me it's safe.

"Okay, okay," I say and move forward toward the plank as he continues springing up and down. Suddenly the dirt under the far side of the board gives way and the end of the board flops down into the pit. Benedict yells, "Whoa!" kind of comically and slides down the falling board, feet first. As the board tumbles, he loses all footing and plunges straight down. The plank flips up behind him and cracks him on the back of the skull. He yells, "Shit," and hits the ground feet first, the rest of his body collapsing like a strand of cooked spaghetti.

I walk over to the edge of the pit. "You okay?"

No answer.

I lean down and try to put a hand down to grab his and pull him out. "Coach?" I get on my belly and reach down further. No hand. He just lies there, out cold. I scramble to my feet and look around frantically for a ladder, a pole to shimmy down, anything to reach him. None of the planks is long enough. Nothing's long enough. In a panic I run in toward Love's house, screaming for assistance, hands waving in the air.

At the far end of the digs a small crew is already sorting pottery shards under the canopy. A fair wind blows. As I get close enough for them to hear me over the whips and cracks of the blowing canvas, they all rise to my shouts. Two of them pick up ladders and then they all run with me back to Benedict. As soon as we reach the edge of the pit, two of the men angle the ladders in and two of the women immediately clamber down.

One shouts up that he's still unconscious, but breathing regularly. The other shouts that his heartbeat's strong.

"He's starting to come around," one of them shouts.

Two more workers go down.

"He's moving both arms slightly."

"He's moving both legs."

"Nothing seems broken. No signs of paralysis," one shouts

"But many signs of alcohol indulgence," the other one adds.

I give a sigh of relief. He'll recover to be paranoid another day.

To haul him up they lower a plank with ropes tied to each end. By now he's almost fully revived. By the time they get him back to the surface, he's sitting upright on the board, groaning and complaining of dizziness. Otherwise he seems fine. With his right hand, he's feeling the big lump on the back of his neck.

"Aw, thet smarts." he says.

"It's already getting black and blue," I tell him.

One of the boys says, "I'll get him some ice," and runs off in the direction of the house.

A familiar voice behind me asks, "How is he?"

All of us who are kneeling before him turn. It's Diana. She's wearing a long, loose, white gown, like a flowing robe. Her hair is pulled back tight into a ponytail, black and sleek.

I stand. She glances at me. Is she relieved, angry, sad, or what? Her face is expressionless.

"Ah'm fine," Benedict answers for himself.

She squats down beside him, holds his chin with thumb and forefinger, and moves his head from side to side, looking into his eyes as they catch the glint of the morning sun, checking his pupils, I guess. Abruptly she lets go and stands over him. Her brows knit. "This pit was hosed down last evening to keep the dust settled. In that condition it was unsafe to move across. You knew that. You've been warned about it before. I gave strict orders that no one, and I mean no one, was to go near this dig after hours without my direct, written, permission. You knew that, too. Especially this pit which is always off limits until it's dry enough to be safely worked. But no, you deliberately violated my direct orders, and have done so many, many times in the past. Snooping around after hours, one time even destroying a newly laid grid and perhaps removing valuable archaeological evidence in at least one of the decoupages before it was properly documented. Why Benedict? What are you trying to prove? That you're a tireless worker? That you know more than us? That you're enthusiastic? A plunderer in the name of science?"

He says nothing, just stares at her. Then he turns his head and winks at me.

"I honestly believe your motive is good," she continues. "That you only want to help. And we appreciate, we all do, your voluntary efforts. But your enthusiasm is hurting our work here more than it helps. Much more."

He raises one brow.

I don't know what, or who, to believe.

She continues looking down at him. "I'm glad you're all right. Very glad. But you cannot work with us here on this project anymore. We're shipping you home. As soon as you're in the right shape for us to do so."

She turns on her heels and starts to walk away. I trot after her. "Is that fair?" I ask.

She stops in her tracks, turns, and stares at me. "Yes, that's fair. To me. Now. Let's go to bed."

She begins walking again, this time even faster. For a moment, I just stand my place, startled. Then I catch up again, and trot beside her.

I'm exhausted, elated, in a daze. She is sexually aroused. We fall into bed and make passionate love, many times.

# TWENTY-THREE

The moon's so bright, it dims the stars. Diana is sleeping next to me. Has she been sleeping all the time I have? Or did she rise to go prowling in the dark after I fell asleep? Something tells me she has. The French doors leading to the terrace are open wide. A soft, warm breeze blows through the room, billowing the sheer curtains. The moonlight shines through, and around them. A white terrycloth robe has been draped over the wicker chair by my side of the bed. It's the same robe I have worn each night I've spent with her. The same one I had worn when I showered. I put it on.

My wallet is in the pocket of the robe, along with my key chain. Did I really leave them there? Or did someone place them there this evening? I slip them into my pants pocket, leaving the pants on the chair, and stroll out to the little table by the terrace rail.

Beside the table is a silver bucket filled nearly to the brim with shaved ice. Nestled in the slush, two bottles of champagne hibernate blissfully. On the table, a cold collation under glass awaits us and, in insulated carafes, hot coffee, cool cream, and chilled orange juice.

It doesn't look too sinister. I pour myself some coffee, sit, put my feet up on the railing, and stare out at the moon. I'm feeling uneasy, but well, physically.

Diana strolls out on the terrace. She's wearing a robe identical to mine. We uncover the dishes, eat everything eatable on the table, drink all the wine to be had, rise and fall into bed again to make love and fall asleep.

When we wake again the moon is gone. But it's still night. Diana takes out a small plastic bag of marijuana from her night stand and deftly rolls some cigarettes. We smoke it in bed. I start laughing. Then I'm kissing her knees and thighs. My head and her body swirl together in a vortex of sexual pleasures. As we lie together afterward, she says there was wave after wave of orgasm and she was on Pluto.

We sleep again. When we wake it's late morning. I squint and struggle to focus on the figure looming in front of me. All I can make out is a silhouette against the light streaming in through the open French doors. I turn my head toward Diana. She is shading her eyes, too, trying, as I am, to see who is standing in the light. I look again. The silhouette moves into the shade. It becomes Abis. He looks grim.

"Benedict is dead," he says.

"What?"

"No way to say this nice, Manny-man, he is very dead."

"But how? What happened?"

"Abis does not know. Nobody knows. Maybe shock. Maybe heart. He had one, but it was not very good for keeping time. Maybe infernal injury?"

"What does the doctor say?"

"No doctor here, Manny-man. You know that."

I jump out of bed. "I want to see him! I want to see the body!"

"No, Manny-man. This is no good. This idea of yours, it sucks mud through a straw."

"I want to see the body!"

Diana sits up now. Why Manny? Why? What can you do for him now?" she says and tries to pull me down by the shoulders.

"I need to respect his fears," I tell her. Then, quickly, to Abis, "Take me to him, please!"

Abis looks at Diana. She shrugs. "Why not?" she says.

I dress hurriedly. Abis leads me down the hall. We enter a large bedroom, larger than mine and Diana's combined. Hume is sitting in one of the ornate Italian Baroque chairs by the bed; a four poster, likewise Italian Baroque, contains Benedict's body. Hume rises when we enter. Without speaking I stride straight to the body and uncover it to the chest from its winding sheet.

The face is not serene. The eyes are wide open, pupils dilated and corneas slightly clouded over. His skin is grayish-white. The color of moldy library paste. The lips, tight and nearly colorless, are pulled back from the teeth and the gray-brown gums. No fluid stains the sheets. No leakage from the ears, nose or mouth. No blood visible anywhere, no bruises, no discoloration, no post mortem lividity I can see. He died as he lay, face up. And in horror.

"Who was with him when he passed away?"

Hume says, "He was alone, sir."

"You left him unattended?"

"We did not believe he was in any mortal danger."

"But you left him unattended?"

"I believe, sir, I just told you that we did."

"Where the hell were you?"

"Serving your dinner, sir. Where the hell were you?"

I begin uncovering more of him. I want to see his hands and wrists and feet. But Abis stays me with his powerful grip.

"I want to see the rest of him."

"Why, Manny-man? He is dead now. Give him dignities."

"I want to see the rest of him." I snatch my wrists from Abis's grasp.

He grabs me again. This time more forcibly. I try to push him aside. Hume shoves me backward, very hard. Abis grabs me from behind. I feel the roughness of his morning stubble against the back of my neck as he wrestles me aside. Hume grabs my shoulders. I reach out and grab at the rubbery substance of his false face. It gives way to reveal once again the full horror behind the façade.

I yell, "No!" but they wrestle me out of the room and into the hall. Hume roars and kicks the door shut with the side of his shoe. Desperately, pathetically I stretch my fingertips toward the doorknob, shouting, "Stop it, both of you! I want to see him now! I've got to see his toes! His toes!"

\*\*\*

I wake up in my own bed, then, alone. The lights are on in the room. Outside the window, it's dark. My body feels so heavy that I can't seem to lift it off the mattress. So I roll to the side of the bed, then slide my feet to the floor and try to stand.

I fail. Two times. I had no idea I would feel so woozy. They must have me on sedatives. Or powerful Class II drugs. I suppose I can't blame them for that, but it makes me feel as if I'm in a boat on the open sea. The room pitches and yaws. I'm seasick, holding onto the bed, then crawling along the floor, inching my way to my feet by using the wall. I lean against it until I feel steady enough to go on.

Now what? I'm fully clothed. They hadn't bothered to undress me. I hold onto the doorknob until I feel some strength coming back into me, and the vertigo abate. Then stealthily, I open the door and on unsteady pinions feel my way along the wall to the hallway, moving through the thick, palpable, visible dark.

I'm pretty sure I'm moving toward the door of the big bedroom, but I must stop many times and hold onto the wall as wave after wave of nausea and dizziness lift me up and set me down. At the crests all I can do is stand perfectly still and pray until they lessen. Thankfully, each crest is less severe than the one preceding it.

My senses are so out of kilter I have no idea how long it takes me to reach the light switch or even how long I rest on the floor under it before the throbbing pain in my ribs subsides enough to let me stretch out my hand to turn out the light.

I'm less dizzy in the dark and feel well enough to try my plan. Quietly. No sense alerting the guards, if there are any, that I'm up and on the loose. I try the door. It's unlocked and just like that I'm in the hallway, straining to pick up a scent or sound or any sign of life. But nothing seems to penetrate this dark. My vertigo's so bad I cannot even sense direction. It's as if I were submerged in a tank of body-warm ink and spun slowly about in all directions, all dimensions.

My only reference point is the wall. I'm afraid to let it go. Is this the terror of the blind? No, only the terror of the newly blind. That's a comfort. I move forward, or rather sideways, like a crab. With my fingers lightly touching the paneling, one foot slides out, parallel to the wall, then both hands slide along the wall in the same direction. My other foot follows until shoe clicks shoe. Next, the lead foot slides out again to repeat the process in a grotesque parody of dancing.

Where in hell am I dancing to? Are those voices? Or just modulated sounds? They're so far off, and so muffled, it's as if they come to me from behind closed doors. Are those scuffling feet? I keep moving through the unrelenting dark toward the unclear sounds.

My fingers disclose that the wall has come to an end. Or at least it proceeds no further in the direction I am traveling in. I slide one foot to the edge until my fingertips curl around the corner, then I grip the edge with both hands and peer around.

Far off in the distance, almost hugging the floor, is a single, glowing bar of light about the length of a thin, dim, neon tube. I move toward it as if it were my single goal in life and as I approach the neon light, it becomes the crack between a door and the floor. Sliding only one hand now along the wall, I hasten toward the light. And soon I do not have to hold onto the wall at all.

The nearer I get to the door, the more I have the impression that the sounds I heard, and am hearing now, are truly voices. Still the words are indistinct. On the other hand, those other sounds are definitely footsteps and scuffles. There is no doubt about it now. They're as real as the whispered voices, and I move closer. But the meaning of the words is still beyond the threshold of my comprehension.

I move closer still. I can almost understand a word or two. It's so frustrating. Do I recognize the voices? I want so desperately to understand. But it seems the closer I get the farther out of reach the comprehension. God, I want so desperately to understand. To know. Despite the lingering dizziness, and the inability to focus I attempt running to the door.

I fail.

Maybe it's for the best. It's easier just to stay on the floor and crawl. The floor is my faith and I rely on it until I arrive and press my ear to the door so hard my cheekbone aches. Still I can't comprehend one word. I try to peer under the door. This is futile, of course. The crack is always below eye level, no matter what position I try. A strange, sweet fragrance like ripe honeydew wafts out of the room. Maybe its marijuana. I breathe it in.

I remain there on my hands and knees. My fingertips are visible now in the light from the crack under the door. The voices in the room are almost comprehensible and I concentrate so hard on them I almost stop breathing. But it works! Suddenly the murmuring voices resolve themselves into comprehensive speech.

It's Diana. And Abis. And someone else. Dear God, could it be? My stomach churns. I feel cold. And so scared. Yet for all I'm worth I press so hard against the door my ear begins to burn and make a crackling noise in my head that thrills through my whole body like a shiver. Even so I'm compelled to press even harder. So hard, in fact, that it is painful and interferes with my hearing. But I can't help myself. I want to push my ear right through to the other side, to the room beyond, to become all ears, so to speak, and to *know*, without being seen or perceived in any way. So I listen with such intensity it seems my soul will wrench out from my body. And I hear the third voice speaking.

It says, "So what do you propose? Either of you? Attis? Cybele? I mean now that we have another body to contend with."

Without trace of any accent, save my own, Abis says, "And what of the other?"

They're deciding my fate in that room! Planning how to do away with me!

One of them is coming near the door! My heart begins to pound so hard I hear it thump against my breastbone. My hair is wet with perspiration and the skin on my back is tingling. I want to run away but I cannot move! I can't control my arms or legs, or even catch my breath. They'll hear me soon! They'll fling this door open and discover me cowering on the floor, burying my head in the tile!

Then the footsteps go away, cross back, and go away again. He's pacing! Not going to the door at all. I'm saved. By his footsteps I can tell he's a huge man, a heavy man. Up and down he paces. Up and down. Like my towering nausea.

"What do you propose to do with him?" he repeats. "I still await your suggestions."

His voice is deep, sonorous, and thrilling.

Diana says, "Well, we can't keep him sleeping forever."

"Actually, we can."

So they are talking about me. Or are they? Who else could they have given narcotics to? But of course, to Benedict! They were trying to fool me about his death. That explains why they wouldn't let me look at him too closely. My God, he's alive! But why should they do that? What would be their motive?

No, it's only a story I'm making up in my head, like the dream I used to have when I was a kid about my dad, that he wasn't really dead, but only on an airplane, and would soon come back to me, down the ramp, waving, then hugging me. But always in the next frame, he was gone again, and I was alone in my dream, and crying.

Well, now I've done it. I've lost my concentration and missed some of their conversation. When I listen in again, Abis is suggesting. "Ship him home?"

"Yes, that's it," I say to myself, "ship me home."

"Then you're giving up? Seems hardly fair."

I hear a shuffling of feet. No one says a word. No one breathes. He must be making some sort of gesture. A nod, perhaps, or a shrug of the shoulders. Then Diana says, "Attis?"

Abis says, "He can go back to the mainland, too. Ship them both back home. It's no use. Too late. We can do nothing for him now."

"Not too late. Not for him. Any of them. Really."

Diana says, "What about you?"

The deep voice says, "What about me?"

"You are my husband."

"I cannot be your husband. I am not a physical man. Let him perform those rites for you."

My jaw drops open involuntarily. My forehead hits the tiles of the floor. Immediately I hear some mumbling, then some scuffling and pacing footfalls toward the door. They're lighter now. Less ponderous.

Oh, God, what have I done? What have I gotten myself into? Who have I sinned against this time?

And then the light! The horrible light! I try to hide from it, to bury my head inside the bathroom tiles. A thud. And pain as the door bangs my skull. I cry out in the light and turn over on my back like a bug. Oh, God, I'm scared! But I look up and squint at the horrible light!

Abis, I think, stands over me in the open doorway. All I can really see is his silhouette, a looming loss of light like a partial eclipse. Even so I can't stand all the illumination that is left to me and I cower in shame. In mortification. In dread. And the horrible pain in my head. Covering my face with the crooks of my elbows. Turning on my side and trying to tuck my knees up to my chin.

But it doesn't seem to help anymore.

"Look who's wakened from the seven sleeper's den."

He continues standing over me.

I uncover my eyes and try opening them all the way. I didn't even realize just how tightly shut they have been. My body's still supine. I turn my head and try to look at him, squinting like a myopic. But even with that I have to cover my eyes again with both arms. The pain is like having an ulcerated cornea.

He helps me to my feet and brings me forward, guiding me and holding me up when I want to be down. Each one of his hands is under each of my armpits. I pity him because I am sweating so much.

He removes one hand. Apparently to make a gesture, because immediately the room becomes darker. When I dare to open my eyes again, all but one of the lights in the room has been extinguished.

Abis lets me go. Weak in the legs, I go down on one knee and look about in the gloom. In the darkness. Transparent darkness. My eyes can penetrate it with little pain, though I want to be blind.

Diana stands before me now. Her hair is unpinned and free to move with any wind. But the air is stifling and her hair drapes down to her shoulders and her thin, gauzy gown drapes over her slim body like a stage costume. She wears a headdress that must be a part of the same costume, for it's like the clothing of the women of the frescos of the library wall.

I wish there were more air in the room. I feel nauseous. But I try to think rationally. These people will probably kill me as they did Coach Benedict. But why are they trying to make a fool of me as well? I can't give in. I must fight the fear as I did when Sara was dying. But my heart is beating so fast. The moment is come. I can't put it off any longer. I have to ask the eternal question. So I take one deep breath and finally do. "Who is he?"

"I," the seated one says, "speak for myself. Look at me."

"I can't. The light."

But it isn't the light.

"And yet we cannot make it any dimmer for you. You would not see at all."

"Oh, sir, it's me," I say. My voice is cracking. "I'm sure it's me. My eyes. Did you give me drugs?"

"No. You are as you came to us. Unaltered now by chemicals. Or anything else."

"But my eyes are so sensitive. I'm so sorry, but it's not my fault."

I take in another sip of air and savor it, trying to force my voice to sound calm. I can't. But I ask my question anyway: "Are you William Love?"

"I am."

"Please, sir, let me go. I just want to go home. And work on my book. I won't tell anyone about anything that happened here, or about you, or anything. I swear. Oh, please, sir. Please don't kill me. I know nothing."

He laughs heartily. "If the length of your life depended upon what you know, and what you need to know, Mr. Markovitz, you, like everyone else, would be immortal."

This hurts my feelings. But already I am on my knees, trying to look up at him, which I can't do. All I can manage is to stare down at the ground.

His sonorous voice is as deep as a lion's purr. It seems to penetrate my very soul. Each word is as distinct as a Shakespearean actor's. Yet I hear him indistinctly. Like a memory.

He demands, "What know you of me?"

"Please, sir, let me go. Choose someone else."

"Answer my question."

"Only what I've been told."

"And what have you been told?"

"No. That isn't true. Only what I've guessed."

"And have you guessed right?"

"I guess not." I feel like a fool. This time I answer, "I know nothing."

He says, "A guess is a guess. And an inadequate bases for a system of philosophy. Even if a system be as delicate and as beautiful as Plato's. My servant Hume could have told you that. Even good reasoning is not always good science. What ought to be seldom is. Science is littered with the debris of good logic. Perfect spheres, perfect circles, perfect nonsense. If your reading, if your understanding, were broader and deeper and more tolerant and less proud, you people would not keep wasting my time or yours trying to reinvent a creation you were meant simply to live in and enjoy. Why try to second-guess me, Mr. Markovitz? Why not simply observe and enjoy? The heavens will not come to you by logic. And surely it will not come to you by Revelation."

"So how can I know? What's left to me?"

"What has always been left to you, time, precious little time, observation and intuition."

I think it is the sound of the laughter he makes. But I can't be sure. I seem to be hearing it all, hearing everything, at a distance beyond my certain comprehension.

"I am here, if I am. What do you want to know? Do you know enough to know you don't know? Do you know enough to ask the right questions?"

I can say nothing. My tongue is stuck to my palate.

We gaze on one another for a very long time. Or rather, he gazes. I gawk. But I can't quite see him for the glare. Finally his great chest heaves in a sigh. "And thus the proof," he says. "Well, do not expect me to simplify the questions at this stage of the game, Manny-man. I have no need to question you. You are the ones with that compulsion. And yet you are incapable of listening when I do speak. The answers would be simple if you were capable. How do you account for it? Stupidity? Lack of will? Attention deficit?"

I sort of hear his words but can't quite comprehend them. It's as if I were back behind the door again. Like a child trying to fit his first jigsaw puzzle. The pieces are the words. I don't really understand the shapes and forms. They are getting in the way. I can't make true sense of it. Partly I don't have the dexterity to fit everything together. My fear is robbing me of my manual skills. And awe is stealing my comprehension.

Time whirls in a different span and I cannot function now in time. I know I'm standing here in front of him. In a dream of him he is waiting for me to speak. I have longed for all this time to ask the eternal questions. Now that I can, I can't. I've been betrayed by my own paltry intellect. I am inadequate. I'm too ignorant. Too unprepared. I don't even know the questions. If I knew them I wouldn't have to ask them. Only great wisdom begets great wisdom and he has chosen a fool to stand in this place before him. Too stupid to know what to ask. And I have been trying for all these years to teach others. Unworthy to even ask. The serpent of my ambition seducing me, squeezing me, to know more than I am ready for. Preying on my desire to know, to hear what I cannot comprehend.

"I am waiting, Manny-man. Will you ask nothing?"

"Please don't hurt me."

"Why do you think I would hurt you?"

I'm startled at this. And mad. Why did I have to spell it out for him? I spell it out for him. "For what I've done to you."

"You done to me? My, my, what a proud little creature you are."

"I beg your pardon, sir?"

"You can do nothing to me, save what I want done. And what I want done I certainly don't need you, or anyone else, to do for me. I'm quite capable of running things."

"But Diana?"

"Here she is Cybele. What about her?"

"We, that is, she, violated her vows."

"She has kept her vows. She has always kept her vows."

"But isn't she your wife?"

"Oh. I see. Well, if she's anyone's wife, she's yours."

"My wife?"

"But she isn't," he adds. "She can't be. She hasn't the time."

Diana laughs bitterly. She sits down by his chair, her elbow resting on his knee.

"But we...."

"Ah, that. Well, you have your own sense of ethics. Self-imposed. Unauthorized. Without religion, and without good authority. Certainly not the authority of self-examination. Pity you didn't listen more closely to Hume. Or even Benedict. You know what Socrates said of the unexamined life? You prefer the translation, 'unaware life?' I do."

"Never mind me, damn it. I don't want to examine my life. I want to know about you."

He laughs. "The way in is the way out."

"What's that supposed to mean?"

He shifts his great body in the chair, smiles and says, "What do you want to know about me that you either do not know already or do not need to know?"

"For starters, what do you do?"

"I run things here."

"Why did you bring me to this island."

"I did not bring you here. People are always saying I did things when they know perfectly well I did not. You came of your own accord."

"You sent Abis to bring me here, sir."

"Here he is Attis."

"And that's another thing I want to talk about," I say, falling into his trap and going off on another tangent. "Why is his name always changing? What's his real name, anyway?"

"He stands here before you. Ask him."

I turn to Abis.

"Yes, old chap," he says in an accent exactly like Hume's.

"Well, what is it?"

"Whatever you want it to be, Manny-man, or Manny, Emanuel, man-man."

"And why the phony accent?"

"Which one?" He laughs. "I gave you what you wanted. What it took for you to be my friend." I wanted to teach you things. Shouldn't a body try to get something into your thick skull? But Manny, Manny-man, man-man, you always seem to get off the subject. Where was I?"

A pause. Then he says, "Well, here I am Attis of Athens."

"That's your real name?"

"Here. Yes."

"I don't believe you."

"Ahh. Well the answer then is 'no.'"

"What were you doing at Delphi?"

"Listening to the oracle. I try to do so every few millennia or so. She left you a message, by the way."

"Oh, really? What was that?"

"Oh, dear, dear, dear," he says in that affected British clip, "I don't think you're ready to know."

I take a deep breath. I'm getting confused again. Every time I get close to asking the right questions, they get me off the subject. I take a different tack. Sounding a bit affected myself, "Benedict says you are all involved in Cybele worship, and that it's unspeakably evil."

Diana says, "I could hardly worship myself, could I, Manny?

"You're not a goddess."

Her head tilts slightly.

"I mean, you are not Cybele."

She shrugs.

"No more than Abis is Attis."

"And I am not Willy Love."

"Oh, yes, you're William Love, all right. That I can believe."

Love says, "You have no religion and you have no moral authority. No self-examination. Yet you persist in examining others. And, lo and behold, you come to conclusions."

But I'm not listening to him. I'm too damn mad. They're trying to put me off again, trying to get stuck on the subject of me. Putting me off about Benedict. About Love. I say, "I will get to the bottom of all this. You know that, don't you? I mean, as soon as I free myself of whatever you've injected me with. I am going to find out what really happened to Benedict. You can count on that."

"You already know what happened to Benedict. He died. It's not unusual."

With that I get even madder and decide to show them then and there what I'm really made of. I turn on my heels to leave. But my foot goes out from under me and I fall right to the floor as ridiculously as that T.V. comic who's always slipping on imaginary banana peels. I feel the impact but not the pain. Then everything is dark again.

# TWENTY-FOUR

I wake in my own room, which they seem to have redecorated and freshly painted while I was asleep. The paint odor is pervasive. As I sit up to inspect more closely, I realize just how sore the muscles of both my upper arms are; it's as if I've been given a pair of tetanus shots. Other than that, and the fact that my face is swollen from too much sleep, I feel remarkably well. How long have I been sleeping?

The sun shines brightly, through I wish it were night. If I'm going to carry out my plans, vague as they are, I'll have to do it under cover. All I can do now is bide my time. Then I can sneak out and try to find out what really happened to Benedict. I owe him that. I don't believe there's a mass grave out there. But there must be something that made him so afraid. Something that cost him his life.

The western breeze blows in through the open terrace door with a hint of autumn chill. The seasons are turning back upon themselves again. The change continuing in the same old way. I rise to shut it out and through the window see the children of the digs playing. Digging up their bones. It reminds me of the lines of an old poem,
"My father's bones are my bones, too.
And I am something, something."
I think it's from Shelly, or one of those modernists.

The students' laughter is like the peels of children. I imagine what it would be like to be in my own living room, listening to my own children playing in the yard. If I had children. If Sara had been well. If she had lived. Dreams, too, can break a heart.

At this distance, their once sensual, khaki-colored bodies are only indistinct, androgynous forms. A tall, slim figure in khaki uniform is standing over them. It could only be Diana, their Goddess of the hunt.

Behind me Hume says, "My, what a nasty bruise you've received."

I turn and look him in the eye. "Almost as nasty as the bruise Benedict got?"

Hume sets the tray down on the table. "Hardly sir. His was fatal. Yours hardly knocked any sense into you."

"You're right. This is ridiculous, isn't it? Here I am thinking the worst of you, all of you, and here you are, being nothing but kind. Handing me coffee, thank you, in hand-painted china cups. Please accept my apologies."

He gives a slight nod. "Indeed, sir, one would say your attitude had been, shall we say, less than estimable. No, let us call it for what it is. Shitty. I mean, really, sir, look around, for God's sake. Do you not realize how you have been blessed? You are in paradise, the earth, and enjoying your only immortality, your mortal life. And here you are, letting the blessing pass you by because you are too busy looking on the underside for crawling things underneath the rug."

He uncovers the breakfast plate. I smile at him, nod, and eat.

"You have this life, Mr. Markovitz. And little time within it. Didn't your wife's death teach you that? Enjoy the time you have left. Enjoy your short eternity."

I tense up again. "Is that a warning or a threat?"

He sighs. "Sir, quite frankly, you are not important enough to harm. No one would bother. Except yourself. I merely wanted to point out that the earth is not ours. Nor are our bodies. They are only loaned out of the elements of the universe. 'Men and boughs break,' as the poet says, sir. 'Praise life as you walk or wake. It is only lent.' We own nothing. We merely borrow and pay back. In a fleeting instant. The elements that make up your body made up the bodies of our ancestors and, shall make up the bodies or our progeny. Every third breath you take contains at least one atom once breathed by Jesus, Moses, Mohammed, Buddha, and Hitler, sir. Every third breath contains an atom that once comprised the shit of your worst enemy. The elements of every person, every race and nation enter into us minute by minute and become for a time a part of you. And some will remain a part of you until you die and your decaying body releases them once again into mother earth to be resurrected and become a part of the following generations. Do you believe in God, sir?"

"Certainly not an Omnipotent One, Hume. That's a hard concept for me to swallow anymore. I've spent too much time in the halls of a cancer ward. If God is omnipotent, then He is, as Randolph Churchill said, a shit. Even Hitler couldn't do worse."

Hume straightens out and looks about. "I believe in God. I see His manifestations everywhere. On this island. In the rain. And in you. I believe God is what is. But I do not believe we were put on earth by God. That is my definition of Him. I believe we are created here, ultimately, out of stardust, by God in His manifestations. And we are here for so little time. For what? To share the earth with each other and enjoy the God-given rain and the God-given sun, and the God-given others of this earth."

I say nothing, just fold my napkin.

His next move is extraordinary. Just as I finish eating, he sits down in the chair next to me and removes his mask. He leans forward for me to get a close-up look at his burned, stretched skin that has healed into shining pink-and-white vacancies of flesh. And suddenly I realize this isn't horrible. It has its own form of plastic beauty, hidden beauty, constantly emerging, the beauty of creation.

His false face gone, I smile at him and hand him the other coffee cup. He fills it, lifts the rim to the shiny, burned accretion of scar tissue that forms his lips, and with much difficulty, drinks. I have never seen him try to suffer meat or drink before. It is an extraordinary treasure.

He smiles his smile and says, "We have enough burdens imposed on us, sir. Why add to them with self-imposed sorrows?" He stands, strolls over to the terrace, spreads his great arms out like angel's wings, and brings them down to rest ever so lightly on the terrace balustrade.

I'm drawn to his side like iron to loadstone. Together we survey the bright flowers of the garden. In the formal part they are arranged in rows like stripes the same colors and design as the canvas canopies that cover the digs and the deck of Mr. Love's launch.

Looking out at the formal rows or flowers, Hume says, "We have subdued nature far more than we have civilized ourselves. And corrupted it. Forming the word. And making it into corrupting flesh."

"I'm not following you at all."

He smiles his smile. "In the beginning was the Logos. Plato claimed reality was but an idea, that essence precedes existence. We believe otherwise." He turns to me. "Or nothing at all."

"I'm still not following you. I'm a sociologist. I have no training in philosophy."

"Then simply look at the garden, Mr. Markovitz, as a child would. Is it not beautiful?"

"Not my kind of garden, Hume, too formal. I just can't appreciate this kind of French formalism. I'm too philosophically opposed."

"Screw your philosophy, Mr. Markovitz, and enjoy the fragrance and the color and the remarkable beauty of the flowers, whatever their form. However they grow."

"Well, I suppose this garden is pretty in its way."

"It is beautiful, Mr. Markovitz. Exquisitely beautiful in its own way. In the way that it is. That is God, Mr. Markovitz, in the way that it is. Enjoy it, sir. Breathe in the fragrance and love it as it is. It is part of our eternity. The only manifestation of God we can ever know. A garden whose form you philosophically oppose is far more beautiful than the dust from whence the flowers and their fragrance came and to which they will return. Enjoy them while you can. Neither you nor they will be here long. And that is not a treat, sir, merely an Old Testament style prophecy. Meaning, not long as we measure things."

"I suppose you're right. Nothing lasts, does it?"

"Nothing needs to. Everything born is born to die. We make progress. But we still die. Slowly. By degree. Or violently and suddenly and painfully. With dignity or without. In shame or in heroism. Whatever the means. By natural causes or unnatural. Life is terrible. Life is wonderful.

You have seen the savage fury of cancer. Do you call that natural death? And if we escape disease? If we survive the danger and the misery of this world, we still grow old and die."

"That's the point, Hume. The point is death."

"Oh, no, sir. The point is life. And in the farther reach, transcendence. What I am telling you is this; the spirit has such difficulty becoming flesh. Applaud the effort, the effect, no matter the form. Applaud the magnificent results."

He backs away, toward the open door.

"Wait, Hume."

"Yes?"

"What are you people going to do with me?"

"Do with you? Has any of us treated you with anything but kindness and respect?"

"But I have this terrible feeling you are out to get me somehow."

"Perhaps sometimes it is good to trust your paranoia. Especially if you're a politician or a king. But in most instances by far, and most certainly in your present one, the only one out to get you, sir, is you. Or, if you prefer the metaphor, the only one out to get you is God. And, God bless Him, He will get you, as we have already pointed out. So you might as well cheer up. When He does, more likely than not, He will do so in a loathsome manner, robbing you of the dignity you think you deserve. All any of us can do is enjoy the time we have between then and now, sir."

He starts to leave again, but stops in the door way.

"Oh, by the way, I almost forgot the main reason I came. Mr. Love will grant you an audience today."

"He will? When?"

He looks at his watch. "In two hours."

***

As soon as Hume closes the door behind himself, I actually turn to the mirror and say aloud, "My God, I must be dreaming! William Love in two hours! What will I wear? I don't have much to choose from. White. That's the ticket. Dazzling white. White duck pants, white shirt, white socks and white canvas shoes. Besides, that's all I have that's clean. I have to be clean.

I put on the pants and shirt, but can't find any socks. I'll have to borrow a pair from Abis. I hate to ask him, but this is desperation time. No other way. I have to appear my best when I confront William Love. So I run down the hall barefooted, holding onto my canvas shoes. As I knock on his door, I'm thinking, "God, you've got to be in. Please. Please."

I knock again, louder. No answer. Again. No answer. Might as well just help myself. As I fling open his door to search his drawers, I find myself mumbling, "Oh, oh, excuse me," when I discover one of the students in Abis's bed. She is lying on her voluptuous stomach, naked, moist as a jellyfish.

She casually turns on her side to face me, making absolutely no effort whatsoever to cover her nudity.

"I, um, um..."

"Want me?" she says, finishing my sentence with a verb and predicate nominative not in my current vocabulary.

"Well, I, I mean, that is, actually, it was Abis I wanted."

"Oh?"

"No, no, I uh, I mean, that is, to uh, borrow a pair of socks."

"Borrow my bod," she mock-whispers.

"Well, that's very sweet of you to offer, I'm sure, but, um, no, really, I've got this rather important business meeting in a few minutes and I really do need, um, white socks."

She makes an exaggerated pout and a sort of shimmying maneuver that makes her breasts shake and sway with incredible momentum. It occurs to me instantly that such a gesture somewhere in humanity's distant past by a woman of similar physical endowments may well have given birth to the by now familiar term, "knockers."

While I stand dumbstruck, she rises, goes to a drawer, reaches in, and tosses me a nearly weightless, black, fuzzy ball. Upon inspection, it turns out to be a wadded pair of socks. "Thank you very much."

"You're very welcome. Now, let's do it." She shakes her nether parts, which do well by shaking.

I blink hard, smile, and back away toward the door, holding the now unfolded socks up as if they were the Golden Fleece and she, the well-known priestess of Hecate.

"Honest," she says, and moves one eyebrow up, "he won't be back for at least twenty minutes. That should be plenty of time for a man like you."

"Thanks again for the socks. I'll, I'll be going now." I back into the hallway, bowing and scraping repeatedly all the way. Then turn around abruptly and smash right into Abis's chest.

"Hey, Manny-man, so this is where you are."

"I was, uh, looking for white socks," I tell him, holding up the unfolded black ones like two dead fish. "To, um, go with these shoes." I point to my bare feet. "Oh, and by the way, you have a visitor in your room. And she's stark naked."

"Virginia? Ha, ha, funny name for her. I have left her there on purpose to get more wine. Look, Manny-man, two gorgeous bottles."

He wages them in front of my eyes. "Also because I needed a break. You know what I am meaning? He rubs his crotch. "Not so young as I used t be. Seven, eight, ten times, is now tops for me. Then I need a five minute break. And wine. Get sore."

He peers through the doorway, grins, wags the bottles three times with one hand, holds up one finger, then pulls me aside and whispers, "She is a killer, Manny-man. Tell you what, there is plenty of room in those pants for both of us, eh? Eh?"

"No, Abis, I can't."

"Nooooooo! Abis did not know this! Diana never, never revealed this terrible secret to Abis. Never! Oh, this sucks mud through a straw, Manny-man. No get up and grow? How did you break it?"

"No, no, wait, Abis, I don't mean I can't. Really. I, I can. But I can't. I, I mean, I haven't the time right now. I've been granted an audience! With William Love!"

He squints first, then shrugs, then says, "Oh, this is great, Manny-man, great! This is the very thing you wanted! No? But wait, when will you be doing this?"

"In about an hour and a half!"

"Plenty of time, Mann-man. Go in. Have Virginia, three times! Here, Abis will wait out on the terrace. No, no, wait, I will watch! Abis is always wanting to learn new tricks."

"Abis, I'm crazy enough already about this interview. I've got to get prepared."

"Hey, man-man, why are you so nervous? It is just a talk with Willy, not Santy Claus."

"I need to prepare what to say. What to ask."

"It is okay, man-man. He will tell you what to ask. Love is plenty good for that. So. Now that is settled. What will you do, huh? Pace the floor for the next hour? Come with me. Abis will get you real relaxed and ready, set, go. Come, I will take you to his old house. You will look about. Take what you can use from there and bring it back here. Abis will give you the grand central tour. We will ask Diana, too. Come!" He grabs me by the left elbow and begins to lead me away.

As usual, I shuffle forward like a zombie. But after a few paces, I stop, then squirm away. "No. Not this time. I don't want to see her now."

"Who?"

"Diana."

"It is okay donkey, Manny-man. Abis will protect you like I always do. She will not bite you anywhere you do not want to be bitten."

"Not just yet."

"Ptah. I spit. You are such a coward. Always a coward. You are a smart guy, Manny-man. You tell me, why does Abis always must have to work with assholes?"

"Everybody has to work with assholes."

"What? You are right! Even God has to work with assholes. This is right?"

"Nothing but. Unless you mean the angels. And, if Milton is right, probably some of them. Why does Diana have to go to the old house with us?"

"Hmmm, ah, it is because it is she who has the keys to the kingdom, Manny-man. You do not think here everyone is trusted with the keys?"

"Couldn't we just get the key from her?"

He grins. "Okay, sure. That is what we will do, wickedly-split."

He takes me back to my room where I dress, then leads me out to the edge of the digs. Diana is standing over the workers, supervising as usual, wearing a loose, khaki jumpsuit and construction helmet cocked to one side. I stop ten feet behind her but Abis strolls right up without breaking stride or looking back at me. I can hear in the wind their murmuring. They both stride over to where I stand. I take both her hands and we kiss. "So," she says, "You want to see the old house of David, huh? Good. Abis tells me William Love will be seeing you today. Also good. Maybe straighten a few things out."

Together they lead me down the garden path to the old house.

# TWENTY-FIVE

The old mansion is more like the one I would have expected William Love to live in rather than that spare and sterile hotel dwelling on the cliff. The roof is red Mediterranean tile. The exterior walls, white stucco. Large, old-fashioned, diamond-pained windows overlook the sea. It looks like one of those old millionaires' row homes that used to dot Biscayne Bay in Florida before they were demolished to make way for the high rises. Only larger. And as magnificent as I had wanted it to be.

The tiled entrance leads to an enormous hall with wood parquetry floors, polished perfectly, and high, coffered ceilings with hand-carved moldings. The Renaissance and medieval furniture has to be authentic. It has a grand aroma.

"God," I say looking around, "why doesn't he live here?"

"He does," Diana says. "He has never abandoned it. I believe he will eventually reside here exclusively again once the other house is reconverted solely to commercial use. And as quickly as that's going, it should not be too much longer."

"To tell you the truth, it seems as if he lives here full-time now. No musty smell, to say the least, the air conditioner is on full blast, none of the furniture is covered over, and there's no dust anywhere. I mean, it looks like he could walk through that doorway any second."

"Hmm, that Willy, he will not walk through that doorway anytime, Manny-man. Why you think he needs us angels to do his bidding," Abis says, pouring each of us freezing-cold champagne from one of his two bottles into three old fashioned, thin stemmed, wide-mouthed crystal glasses.

As we continue the tour I become more and more amazed. The building is miraculous. "It seems so old," I say. "How do they create that illusion?"

"It is even older than you can only imagine, Manny-man."

"Allow me to translate that Abism for you," Diana offers. "What he means, or what I think he means, is that the place is, more or less, an assemblage."

She slides open a ten foot tall pocket door and we enter another room. "This library, for instance, was salvaged from a demolished manse that formerly sat atop one of the Seven Hills of Rome. Though it is over four centuries old, it happens to be one of the newer sections of the present house."

I look up at all the leather-bound books and say, "here's the real wealth."

Diana nods enthusiastically. "Greatest private collection on earth," she says. We're two pedants on a roll. Abis raises his eyes to the high ceiling, then shakes his head and urges us to continue the tour. "Likewise and also, Manny-man, every room is part of someplace else."

Diana takes me by the arm. "He's right. The pillars of this portico are from a temple of Abraham. These steles are from Egypt. A gift from the old regime. This bronze David was cast directly from the original by Donatello. On the terrace above us is a table from the ruins of Herculon, probably brought there as an antique from Chaldea by some wealthy patrician whose family died in the eruption. The vaulted hallway out that way leads to a man-made grotto partially filled with water. It forms the indoor half of the indoor-outdoor swimming pool, and it's lit from above with oil lamps, now converted to electricity, of course, that date back to King David's time. Wading or swimming through the grotto will lead you to various parts of the house as well as to the indoor section of the pool in the spa area. Continue to the end and you emerge in the outdoor section of the pool"

"It leads down to the sun-lit sea," Abis says, topping off our glasses once again with icy champagne.

As we drink it off, he opens the other bottle. We polish off that bottle, too, and the greater part of a third one he somehow finds. "Indoor part of the pool is just great. It leads to the re-creation room. And the bar, Manny-man."

"He's talking about a small Roman bath," Diana says. "Excavated in the middle east. The outdoor section of the pool is surrounded by an Oriental garden, with genuine Ming, and earlier vases, Han ceramic garden seats, bronze dragons and dogs, turtles and lions guarding the entryways and exits. The concrete pier beyond the garden dates from early Roman times, and until the day it was moved here from the small Mediterranean port where it was built, it had been in constant use for well over two thousand years. When we removed it, we found evidence of an older, wooden pier that had stood on the same site. It was perhaps as old, or older, than the excavations we are making here."

"And it all forevermore is and was in the control of the family of Love, Manny-man. Here, drink up before the bubbles burst forever."

I steal a glance at Diana's watch.

Abis catches me. "No good, Manny-man, always watching the watch. Time goes by without you worrying it along."

"I need to keep my appointment."

"You will," Diana says, gently. "Some appointments you have no choice. We won't let you forget it. Now, do as Abis says. Drink up your champagne. Calm your nerves, and mine as well."

I drink off the glass directly. Abis fills it again, wetting my fingers with the overflow. We drink a toast to William Love, and one to all his houses. Of course I'm already feeling dizzy and sleepy, disorientated, but heartened by the prospects. Abis wanders off to look for his dog.

Instead of returning with his mutt, Abis shows up with wonderful black caviar and toast. As I smear some of the Beluga thinly on the thin, warm crust, something occurs to me. "Hey, wait a minute, somebody's been liv here all 'long!"

Abis snickers. I take this for acquiescence. Diana crooks her finger for me to follow her to the entrance to the grotto. At the edge of the artificial waters she rolls up her pants and removes her shoes.

Abis does likewise. "Come on, Mann-man. Now it is time to reveal to you the whole truth. Show to you the true dweller."

I remove my shoes, too, falling over once in the process. Abis and Diana enter the water and begin wading. It's up to their knees. Reluctantly, as usual, I follow. But when we get about ten feet out from the steps, I say, "I can't go on. 'Tis gettin' too deep. We'll get our clothesies wetty-wetty-wet."

"It's worth it plenty big, Manny-man."

"No, no, no."

"We go on."

"How much deeper?"

"Only halfway up the thigh."

"Too deep."

"Not too deep. Small sacrifice."

"Is this salt water or fresh?"

Abis shrugs. "Taste."

As I bend down to do so, he kicks me hard in the posterior. Suddenly I'm gasping for air, totally immersed in the water. Wallowing like a lemming. Drowning. Trying to reach the pool floor with my feet. But I'm in over my head. He's kicked me over a precipice. Then I realize the water is only up to my eyebrows. I can get air and move forward, too, just as they are doing, by bobbing.

"Salt or fresh, Manny?"

"Forgot t'taste."

In a few yards, the water starts to become more shallow again. We all begin to wade. Diana is in front of me. Abis behind. But no sooner do I relax when the water is again up to my neck.

"Damn it, Abis, you said th' water'd only come up to my thigh."

"You must grow, Manny-man. No big deal. Okay I lied. We must blame it on my tongue. He lives in a very wet place. It is easy for him to slip. No, no, wait, I do not lie! The water is truly only up to the middle of the thigh. But not your thigh."

"Whose, the Cyclopes'seses?"

"Hmm, God's thigh. He is way bigger than you. Wrestle him and you got big problems."

The last bottle of champagne floats before us like the stiff carcass of a small animal. When Abis's wake hits it, the bottle gurgles a few times, bubbles, turns bottoms up and goes down. Caviar and soggy toast spread before us in the water. It looks like an open sewer. It smells a like an open sewer that someone dumped fish eggs into.

Diana swims next to me. Her limp, wet hair nearly covers her face. She tries to smooth it out of her eyes, but is unsuccessful. So she dips her head back into the water. This helps, except now she has fish eggs in her hair. I realize that I, too, have caviar sticking to me. She submerges herself completely, then shoots up, spilling water like a naiad of the ocean spray. When she catches her breath, she says, "Fresh water," and squeezes out her long, long tresses. "Manny, you should get some of those fish eggs off your face."

"I can't dunk my head completely under water. Wooden come uppence."

"It is like a womb on a windy night," Abis says.

"Wha's that supposed to mean?"

We push forward. The water is now only up to our waists. Abis shrugs. "Never done this before."

I push him. He falls forward, scrambles to his feet and pushes me. Soon we're all three thrashing about, laughing and gulping in water with bits of wasted caviar in it. When we tire of our sport we wade out. Diana leads us up some steps into a darkened room and an artificial, starlit night sky. I'm guessing it's a planetarium, an enormous, private planetarium. Soon a tiny but powerfully bright artificial moon rises over the silhouette of an ancient city, whether based on the skyline of a real or imagined one, I don't know.

We seem to be standing on the concrete shore of a concrete beach, almost completely covered over with a thin layer of real beach sand.

A deep, sonorous voice booms out, "Look at you! All of you!"

We are a sight: wrinkled, dirty, sand-covered animals smelling of stale alcohol and smeared fish eggs.

"And one hour late, besides!"

"You and you. Go on now. Get dressed again. Clean up."

"I have an excuse," Abis says. "We are very, very drunk."

"Go now."

Abis and Diana quickly leave his presence. I straighten my back, shiver a bit and fall flat on my face and barf before getting to one knee. I'm dizzy, disheveled, drunk, dirty, frightened, and alone.

He nods subtly in the direction of a chair. I sit in it. His movements seem so awkward, as if he were an amateur's marionette. The lower half of his body, tightly covered by a lap quilt, does not move at all. His seat is on the raised platform that supports the control panel and the machine that projects the heavens. He looks intently at my face and, I think for just a faint moment, actually smiles down upon me. It could just be a trick of the light, the shadow of his artificial moon and the dim red glow of his control panel.

His face seems worn. Not like Hume's, but more like the sea worm eaten statues in the basement of the Athens museum.

He does smile then. No doubt about it. The lap quilt drops to the floor. At once I understand. He's paralyzed from the hips down. His flesh is wasted away and useless. With all his powers he is bound and unable.

He says, "This canopy, this place, is my passion. My own tiny universe. I create the stars and move them about in their higher spheres. Here is no beginning and no end. Here, as out there, in the outside universe. Knowledge is intuitive, not logical. I believe my servant, Hume, tried to tell you so. I can move my stars and my little cosmos forward or backward. It makes no difference to me, save my penchant for order. And so I keep the arrow of time moving forward. Out there, too, in my larger universe as well. Let us say I pretend the harmony I keep is reflective, is important, and keeps the nearly countless, except of course, to me in my imagination, inhabitants of my universe secure, happy, and religious."

"Religious, sir?"

"The stars in their due course give my imaginary souls something to count on, something to believe in, namely order in the universe. Hope of a predicable future. The avoidance of nasty surprises in the macrocosm and the anxiety they would cause. The future variables in their own personal lives are nasty enough, but I don't have to tell you that, without having to worry about the regularity of the stars, don't you think?"

"Sir, I, I don't know what to think."

"I thought you were the one who liked to create conundrums, Mr. Markovitz. Isn't that what you have been trying to do ever since you came here?

"I don't think I know what you mean."

"Let me pose a parable to you. Should you riddle it out, I promise that your own personal problems will be solved and you will be able to return home tinged, ever so slightly, by wisdom. Braised by the fires like a good beef steak. Here it is: Somewhere out there among the temporary stars a mad man is thinking, 'life's unfair. You eat right, avoid sin, get plenty of rest, and still God gives you a hard time. What does God want? Why won't He say? Why won't He show Himself? The stars move about with such order and precision. Why won't my life do the same?' Now, how do I answer the mad man?

"I guess you tell him to do what God said to Job, to keep his mouth shut and just do his work," I answer.

"But the Book of Job is merely a parable. In this case, a parable inside a parable. What about me, Mr. Markovitz? What about my mythical, my projected reality? My real, so to speak, problems? I speak, but the mad man can't hear me. He doesn't even know for sure I exist. He only suspects that someone is making the stars go 'round."

"Then give him a sign. Turn the lights out for a minute. Make the stars stand still for an hour. I don't know. Make them back up a foot or two."

"That would only frighten him and provide no proof of a benevolent one keeping order in the universe. In fact, it might do the opposite. At best, it might ignite scientific speculation in his world, or apocalyptic fervor, but no proof. "

"So I guess you just let things go on in the same old way. Let him infer your existence by the order you keep."

"So I become the order and nothing more. Besides, I don't keep the order. The exquisite machine does that all by itself."

"Wouldn't he infer that you built the machine and made it run?"

"Inference isn't proof. He'd still have to take it on faith. Besides, who says I built the machine?"

"Why not rearrange the stars with your machine to spell your name?"

"Exactly. You catch on fast, Manny-man."

But I don't catch on at all. So after a long pause, I say, "So there's nothing you can do for him? No way you can allay his fears or answer his doubts?"

"I don't have the answers. And he's asking the wrong questions, anyway. He's on the wrong track. You see, Mr. Markovitz, you've come to the crux of the problem. I'm too big for him to see. The only way he has of knowing me is by inference. And he has made the wrong inference. He says, 'my universe is orderly, therefore someone must be running the show.' But am I not independent of the show? I am trying to help, but all I seem to be able to do is keep the machine running as long as I can and allow him to draw false conclusions."

"Why let him blunder on like that?"

"Because his false conclusions at least approximate the truth. Do you understand?"

"No."

"People need regular laws of the universe. Moreover, they expect them. They count on them. They have built around them a hundred thousand scientific, religious, philosophical and psychological systems they must accept as true or become mad men. Look at it from my imaginary mad man's point of view. Let us suppose he is a man of the soil. He has this advantage over mad men of the city such as you, Mr. Markovitz, he observes nature better. His unshod foot feels the grass. It knows the dew and the condition of the blades it trods upon. Your shod foot, Mr. Modern City Man, must rely on agricultural reports, on instruments, to know the state of the earth. His unsophisticated eye sees the movement of the stars in the heavens and what he surmises is being written there by God. To him, a new moon in the old moon's arms is proof of a coming storm. He knows the hours by the position of the sun and the stars, not a glance at his wristwatch. He finds directly in the world of things what you must try to recapture in the world of ideas and machines. He sees and admires trees. You see and admire paintings of trees. Those that live in the world of the imagination, the poets, priests and seers, they are the true intermediaries, they see trees and picture them for you, *n'est pas?*"

"*Oui.* Is there a point of this?"

"Is there point to this? Oh, Mr. Markovitz, you are fun. Yes, of course there is a point. These people observe. And what does my, let us say, imaginary mad man learn by his naked observation? That the universe is orderly. That it moves in great cycles. Days follow days and seasons follows seasons. That is what people count on. A predictable future. It gives them comfort, even if the end of the cycle is death. Which, of course they don't believe in. They expect another cycle. They believe in it. They have faith, the mad men. Belief in the afterlife, the next cycle, allays their most primal fear."

"So what's the problem?"

"That from this inexact observation, this observation of the unobserved, my madman makes another false assumption, seductive in that it seems logical. But logic is not truth."

"So what's the deduction?"

"That if the movements of the stars are regular and recurring, they can predict the future. He confuses the great recurring cycles of time with the linear arrow of time. 'After all,' my madman says to himself, 'the stars predict accurately the four seasons and the coming of hot and cold weather, why not everything else?' He has complete faith in the premise that the general future can be told, which my servant Hume has certainly tried to point out to you, is false. My madman builds all his future deductions upon that false base. He is led in circles following his logical nose. Let me illustrate by predicting your future with perfect, unfailing accuracy, Mr. Markovitz"

"Please do, sir."

"You, Mr. Markovitz, will die. From this time forward you will grow older until you do. Your hair will continue to turn grey and fall out. Your gums will recede, your eyesight diminish."

"Could you be a bit more specific?" I ask. "What do you plan to do with me?"

He laughs. "Always the paranoid. Always the egoist. Ah, but they amount to the same thing. Madness. The point is, I cannot be more specific. If I tried, I would become either a false prophet, or simply a lucky one, which is worse, since it leads to a completely false sense of accomplishment and hubris. In truth, all one can predict is trends, climates, if you like. But what if I did predict your future with exactitude? And what if I were wrong, as I almost certainly would be? Should I then abandon the first premise? Of course not. But I should. After all, I will not know you are going to die for sure until you are actually dead, because there is, of course, always the ever so slight chance that an exception will be made in your case. But were I a betting man, which I'm not in either case, I would bet the other way. If you lose, how could the other side collect?"

"So you don't abandon your first premise. Then what?"

"Then you are in trouble. For the only logical step is to assume you *can* predict the specific future, if only you knew the correct formula."

"Like alchemy," I say. "Like thinking you can change lead into gold if only you can get the recipe right."

"Very good, Manny-man. And remember the other part of the alchemists' dream: if you find the elusive elixir that transmutes changeable lead into immutable gold and drink it, you, too can become unchangeable, immortal. If one truly believes the formula is out there, one is driven like a madman to find the fountain of immortality. And the rallying cry of madmen is 'who knows?'"

"Only the gods, sir."

"And thus you have just formed the madman's third premise, and so all the madmen out there in my little mechanical universe give to their God..."

"That would be you," I interrupt.

"That would be me. They give to their god an attribute beyond even omniscience, the attribute of knowing not just all there is and was, but all that shall be, as well."

"Well, what if our metaphorical god does know the future but simply will not reveal it?"

"Then it amounts to the same thing. We cannot know God, or what God knows, but continually try. We reason by analogy. It is not science. It is not even reason. It is error built upon error. It is non sense. Castles built on foundations of clay. Systems floated on the wind. Sunshine from cucumbers. And so we float, Manny-man, when we should reflect. We float and float and float on vast seas, on flying clouds, all of us, from Alexandria to Zimbabwe. It is error that links us all. We cannot know the God that dwells outside of us without seeing inside, and our idea of God is the worst idea of all. Do you know why? Because people hurt others In God's Name. They lie to themselves In God's Name. They kill in His Sacred Name. What presumption, to think you know the mind of God and dare act accordingly. And what does He do while we are so occupied? Does God cry in impotent rage as we create in the name of the virtue of the Lord His opposite on earth? Does He simply watch in benevolent understanding while we act the devil in the name of God? We have no idea. We cannot know. Because God is the neurons hard-wired inside of us. And yet we are continually preoccupied. Take yourself, for example. Aren't you seeking to hold the wind? Aren't you always making yourself sick trying to be the center of the universe, trying to know the unknown, to know what cannot be known? Looking for the philosopher's stone, the elixir of life? Making and living inside the myth you made yourself, when you can drop all illusions and live in the present and know the knowable? When you can be aware?"

"How am I supposed to know what's knowable and what's not if I don't try? Making mistakes is the only hope I have."

"Hope is a mistake. It's a desire. You went to the oracle of Delphi but you only heard the wind. Did the wind whisper to you, 'know thyself?' Well, never mind, man-man, I merely sit and speculate and watch my machine whirl the stars around. I project theory as easily and inconsequently as the stars are projected onto this domed ceiling. But at least it explains to you why I keep the old machine running in the same old way. It makes me God. This history of this religion I have projected onto my cunning little universe is a movement from idolatry of the stars to worship of the mover of the stars. An attempt to pierce the impiercable veil. The trouble is, out there, in what we are pleased to call the real world, things are not so regular. Mistakes occur and no true miracles. And so, as scientific instruments advance and become accurate enough to reveal the irregularities of nature, why then religion, which is unprepared for even minute change, often recedes only because faith was built on the wrong foundation, namely the insane belief in a regular and orderly universe. But what if God, so to speak, were lame? What if He were just the circumference or the center instead of both? What if He were merely a metaphor? The hard wiring, as I say, of the mind? What if he were on a random current, while we were thinking the current was direct or regularly alternating? What if God did, in fact, play dice with the universe? Physics would be too complicated for the physicists. It may be, anyway. That is why they are always re-measuring."

Sandy Cohen

"You're not telling me what I want to know."
"You're not listening.
"Two things, sir."
"One?"
"Where is Benedict?"
"Home."
"Alive?"
"You know better than that. There are limits, after all. Limits to life."
"What exactly did he die of?"
"We examined his heart."
"What's that supposed to mean?"
"Sorry, I forgot; you're a literal knave. We must speak by the card. An autopsy was not performed, if that's what you mean. There are no doctors on this island. You know that. At least you were told. The people here are sick of doctors. They have seen too much of doctors. They are beyond the considerable skill of the doctors. Even in this modern age doctors cannot stop any illness once it has gotten hold of us. All they can do is try to prevent their taking hold before it's too late. Here is the general law of nature. It has never failed, so far. All doctors lose all of their patients eventually. We shipped Coach Benedict's body back home to his ex-wife in Texas."
"May I get her address? I'll want to pay my respects to the family after I return."
"Hume will bring it to you, though you shall never use it."
"What are you planning to do to me?"
"Is that your third question? I have been trying to tell you, Hume and Diana have been trying to tell you, we are not planning to do anything to or with you. I am merely making an observation based upon my knowledge of human nature, and yours. What you actually do is up to you, is it not? As always, when logic and experience fail, you will end up following your emotions, anyway. Above all, people do what they want to do. While we, and certain members of our household especially, are more than eager for you to stay as our guest for as long as you like, even the rest of your life, however long, or short, that may be, you may, of course, leave us at any time you wish."
"I would like to stay a while longer and find out what's really going on around here."
"You may be uneasy with the truth you learn. Ahh, but we have told you. You have observed. You should have guessed the rest. But you have simply refused to understand. Life is in reality a poem without metaphor."
"I refuse to believe that."
"I know."

242

"What about Diana? Is she your wife?"

"Look at me, Mr. Markovitz. I have no functioning body parts. No physical presence. I'm not here. How can I be husband to anyone."

"You can still be married to her."

"Life is a poem without metaphor."

"No, goddamn it, life hints. Life symbolizes. It suggests. There *is* life beyond the physical. There's love, compassion, hate, virtue, and the seven deadly sins to name a few."

"These are mere functions of the mind, not life. Life is physical. The glorious beating heart. Mr. Markovitz, my mind is connected to my body by its neurons, and in my case, to very few parts of it. But unless you accept a higher consciousness, that is, one higher than your own Cartesian ego, my mind has no connection whatsoever to your body, nor your mind to mine. There is no dialogue, save the paltry, possibly lying, words."

"Yes!" I say, "Yes! The soul expands. It can include others! I am witness!"

"Life is a poem without metaphor."

"Are you married to her or not?"

"What is mine is hers. We have that agreement. Legally and formally. I have no other family or issue. In a sense, she would inherit my estate, yes. Though, of course, I shall be here long after she is gone."

"What's that supposed to mean? Are you planning an accident for her, too?"

"Merely an observation, a prediction, Mr. Markovitz. Based on facts. Based on human statistics. Not a threat."

"I thought you didn't believe in predictions."

"What's not to believe in? A prediction is a prediction, not a foregone conclusion. Like an old testament prophesy: if things go on as they have been, then such and such a result is sure to occur. Mr. Markovitz, Diana is dying. Didn't she tell you that?"

"What do you mean?"

"I mean she is dying. Rapidly. She has cancer."

"I don't believe you."

"But you've surmised.

I take in a deep breath. I have surmised.

"You would be better off believing everything I say."

"And why is that?"

"Because I know *all* about you. Everything. The truth. I am inside of you, Manny-man."

"Such as?"

"Tell me about your wife. Tell me about Diana. Tell me about love."

I feel as though all the blood were draining from my brain. Could everything he has said be true?

"Tell me what you did for Sara. Tell the truth. Tell yourself the truth."

"I, I loved her with all my heart."

"I do not dispute that in the least, Manny-man. But you abandoned her."

"I didn't abandon her; I just couldn't keep her home to die. You know that. I took her to the hospital. What's wrong with that?"

"She begged you to allow her to stay at home."

"She had health care professionals in the hospital to care for her. Doctors and professional nurses."

"She wanted you!"

"She couldn't stay home!"

"Why not?"

"What if she had died there? In my bed? And just the two of us. How could I have gotten help in time?"

"She didn't need help. She was dying. She needed love. She needed you."

"I had to go. Just a four day trip. I didn't know she would die while I was away. Just a four day trip. My grant was running out. The summer was almost up. I had to get my research done. About love. For my book. I didn't abandon her, I didn't, I didn't! They were supposed to call if she took a turn for the worse. She was in a coma then. I did what I had to do. I did the right thing. Everybody said so."

"And where did you do the right thing? In the library?"

My hands go to my face. I begin to cry all over again. I cannot bear to hear it anymore. But his voice keeps droning on and on and on and it is my voice, too, repeating the blood accusation, adding name by name, like drops of blood falling and falling into a stream: "Diana is dying. Hume is dying. All of the children of the digs are dying. All of them are dying. Didn't you know? Didn't you at least suspect? Of course you did. This island is for the dying. That is what it's for. Only I am and shall survive. And I am severed from the body, am I not?"

"Abis too?"

"Abis is my messenger. My summoner, my Hermes out of Maia. He gathers them in to me. And goes on."

"And I?"

"You are dying, too."

"Only if you kill me. Because I feel fine. And Diana is perfectly fine, too. She looks healthy. And beautiful."

"There is no beauty without death."

"We made love."

"Making love is a function of the dying. If it weren't for death there would be no need for sexual congress, would there? Without death there would be no need for love as you know it."

I remember the last time Sara and I made love. She was already beginning to have the pain as her cancer spread to her liver. I remember thinking even then, this is the last time, dear God, we will never make love again."

"Yes," he is murmuring, "yes."

"NO! I'm getting out of here!"

"Man-man, flowers are the sexual organs of plants. No beauty exists on earth without death."

"I'm not listening to you anymore. I don't want to hear this. I'm finding Abis and making him take me out of here!"

"The other possibility is that I am you talking, or thinking or dreaming, you know."

Calmly and rationally I walk out of the pitch-dark room. I hadn't even realized all this time that he had been dimming out the stars. It's as dark as my bedroom in the middle of the night. I grope until I find the door and open it into the searing orange-golden light of the dying day. I start to run. Blinded by the light, I run right into a wall and knock myself out.

# TWENTY-SIX

I'm in a room I've never been in before, sitting upright in a massive chair of dark hardwood, intricately carved with animal figures. The seat and back are upholstered in wild animal hide, maybe giraffe, with the hair side out. On the floor is a lion skin rug. On the other side of it a companion chair faces me, like a mirror image. Sitting in the chair, hands on knees, staring at me intently, is Abis.

"You are back now to the land of the living, Manny-man?"

"What happened?"

"You passed out. Hit wall. Maybe too much wine?"

"Where are we?"

"In the great hallway, man-man. The trophy room. Nice, huh?"

"It's incredible," I answer, looking up and up."

"This is what is called the pole-vaulted ceiling, Manny-man. Like the cathedral in Notre Dammed. It is called that because it is a tribute to Noah's flood, which dammed up the whole world to the armpits in the year 1066. This ceiling goes here nine feet straight up! No, no, wait, it is more than that!"

"Abis, that ceiling has got to be well over fifty feet."

"No, no, wait, it is ninety feet, not nine. This William Love whispered into Abis's own ear many, many years ago, when he first came here. It is curved like Cupid's bow. Round as Eve's ass. Higher than Scrooge McDucks's money dome. It is the trophy room. Look how it is built like an upside down ark, Manny-man, which is the kind of boat God transports animals in. Better shipping than U.S. American post office, FedEx and UPS combined."

"You're right, it is sort of shaped like a capsized boat."

"Bigger than a cap size, Manny-man. This whole hunting lodge was disassembled and shipped here from a place in Africa named Kuala Lumpor. It is a house within a house."

"I don't understand."

He makes a sweeping gesture with his hand. My eyes follow as he points from the high ceiling down to the tops of the bleached oak paneled walls. A myriad of stuffed and mounted animals hangs everywhere. It's strange that I hadn't even noticed them before. I was so overwhelmed by the high, coffered ceiling and my own groggy mental state.

"God, it's a taxidermist's dream," I mutter as I begin to take it all in. Creatures of every sort from all over the world either smile down benevolently, or grimace, snarl, stare, gape, frown, goggle, glare, or glower as they scrutinize the room, and us, through glass eyes.

"Now this is my idea of civilization, Abis," I say as I move across the rich Persian and wild animal skin rugs toward the dark, carved bar to serve myself a gin and tonic. The perfume of old shellac pervades this room, too, like the aroma of a fine antique shop. "The beauty of the wilds without the heat, the bugs and the bother. Nature subdued."

"It is nature whooped," Abis answers quickly and makes a gesture like a baseball umpire making the "out" call.

My eyes instinctively follow where his thumb is pointing. I'm instantly caught, so to speak, and held, by this enormous stuffed billfish.

"Blue Marlin," he says, as if he were looking out of my eyes, monitoring what they see, and making running commentary. "From my home town of Bimini. In the Bahamas. Lots of fish there, Manny-man. Lots of sun and rum. Lots of women with big breasts like coconuts. Out to here."

But I can hardly take my eyes off the fish to see what he is doing. It's the enormous length and girth of the creature that's so awesome.

"Abis, this thing must have weighed over five hundred pounds."

"Six hundred twenty-two, Manny-man."

"Are you sure?"

"Read the prescription on the plaque."

As I move forward a few feet toward the plaque, Abis says, "now look here, Manny-man."

He points to the wall behind me. I turn. My eyes widen. My jaw drops down. I can't believe what I'm seeing. It is so awesome a leviathan, I can't even comprehend.

"Black marlin, Manny."

In general shape, this fish is like the other marlin, but of such size I can't accept that it could have once been real. I step back three more paces, then glance back at the big blue marlin I had first been shown by Abis. Then I look at the leviathan again. And still, I can not comprehend.

For this second fish could easily, easily, have swallowed the first one whole! It's at least three times the size of the other. The leviathan who eats leviathans. The god who eats the gods. The snake that swallowed the snakes of the Pharaoh's magi.

"Black marlin, Manny," Abis repeats, casually. He is obviously enjoying the effect this fish is having on me. "Belly like a whale, Manny-man."

"And a bill like the staff of God," I add, not taking my eyes off it, except in snatches, to look about the place.

Gradually I become aware that this room is filled with other treasures. It must have been some sort of explorer's club in its other life. Below the level of the stuffed beasts, paintings of hunters, dogs and horses line the room. Each wall features at least one oak bookcase carved with scenes of the hunt.

Under the scattered Persian rugs is a parquet floor of teak. Above one ancient Bergamo a great, warped English Tudor library table is laden with great bronze statues of elephants, tigers and other beasts.

On each side of the ponderous doors, prodigious ivory tusks mounted on massive bronze and turned rosewood bases arch majestically. Heavy chairs and Chesterfield sofas, all upholstered in leather, dot the vast landscape. As I sit in one of the chairs, the faint aroma of birch oil and pipe tobacco rises to complete the image I have of being transported to some exclusive English explorers' club of a past century.

In the farthest, darkest corner of the room, in a Morris chair, wearing khaki jodhpurs, tight riding boots and a tailored shirt with epaulets, sits Diana. Abis nods, and leaves the room.

I take her hands. "Is it true?"

"Is what true?"

"About your illness?"

She nods.

"Are you in pain?"

"Not much yet. But soon, they tell me. It may be intense, soon. But not for long."

I feel sick to my stomach and have to sit down. "Let's leave this island. Travel, see as much of the world together as we can."

"No, sweetheart. I've seen a lot of this world, and now I want to stay here. I need to work as long as I can. And then, well, we have the best hospice care in the world right here."

"You mean on this island? How could that be?"

"Haven't you guessed? You finally guessed about my illness, didn't you? Don't you know what this island is? In addition to everything else, it's the land of the dying, Manny. Almost all of us here are dying. The workers out there, even the young ones, most of them, me, Hume, we're all dying. Only a few, like you, and the hospice staff and Abis, of course, and certain chosen others are not. We all came here to do our work, to be involved in this project, do something good and useful and diverting until we are in too much pain, or too impaired to continue. And then we will be cared for physically, emotionally and psychologically by a loving and dedicated staff of men and women trained in the art of natural, easeful death. Some, like you, were brought here for the opposite journey, darling. To come back from the dead, so to speak. To learn to look about you again, instead of backward. To learn, or relearn to enjoy your now, the only eternity we are certain of, that is, life."

"You're sounding like Hume now."

Sandy Cohen

"He's a good influence."

"And he's dying, too?"

She nods.

"And what about Coach Benedict? What really happened there?"

"His death was an accident. His liver was so impaired it made him do some strange things in the end. He fell before his time, I guess you'd say, but he would have fallen anyway, and soon."

"And you?"

"Four months, maybe six."

"I'd like to stay with you, if you'll have me," I say.

"If you really, truly want to stay. I think it would be good for both of us. Come, let's try to talk about something else."

"What else is there?"

"Everything. Let's wander about Love's house for a while. Let me show it to you."

"This is his real house?"

"One of them. He has many others. Many rooms. Many mansions."

"Like the new one across the gardens where we're staying?"

"That one's for commercial purposes, I guess you'd say. This one's his real home here. Where he stays, this house with its many rooms. Each of us has one here."

"But he was there in the other house."

"Who?"

"Love. I saw him there. With Abis. And with you."

Her brows knit tightly. "Me? Oh, darling, you must have been dreaming."

"Maybe so."

She takes my arm. We walk. "Was she afraid when she died?"

"Sara? No. She had more courage facing her own death than I did. I suppose that's why I had such a hard time facing it, and had to put her in a hospital in the end. I couldn't be there. I was so afraid. She had, or obtained somehow, a peace that passed understanding. I suppose it was her faith that sustained her."

"Do you believe in an immortal soul?"

"No, I suppose not. But how would I know? I have no belief in much of anything anymore. Not since walking every day through the children's ward of the hospital to see Sara every day. But I suppose whether we have an immortality or not isn't a matter of logic or belief or faith any more than the existence of other planets with living, thinking beings on them is a matter of logic or belief, or faith, is it? Either they exist or don't exist, whether we believe or posit them or not. Both France and Shangra-la either exist or don't exist whether we believe in them or not."

"I believe we're losing our souls," she says, "whether they exist or not."

"What do you mean?"

"If you don't believe in the concept of the soul, then you've lost it, haven't you? It's gone, lost to you. Whether you really have one or not, if you believe in it, you have it, whether it exists or not. Just like the existence of God. For the past few months I've immersed myself in work. It's been good for me. Immersed in the past, so to speak. I guess in a way I'm becoming my past. It's a kind of reincarnation, becoming your legacy, that is, however small it is."

"Why not give up work and enjoy what time we have left? We could be together and go places and do things while we can."

"Because giving up my work would be giving up hope. The doctors say my cancer has a five percent survival rate. I'd like to hope I'm one of the five in a hundred. I know, I know, the Buddha says hope is another name for desire and we should rid ourselves of desire. But I can't. Keeping up my work not only gives me hope, it staves off reality. Miracle cures happen five times in a hundred and we can't know the future. Besides, what's the difference whether we know our death sentence has been stayed five months or fifty years? The reward of life is always death, and we have such little time during our eternity between birth and death."

"Isn't that even more reason to do what we want while we can?

"We should just follow our hearts, but don't we usually follow our hollow sacrifices instead? We're so addicted to praise, we non-Buddhas. We do what's expected and we live and we die in the passive voice. Lives of quiet desperation. You have to do what you really want to do, too, Manny. What you really feel. Not out of a false sense of duty or loyalty, or love or even guilt. But a true one. For once, you've got to really follow your heart."

"For once, I am. I didn't when my Sara died. It's been my Gehenna. But now I know I really am."

"Come, let's walk out to the digs."

"Looks like a bad thunderstorm's brewing."

"You're made of sterner stuff; you won't melt."

We walk to the abandoned shafts.

"Where is everybody?"

"It's the weekend."

We stop in front of the pit where Benedict died, or began to.

"Manny, do you remember that passage in Dante where Uberti, the man of God with the soul in hell rises from the flames of his own torment with the lid of his grave thrown back, to speak to the poets and give them the experience of revelation?"

Sandy Cohen

"Vaguely."

"He says, 'I wish the souls of the damned would speak to me.' In a few weeks, maybe a month, I'm going to be almost completely bed ridden. Then what?"

"Then I will be there with you."

"This old peasant woman told me once, 'if you live a good life and do what you should, then when your time comes you will be lucky enough to have someone there for you."

"I suppose there's some truth to that. But to me the bottom line is that living a good life is independent of living a lucky one. Too many bastards get lucky for me to think otherwise. No, I'll be with you because you have become me. No 'because,' no 'thank you for doing this' anymore than you would thank your own right hand for scratching your own left shoulder. So, now, no more word about it, okay? I will be here with you, a part of you, as your hand is a part of your wrist."

She takes my arm again. "Well, then, now that we are free, what shall we talk about?" she says as she turns up her collar against the light, misting rain. "Because I really need not to dwell on it."

"All right. Let's talk about how you decided to become an archeologist for a bit."

"When I was an undergraduate, my hero was Heinrich Schliemann. You remember who he was?"

"Second baseman for the Braves, 1947-52?"

"He was an amateur archeologist, an untutored dilettante, the professionals called him. Because he was such a fool, he made one of the most important archeological discoveries of all time. Instead of following the experts he followed Homer and he rediscovered Troy."

"Okay, sure, now I remember. They had a PBS special about him a few years ago."

"While my friends were out partying, I was home in the dorm fascinated by his account of how he followed the clues in *The Odyssey* back to Troy. I simply could not put the book down. Oh, God, how I wanted to be like him. To uncover such a find."

"But weren't his conclusions refuted by the real archeologists?"

"His conclusions, true, but they couldn't refute what he uncovered. He was the real archeologist."

"The PBS show said he was so obsessed with Homer that everything he found had to relate to the story of Troy as Homer told it, even when it obviously didn't. 'The golden mask of Agamemnon,' 'the spear of Achilles,' and all that stuff that wasn't even of that era."

"But that's the whole point, Manny. His monomaniacal devotion to myth-shrouded Homer led him to the real Troy. He didn't know any better than to trust the original. To become a part of it. And it worked! He uncovered himself. His own past. That is what he became. Has become. Arthur Evans at Knossos *was* the last king of Mycenae. That is as real a reincarnation as we can know, to become our metaphors. Imaginary gardens with real toads in them. Or in this case imaginary toads in real gardens. Our lives are devoted to becoming our images of ourselves. We create what we are."

"Even if it's a neurotic image?"

"Yep. This archeological dig here is some day going to rank with Troy and Mycenae. As I'm being involuntarily separated from my flesh, this place will remain as my immortality, my soul. I can't become One with the Great Spirits of my father. I can't believe in an external God, a Wunder-faeder, as my mother did. So I have to create my own soul in my own way. My second soul, if I have another. My only one, if I have no other."

"I don't think that's the way it works."

"It's the only way it works. We all do it, Manny. Only some are more successful than others. Our God is inside of us. And only the dust is immortal, after all."

# TWENTY-SEVEN

The pattern of every normal childhood, every natural death, is the same. William Love, or my dream of him, was right; death is something we count on, though the pain is more bitter by our knowing. Watching someone you love die is like seeing a Greek tragedy whose final scene, whose final outcome, you know too well, and dread, but cannot change. No matter what you do, the drama still unfolds. Agamemnon dies. You know this from the beginning. Though we wish it otherwise with all our hearts, there can be no other ending.

Agamemnon is just a dream. But the pain of his death is real. For Agamemnon is everyone. And so you ache each time he commits the fatal errors, each time he speaks the fatal words and struts upon the fatal tapestries, each time he is proud and disdainful and commits an act of hubris, you and he are one. You wish with all your heart you could stay the execution. But even if you could, it would only be a stay and not the final curtain. It is the doom that finally and inevitably waits on him and all of us, coupled with the fate that we all have made for ourselves.

When it's someone you love with all your heart that is hurtling toward imminent death and not just some dream of Agamemnon in a play, you know you will not be able to cast aside your pity and your fear along with your ticket stub as you leave the theater. In our pain is the parting place of life and art. Art is the clean wound, the catharsis that leaves no scars and gives us empathy for the tragedy of others and makes us grow. Art teaches. Art heals. Life hurts. When someone you love with all your being dies, it does not sear the intellect. It tears the heart. The act of dying yokes two souls grotesquely, like conjoined twins. At their parting, the death of one is the partial death of the other.

And so it is with the cancer Diana and I share.

At first we sense a slight loss of energy, and some loss of weight. Then she begins to feel a pain in her abdomen that intensifies so abruptly and in such huge, terrifying, savage devouring bites, that we are always caught breathless by its bestial ferocity. Each new level of her agony is so much more intense than the last that there is simply no way to prepare for it.

One night she is so uncomfortable I can no longer lie beside her in bed. And I know then I will never lie beside her ever again. Never. Hume brings a cot which we set up close enough to her bed so that if she moans in the night I can reach out to her.

When I run my hand ever-so-gently on the side of her abdomen one evening, I can feel the hard tumor inside of her. Soon after that, I can see it under the skin, like a coiled snake, devouring her at its will. In my dreams and in my waking dreams as well, I can imagine it enlarging, slowly, inexorably, minute by minute, writhing and growing, pushing aside the internal organs with no more concern than an iron wedge has in riving the cells of a tree. My dreams are filled to the breaking point by images of the tumor rending the cells of her body, tearing at us, ripping us apart, slowly, separating body from soul, independent of the will. What do these cancer cells want? What we all want, immortality. But they pursue their goal mindlessly, irrationally, blindly, unconsciously, at the very price of their own mortality, and of hers.

Each day the tumor protrudes more and more, slowly, but inevitably, like roots against a sidewalk. For five hundred years we humans have outlawed drawing and quartering as vilely cruel and inhuman punishment. Yet nature does this. We say it is God's will. We say He has a plan, and that's supposed to make the barbaric torture acceptable to us.

As she wastes away, she becomes pale, then sallow. We measure life by the low bodily functions. A month ago she could rise by herself and walk to the toilet. Two weeks ago she could barely sit upright and slide by herself onto the portable toilet by her bed. Yesterday I had to lift her onto the pot and lift her off.

And now, even that is too painful. She can only lie without moving, defecate and urinate onto the plastic lined sheets. She has little energy left, and less will. I lift her and clean her and hold her tenderly to cause as little pain as possible as Hume and Abis change her linens. A nurse teaches me how to administer the needle. The bedsores widen and deepen until now they reach the bone. Where is Love? Why will he never show? Morphine cannot alleviate our exquisite pain. God is great. God is good.

***

Through the darkening clouds and the misting rain, the sun's rays stream like golden angel's hair, streaming down to the earth. The sun rays come aslant through the window, hiding the shadows of the sockets of Diana's cheeks and eyes. When I look at her in this light, she still looks beautiful to me. Angelic. It's the only face of God I may ever get to know.

Her lips, thin now, and nearly colorless, are serene. She breathes easily in her coma. The hospice nurse comes to regulate for us the dosage of her anodyne. She's arrived at the last stage of her dying. I do not try to talk to her. I do not think she can hear me. I wish I could say, "I love you," for I know she will not be alive much longer now, an hour, perhaps, or a day, and most likely, will never be awake again to this world before she leaves it. I wish I could talk to her, to tell her what I feel in my heart. I pray for the means to pray and for the belief that brings comfort. But God and I do not seem to be communicating, and so I can not say the words, not to her, or to God. I just sit in the chair next to her, arms folded around myself, rocking, gently rocking.

Her breathing is so shallow now. I don't want to leave her side and so I wait and wait. But finally I must go to the restroom. I have put it off so long I ache, but somehow I know. I know she knows. She doesn't want me to see her parting. So I go.

When I return, as I knew it would be, she is dead. In the hallway, I motion to Hume. He dons another mask, this one of gauze, and enters to minister to the dust. He covers her face with the sheet and turns to me, and nods. Together, we leave the room as the hospice nurses enter. Hume and I are only human. We cannot enter deeper into the mystery. Our human ministry ends with the closing of that door.

I close the door.

Disoriented, out of breath, and alone, I wander out of Love's house and into the rain, turn my face skyward to catch the full force of the warm shower, but soon find my hands are over my nose and eyes, trying to protect them as the storm begins to rage in thundering heaps. Wishing I could cry. I am beyond any inadequate emotion. I think about seeking shelter, but I don't. The clouds barrage me at first with a heavy, freezing torrent, and then ease into a gentle drizzle, warm as a baby's breath. On the horizon comes the true storm.

Grateful for the respite, I look about and am surprised the sun is close to setting. Some miles off in the distance, fire trails of lightening pierce the gathering gloom. Great claps and rolling rumbles of thunder roar and crackle after them. The hair on my arms and chest bristles with electricity. This is a sign, I suppose, that I will soon be hit by lightening. I know I should take cover now, but I cannot move. I cannot comprehend. Suddenly, as if pushed by someone else, I am swept away until I find myself standing on the dock.

To my left, Abis's life vest hangs like a war bundle from the piling that holds the pathetic hawser of his pathetic little boat. I put the life vest on and frantically begin to untie the rope, fumbling, hardly able to move, moving in slow motion, as if through thick molasses, like the man in my own dream again. Horrible.

Chufee barks and snarls at me. Abis calls to her. His hands are on my shoulders, pushing my hands from the rope that holds his little ferry boat to the mooring, throwing me back onto the dock. His eyes are on fire. He shouts at me, "No!"

I seem to be shouting, "no!" as well. But somewhere in the distance.

"What are you doing, Manny-man?"

"I've got to get away from here. You don't understand!"

"Only I understand, Manny-man."

Sandy Cohen

"Let me go!"

But he holds me fast, hard against his chest, against the wind, the rain and the noise of the thunderclaps. I try to push away. But I can't. "No, Abis, please, let me go."

"Cannot let you go, Manny-man. The storm," he answers with such calm. His voice is deep and rumbling in his chest, like the voices of the thunder boys. "Manny-man, I will *give* you this ferry boat. It is yours! It has always been yours. But after the storm. It is no good now! Useless boat with the waves so high. It cannot save you until the calm. You must trust in Abis now, this very darkening night."

He lets me go and turns his back on me to tie the boat back up. I break away, toss the life vest into the boat, and run and run and run until I find myself in front of the little tavern where I first met the three fishermen.

What a great impression I made on them my first visit here. I imagine what they will make of me this time. Legends forever of the madman of the storm. Eyes wild and wide. Thin hair plastered to the side of his face. Bald spot fully revealed. Shirt and pants slick to the skinny body. Nothing hidden. Standing before them like a model for an icon of the Byzantine Church, dragged up for the occasion out of the Jewish ghetto, out of pissing lane and set down here to pose and ridicule for the price of a beer.

I can see my nightmares reflected now in the their eyes as I stagger through the door, my nightmares casting light in the set of their jaws, but still I say, "Please let me hire your boat for tonight. This time I'll pay; I swear I will pay you when you put me ashore!"

They laugh at me.

"I'll buy the boat, only, please take me to the mainland!"

That sets them laughing even harder and I find myself outside in the raging storm again, weeping.

"I don't deserve this, Lord! I'm not that bad! I don't deserve this, Lord, oh Lord, oh Lord, oh God!"

But still the storm rages in a frenzy of hot thunder and blowing wind as I slide down against the side of the building with my back against the wall until I'm sitting sprawling in the mud, weeping like a madman. Like a child. Like the man I wished I were at Delphi.

I feel his presence at my hip, the warmth of life, Abis's leg against my own. Down there in the mud, his arm winds about my shoulder, like a snake about to squeeze. He squeezes my shoulder like a friend.

With his hand he points up toward the sky. "Oh, Manny-man, it is greatly, greatly wet up there tonight, *n'est-ce pour?*" he shouts above the bursts of thunder. "It is a magical world of fireworks, Manny-man.

Makes Abis think of home. That world up there is full of spirits, Manny-man."

The rolling thunder makes me shudder. But Abis is enjoying it. He is unafraid, and takes his arm from around my shoulder to applaud each burst of lightning. Then he sees that I am shivering and holds me tighter than before. "It is great, Manny-man. Abis loves this, huh? The spirits down below are sucking mud tonight!"

"Abis, I want to go home. I have to go home. Tonight."

"Me too."

At once I stop and look at him. He is smiling. But I find myself weeping once again.

"It is okay-donkey, Manny-man. All right. And true. We will go. But can't we wait until the storm is over?"

"I've got to go home now. I can't stand the pain any longer."

"You hurt?"

"I can't stand the pain."

"Need nurse?"

"Can't stand the pain."

He looks up to the raging storm. Then at me. "I am first giving you this advice, man-man, for soon we shall be whole again and one. Remember this, there are four rules for life. You are ready to listen now? This is the last time I give you wisdom words. Do not hate anyone. Try to understand. Try to mind your own business. Try to be aware of everything. This you must do from now on. Come, now, Manny-man, we go."

"Just give me the keys to the boat. I'll tie it up to leave for you on the dock at Love's house on the other side. Or I'll pay you for it. Here, look, I swear. I'll write you out a note. A will. Leave everything to you in payment if I don't make it. Let's go somewhere to keep the paper dry so I can write it out. Not in there, though, please. Not there."

He shakes his head and smiles. "No key, Manny-man. No will. I have already given you the boat. It is yours. And now I will take you to the other side. Me. Abis, Ferryman to the fragile. And his faithful part-coyote, Idiomene."

I see movement under his tattered coat and for the first time realize she has been hidden there all this time. She pokes her little head out now and doesn't growl at me or even bark. She seems used to me at last. Or resigned. Her yellow irises strain to look at me. The whites of her eyes show bloodshot pink. Her body is shuddering, like mine. But she's not shivering; her master's body is still warm against her own, shielding her from the rain. It is only the blowing rain, and not the air, that is cold. She is merely afraid of the thunder.

Sandy Cohen

Abis holds the top of his coat closed with one hand. He cradles the dog in the crook of his other arm and rises to his feet. I rise after him and follow back toward the dock, and his little ferry boat.

"Come, Manny-man, we are going home."

The storm is all but over now. Between us and home is protected water and the waves can never get too high. I will be sick, but safe. Despite it all, Abis is a practiced sailor.

But by the time we get to his little ferry boat, the rain is sheeting harder. He steps aboard The boat sways erratically and sinks down into the water. He waves me forward and reaches out to help me board. Hard stings of hail and shuddering buckets of freezing rain take my breath away. Then bands of lighter, prickling, warm, soothing showers fall.

"Abis, let's wait a bit."

He pushes his dog through the cabin door, yelping, "Out of the way, little bitch!"

She yelps, too, but obeys, reluctantly. But soon we see her head poke out from the hatchway, as ridged as if it were mounted on a stick. She whines and starts to come back out to be with him.

"She's too scared to go," I say.

But he says to her, "No, little sister. You must stay dry and warm as long as can be."

At once, she does as she is told. But two minutes later her whole head and shoulder are exposed again, and getting drenched. She shivers to the bone and looks so forlorn.

Abis gives her a stern look. She doesn't move. Finally, he points toward the hatch again and she backs down into the dark, damp, secure hold. The dog stench dissipates.

"Now she will be comfortable for the journey we are about to take, Manny-man," Abis says as he begins to untie us. As he does, I casually stroll to the side and vomit. He ties the boat back up and comes to me.

"You are sure and certain you really want to do this thing, Manny-man?"

"Yes," I say calmly, and calmly turn and vomit again.

"No?"

"Yes."

At first I think his arms are on my shoulders to hug me again, to reassure. Then I realize he's really lifting up each of my arms one by one and lacing the life vest onto me.

"You must wear it, Manny-man. It is the official circumcised law of the great state of Georgia, one of the original thirteen colonies of the United States of America. Abis can scuff at, and break this state law with impudence because he can swim like an abalone-eating sea otter and you cannot. Idiomene, now we must call her Cereba, does not need such a

260

safety device about her because she can paddle like hell. She is a great and versatile dog on land and sea. Abis has not revealed this thing to you before, but she is part water spaniel. I think two-thirds. No, no, really, Manny-man, this is the truth this one last time."

He gets the vest tied around my waist and chest and turns me around completely. I manage to sit with my back against the side of the boat, my legs straddled out on the floor.

"This *can't* be the only life jacket on board."

"Yes, for sure. Abis never needed more than one before. Who for hell would go out sailing with a crazy man when the weather is as bad as this, eh? Eh? So far so good, Abis only needed one. You bet. Do not look so gloomy, Manny-man. I will look about. Everything abroad can float. The safety paddles float. The stupid old man, who is Abis now, he can float too, given much encouragement. Besides, I have many, many friends out there. Look here, Manny-man, the cushions float."

He throws the biggest one out on the water. It bobs on the waves a bit, then kicks about and starts to swirl away on the mounting waves.

"Grab it quick, Abis! We may need to hold onto it in an emergency!"

"I will get it later. It can go nowhere that Abis cannot find. This is a protected harbor. Look here, Manny-man, the beer cooler floats!"

He throws it into the water. "Shoes float. Compass floats. Maps float, too," he shouts above the roaring wind as he throws each item in turn upon the waters. "Want to see if doggie floats?"

"NO!"

"No worry, Manny-man. Doggie *will* float. I have tested her many, many times."

I throw up on the deck.

"Hmm, try to do that very thing next time out there in the water, man-man. No, no, do not frenzy yourself about it now. Mother Nature will clean the mess up pronto-quick. See, she is already hosing the deck down as we speak of it. Look out for her sprinkler hose, Manny, she will drench you plenty!"

"Too late," I say and laugh with him as the rain falls harder.

Then I dry heave as he fumbles with the rope.

He turns to me and says, "No use, Manny-man. I must untie it permanently." He cuts the cord with his pocket knife, then throws the knife overboard, too, along with the bits of rope he cut.

"Look at that, Manny-man; the knife does not float."

He pushes us off with his boat hook, then plops that in the water, too. At once we begin to drift uncontrollably into the bay.

But soon he gets the sail partially up and it pushes us forward in a parody of control. I struggle to my knees, holding onto the sides of the rocking, pitching, yawing boat and look about. We are actually churning up a wake of white water as if propelled by a motor. I lie down again on the deck and dry retch. It is the only dry about me.

Abis thrashes about at the tiller, laughing and turning his face toward the rain. "Manny-man, this is great! Just great!"

Thunder crashes and the clouds spit fire. As we clear the little harbor, Abis loses his grip on the sail ropes. My nausea overwhelms me. Abis giggles like a three-year-old as the storm rages harder. Suddenly he leaps forward the same way he did when he caught that bird on the playing field of Delphi. "Oh, Manny-man," he moans, and holds up a red-tipped feather.

"Wha?"

"Oh, Manny-man, it is Red! It is Red! He has been on my very boat! See? It is his other feather!"

"Throw it away!"

"Oh, Man-man!"

"Abis, throw the feather away! It's just a superstition! Do you understand?"

"It is Red! It is Red! He has changed my tobacco!"

"Throw it away. Here, give it to me!"

"It is too late, Manny-man!" He turns his head and shouts into the wind, "I come!"

My skin begins to tingle. At the same time, lightening hits the mast, blinding me with its intensity. My bones shiver with the explosion of the thunder, but my ears seem to refuse to register it on my brain, as if all sound and all movement in the universe were banished for that instant.

From front to back, the whole boat spins and is awash with steam and fire and light. The mast splits up the middle. Then it vanishes and I realize I'm floating in the water. Two feet away from me, Abis thrashes about. He's screaming for his little dog. Blood gushes from his face as he tries to lift himself out of the reddening foam to catch a glimpse of her. He turns, searching frantically in the swells for a cushion, or for anything to hold onto. I reach out to him, stretching with my fingertips, kicking with all my strength, trying to propel myself to him. The sea is whipped into flying flecks of foam. In the distance the dog screams like a human baby. We can't see her above the swollen, bloated sea and the sheets of rain.

"Idiomene!, Abis shouts, "Cereba!"

"Please, Abis, please, come back to me!" I scream, but my voice is choked off by the wash of the waves. Desperately, I cough and flounder about, trying to reach out to him. But he continues to swim away. I can see that his strokes are not powerful enough to propel him very far. He seems to be in such great pain. He's not going to make it. Oh, God, he's going to drown!

"Abis, come back. Cling to me! Oh, God, cling to me!"

If he does come back and tries to hold onto me, the rotting life vest he attached to me will not hold together. It can't hold us both. Does he know this, too? We will both go under and die.

I see the sharks. Great, grey, shadowy masses below me and the fins across the surface of the water, rolling on the waves, then going down again. One of them raises its head completely out of the water and its black, beady eyes see me and its great, beaked head rises out of the water once again and pushes at my leg and back as I wince in terror.

Then I realize it's a dolphin, and she's pushing me up, holding my head at the surface as the rest of the pod swims off as quickly as they came, headed in the direction of Abis and the barking dog.

I continue screaming out to Abis. But he's gone. The barking dog is gone. Only the sound of the wind and the waves remains, and one voice screaming in the dark.

That voice is mine. In my terror of the storm and the dark water that surrounds me I continue to scream, though the waves often overwhelm me, with all the lung power I have left in me I cry out into the dark as long as my voice lasts.

# TWENTY-EIGHT

When I wake, it's morning and the waters that surround me are still. The sky is blue. Unclouded. Hot. My face is dry, blistered, caked with salt. I'm dying of thirst, slowly, but don't care anymore, even about the dark, grey shadows undulating under me. I think this time they are really sharks, and I wish that I could be terrified of them, but I don't care anymore.

By the morning of the second day, or the third, they rescue me. Three fishermen in a sleek, fiberglass boat, three sport fishermen who pluck me out of the water, incoherent, probably delirious, somewhere off the Carolina coast, hundreds of miles from my original course.

*\*\**

"We were lookin' for seaweed. You know, for the shade. For the fish below the shade. Where the big ones hide."

"That's what we thought you were. Seaweed."

"Why we first came to investigate."

"And I said, 'Look, Ed, it's a man.'"

"Actually, he said, "Look, Ed, it's a corpse.""

"And we rushed on over."

But I don't care.

I lie on the sheets in the hospital room, looking out at them through bleary eyes, thinking, "this is how it was for Diana and for Sara." I am seeing now from their eyes. But they're gone. Then it's Abis that I see. His soul stands before me, astride the floor. His bloated body floats on the waves, as worn as the worm-eaten statues in the basement of the Athens museum. The round, puffed body of his little Cereba floats not far from him and the two bodies and my own fade and become the man and his two sons who rescued me. The three of them are standing beside the bed and the father is saying, "You're very lucky."

"No. Not very. Maybe just lucky. If I were very lucky I wouldn't have been floating on the water in the first place. I would have been riding over it in a boat."

All three nod, I think, and I drift off again. Then back. One of them is saying that my boat has been found and towed back in for me. I forget to tell them that it is not really my boat. But I suppose it is.

"Mast's a goner. But that can be replaced."

"What about Abis and the dog?"

"No trace, so far."

The father shakes his head. "Washed out to sea, probably."

"Maybe they washed ashore somewhere."

"Or were picked up by somebody else."

"Did I tell you the dog was a sort of miniature coyote from hell?"

"Listen, maybe we could come back later, when you're more rested. Don't want to tire you out."

"Wait, don't go yet. Please. What about the island? Surely they've found that."

"Could be any one of a hundred or more out there."

"I think they said they're still searching. Trying to figure out what your bearings were. But they haven't much to go on."

"You weren't too lucid when you gave 'em the descriptions. But I reckon they tried best they could. I still have the newspaper clippings, if you want 'em."

"No. But what about the name? I gave you the name. Didn't you check it out on the maps? You have nautical maps of Georgia? Did I give you the name?"

"Well, sir. You gave us *a* name. And the name you gave us wasn't necessarily on the map. See, most those islands are privately owned, or parts of corporate estates. You would not believe the money floating around out there."

"An' being private, lots those rich folks just call 'em whatever they want to. Makes no difference to them what th'official name is, or was."

"But surely with an operation like that. Those digs. I mean, that has to be registered with the government, right?"

The father laughs. "Not if they're sellin' stuff off to collectors."

"But he wouldn't *do* that. He's setting it up as a tourist place."

"I doubt that seriously, Mr. Markovitz. See, those Indian mounds are always kept private, 'cause, number one, they don't' want government restrictions placed on land usage, and number two, they don't want any militant Indian interference. You know, 'how dare you go diggin' up grammy's bones,' and such."

"But she is an Indian. I mean, she was. Part Indian."

"Which part? And the other thing is, most of those private excavations are as illegal as pit bull fights. Which they also got out there on those private islands. If it's a real good find, I mean with lots of old Indian dishes and stuff, see, they'll sell it off 'til it's clean gone then close up shop and head for the bank, happy as a hound dog in a garbage pail. Let me tell you something, buddy, selling off a Indian mound as loaded up as the one you claim you saw'll make a man rich quick."

"But William Love doesn't need to do all that. He's already rich."

"And the already rich don't do things like that, right? Don't wanna become richer?"

I put one hand over my eyes. "I really appreciate your visit, but please excuse me, I'm very, very tired now."

When they leave, I wonder, did I tell them about the murder of Coach Benedict? If I haven't, how can I tell them now? They'll think I was a part of it. Or did he die by his own doing? Maybe when I get back home, back in my own study, surrounded by my own notes and books and ideas I'm familiar with, things will begin to sort themselves out again and be normal. I'm in no condition to think now.

As for Abis and the dog, I'm not giving up hope. Maybe the dolphins rescued them. Or Abis did it on his own. If his dog were really drowning, how could she have yelped so lustily? I mean, I got a mouthful of water every time I tried to yell, and I had a life vest on.

The story's generated some publicity. Maybe that'll help. But even if they do find him dead or alive, how will I know? The story might not be covered nationally. And I don't even think I know his real name. And if he is alive he probably won't even know anyone's been looking for him. It's not like he reads newspapers or watches T.V. as far as I know. On the other hand, what do I know? One of these days he'll come knocking on my study door and grinning like a fool when I open it. When I get home I can look Love's island up. Maybe there's some sort of national archeological registry or something. Maybe Benedict was right and the whole thing's just a tourist ploy in the making. But that would mean Diana's life work was a sham and I can't believe Love would do that. And you can't fool science. Wouldn't it be ironic if I ended up there someday as a tourist and ran into Love and Abis that way? Maybe Hume was right and Willy Love, as well; maybe there is no enigma, no metaphor, just mysteries science has not yet solved and things actually are as they actually are. Coach Benedict's death was an accident, and Abis's was, too.

Maybe they were lucky, after all, and avoided a worse death at the hands of God, like the ones He handed out to Sara and Diana and all the others He hands out so readily in the cancer wards and misery centers of the world.

# EPILOGUE

William Love, Benedict, Hume, all of them, they are lost to me now, unreal again, in the past. And the past does not exist, save as a dream of reality, a drama to learn by, a metaphor, a myth. It is this lesson that I cannot seem to learn: Letting go. Living now. Letting go. Living in the middle tense.

Because I think of them alive each day, they must die to me each day, each night in my dreams, and I must feel the pain each day even more than the daily dying of my own flesh. It is an emptiness. You add that emptiness to the emptiness that is Sara and the emptiness that is Diana and Abis and the rest. One emptiness is added to another, and another. And that is how you have eternity.

# About the Author

Before *Revelations,* Sandy Cohen published two books in Europe plus stories, articles, poetry, and essays in journals and magazines in the United States, Canada, China, Germany, England, and Greece. His work, critical and creative, has drawn praise from, among others, Norman Mailer, Bernard Malamud, Patrick White and Isaac Beshevis Singer. He has been a professor, jazz musician, bookbinder, actor and, for almost two decades, a humorous commentator on public radio. He appeared in his own mini-series for public television and in a feature film, *Do Not Disturb,* filmed in northern China, where he lived for a year. He currently resides in southwest Florida with his nearly-perfect family.

www.ingramcontent.com/pod-product-compliance
Lightning Source LLC
Chambersburg PA
CBHW071411090426

42737CB00011B/1423